THE LAST FLIGHT OVER THUD RIDGE

The clouds increased and all flights except Art's were forced to turn back. He thought it was his duty to try to make it despite almost insurmountable obstacles. He got to his target—only to find it obscured by clouds and the black and orange overcast of an 85 millimeter barrage.

Down he went, into a hail of automatic weapons that ripped the belly of his aircraft to shreds. The fuel gushed, torched and covered the aircraft from cockpit to tailpipe; the idiot panel turned amber; the fire panel glowed its sickening shade of red; one by one the systems began their bleeding countdown to imminent control seizure and explosion.

The craft rolled and dipped down, toward the green-carpeted hills. She was all done.

THUD RIDGE
COLONEL JACK BROUGHTON, USAF (RET.)

With an Introduction by Hanson W. Baldwin

BANTAM BOOKS
TORONTO • NEW YORK • LONDON • SYDNEY • AUCKLAND

THUD RIDGE

A Bantam Book / published by arrangement with
the Author

PRINTING HISTORY

Bantam edition / November 1985

Drawings by Greg Beecham.
Maps by Alan McKnight.

ISBN 0-553-25189-9

Published simultaneously in the United States and Canada

Bantam Books are published by Bantam Books, Inc. Its trademark, consisting of the words "Bantam Books" and the por-
trayal of a rooster, is Registered in U.S. Patent and Trademark
Office and in other countries. Marca Registrada. Bantam
Books, Inc., 666 Fifth Avenue, New York, New York 10103.

PRINTED IN THE UNITED STATES OF AMERICA

O   0 9 8 7 6 5 4 3 2 1

"To Our Comrades Up North"

—F-105 pilots' toast to the prisoners of Hanoi

CONTENTS

INTRODUCTION
by Hanson W. Baldwin

The fighter pilot is a breed apart; to him, loyalty down is all important, and the men who flew against North Vietnam in aircraft designed for far different missions felt they were always under the gun of official disapproval in Washington and Hawaii. They risked their lives to the enemy, their careers to the politicians. Infractions of any one of the tremendous numbers of restrictions which governed every flying hour of their lives subjected them to inquiry and perhaps to censure and punishment. Yet far from being just irresponsible Gung-Ho pilots out to kill women and children—a Communist-sponsored caricature that has been sold to too many of the American people—they were quiet heroes who tried their best to deliver their bombs on military targets only, and who often paid with their lives for their humanity and their restraint.

The story of these people, and, particularly, of the men who flew the Air Force workhorse—the F-105 "Thud"—over North Vietnam, is scarcely known to the public. Colonel Broughton, a football tackle at West Point in the class of 1945, tells it here.

He is not concerned with the big picture; his story concerns one wing of F-105's based on Takhli in Thailand, and the men who flew with it and lived or died. It is told in the language of the fighter pilot and with all its verve, authenticity, and drama.

Colonel Broughton flies and writes the way he played football, in a tough, moving, fluent, and veracious style. His is a unique story. He tells it as it was, with all the mistakes and frustrations, the tragedies and heartaches, the high drama and the flaming terror. It is rare to find in any book the combination of precise professional and technical knowledge with narrative power that this one possesses.

But *Thud Ridge* has another original quality. It is history-in-the-making. It is the first battle narrative I know of that was, in large part, actually recorded *during* battle. Most battle accounts are warmed over. After-action reports and after-action interviews usually represent the raw stuff of history. *Thud Ridge* utilizes *in-action* records for this purpose; in his flight over the north, Colonel Broughton carried with him in his cockpit a miniature tape recorder, which preserved the pilot talk, the orders, the high excitement, and the tragedy.

There is, thus, about this book the realism, the honesty, the frankness, and the dedication that is the best memorial to those Americans who died in North Vietnam for a country that did not seem to "long remember."

This bitter war in the jungles far away is probably the most misunderstood war—one of the most unpopular wars—in our history. Though it has been mismanaged and overcontrolled at high levels, it has never been the "big bully" war its opponents have charged. Its fundamental purpose—to enable South Vietnam to direct its own political destinies without outside interference and to prevent Communism from conquering another area by terrorism and force—was, and is, sound and in our own interest. But, as in Korea, our fundamental objective in Vietnam has been essentially a defensive one, a negative one, a limited one, and Americans have not yet demonstrated the patience, the wisdom, or the understanding necessary for the support of such a war.

We have allowed the term "limited war" to become a shibboleth. Strategy is the science of alternatives; we have, by our own actions or lack of actions, reduced too greatly the options available to us. Limited war should mean first and primarily the definition of aims and objectives and of the limited political end to be achieved. But in practice in two limited wars—Korea and Vietnam—we have used American manpower and spent American blood while limiting weapons and hobbling strategy and tactics. We have practiced manpower escalation while limiting technological escalation; the result has been frustration, both military and political. The problem of the future is not simply how to limit wars, but how to limit them without frustrating our basic political objectives.

The accomplishment of even the negative purpose of defense would, in any case, have been difficult in Vietnam. The Vietcong were deeply ensconced in the country's social fabric when we first committed our military strength in 1965, and they had the support—voluntary or enforced by terror—of a sizable minority of the South Vietnamese population. They had access to supplies and replacements and had secure sanctuaries, long prepared, not only in the jungle and mountain fastnesses of South Vietnam, but also in North Vietnam, Laos, and Cambodia. And as the war continued, they enlisted the active support of the world's two greatest Communist powers—the USSR and Red China.

Any guerrilla war is certain to be a long-drawn-out war of attrition; the British and their allies fought for twelve years to eliminate a far smaller Communist guerrilla movement in Malaysia. Neither the Administration nor the public understood, when we first committed our strength, that any war in Vietnam, no matter what we did, was bound to be a long war requiring major effort. (Some of our key military leaders had greater foresight. Before a single U. S. combat soldier was committed to Vietnam in 1965, the Army Chief of Staff and the Marine Commandant estimated that a total of 600,000 to 1,000,000 American troops might be required.) But the Administration compounded its failure to understand the difficulties of Vietnam by the policy of gradualism it followed. President Johnson described this policy as the gradual application of increased power to the enemy to force him to cease and desist. This form of escalation sacrificed the great initial U. S. advantage in power. Escalation always works to the advantage of the stronger power if the ante is raised to a degree the opponent cannot quickly match. But the United States sacrificed this advantage; it increased U. S. power and U. S. pressure slowly and gradually—so slowly and so gradually that it permitted the enemy, with major help from its great Communist allies, to match us relatively. The policy of gradualism meant that what was bound in any case to be a long war was now certain to become even more protracted.

Nowhere was this mistake more obvious, nowhere were the results so tragic, as in the air war against North Vietnam. In Vietnam, air power—in large part through no fault of its own—has suffered in the public mind; it has been wrongly blamed for failures that were not its doing; it has failed to win recognition for its real accomplishments.

Never in the history of human conflict have so many hampered, limited, and miscontrolled so few as in the air campaign against North Vietnam. Never has frustration been more compounded. Never have brave men died to less purpose than in some of the bombing forays over the North. Never, in American experience, have the lessons of air warfare, of all warfare, been so pointedly ignored. And never before has an air campaign been controlled, in detail, from thousands of miles away.

The objectives of the air campaign against North Vietnam were defined by Washington as retaliation and punishment of the North for its attacks upon the South and upon U. S. units; a psychological boost to the hard-pressed South Vietnamese peoples; and the imposition of a limitation on the supplies provided by North Vietnam to the enemy in the South.

The air campaign undoubtedly improved the morale of South Vietnam, but it failed to depress the morale of the North in any vital manner, failed to persuade Hanoi to cease and desist, and hampered but never halted the large-scale flow of supplies and replacements to the South from North Vietnam, Laos, and Cambodia.

U. S. memories are short; air power should never have been expected to accomplish all of these objectives, particularly when the restrictions and limitations placed upon the air campaign doomed it a-borning.

There was undoubtedly initial overenthusiasm, among some professionals as well as the Administration and the public, about what air power might accomplish. Americans like to think in terms of an immaculate war won in the wild blue yonder, and some Air Force publicists have encouraged this Madison Avenue fantasy. The Air Force is a young service led by enthusiasts who had had to fight hard to establish its validity against the military traditionalists, and from time to time it has oversold its capabilities. The lessons of World War II, when air power proved to be a vital part—but still only a part—of the military team, and of Korea, when the air interdiction campaign—Operation Strangle—failed to strangle, were quickly forgotten, and some in Washington, including many laymen and a few professionals, anticipated quick results when the bombs began to fall on North Vietnam.

But oversell was not primarily responsible for the disappointing results in North Vietnam. In 1965 when the bombing campaign started the Joint Chiefs of Staff recommended that some ninety-four key military targets be destroyed within two to three weeks in an overwhelming blitz. The campaign was planned in accordance with the military principles of mass, momentum, and concentration to maximize the shock effects of air power to the full. North Vietnam's air defenses then were weak; her gasoline and petroleum storage, electric power, transportation, and other vital targets were concentrated and vulnerable; and the cumulative effect of destroying all these targets rapidly would, at the very least, have materially impeded Hanoi's aid to the Vietcong and might have shaken the North Vietnamese hierarchy.

The recommendation for a planned bombing campaign was ignored, but the bombing was started, hedged around with so many restrictions and limited so severely by the policy of gradualism that it was, except for brief periods, largely ineffective. Instead of striking ninety-four targets in three weeks, the power of the United States Air Force and Navy was applied in driblets over three years; some of the ninety-four targets have not yet been hit. Initially, even the Russian-provided and Russian-directed Sam (surface-to-air missile) sites could not be bombed at all; later, only if the Sams endangered our aircraft. The tank farms at Haiphong were on the forbidden list for months; the enemy had ample time to disperse and conceal his fuel supplies before we bombed them. Power plants were similarly spared until it was too late. Airfields were prohibited targets until late in the war. Migs could and did take off and land directly beneath the bomb sights of our aircraft, and the rule forbade their destruction until they were airborne. Key communication bottlenecks, like the Paul

Doumer bridge across the Red River at Hanoi, and the Haiphong docks, through which funneled most of the food, fuel oil, trucks, bulk materials, weapons, ammunition, and heavy equipment essential to Hanoi's survival, were forbidden targets.

In short, the United States pulled its punches in North Vietnam; Hanoi fought a total war, and Russia and Red China provided the massive aid without which Hanoi could not have survived. The result was inevitable: military and psychological stultification, and an increasing pilot and aircraft loss rate as Moscow helped Hanoi to establish the most sophisticated air defense system ever tested in war—a far-flung complex of missiles, ground guns, interceptors, radar, and communications and control centers.

Targeting restrictions formed only one part of the remote-contol limitations that nullified the efforts of our finest fliers. The permissible targets, except for a brief period of intensified bombing in 1967, formed no part of a coherent pattern. The target list was controlled tightly by the White House, with the civilian chiefs of the Pentagon and State Departments as the chief advisers to the President, and with the Joint Chiefs of Staff (the only body with military experience) the low men on the totem pole.

First Washington and then Hawaii—the latter the headquarters of the Commander-in-Chief Pacific and of the Commander of Pacific Air Forces—controlled such details as flight profiles, armament loads, flak suppression missions, and reconnaissance. Prohibited areas abounded; there was a 30-mile "neutral" strip along the Chinese frontier, a 10-mile prohibited zone around Haiphong, a 30- and 20-mile circle—each with its prohibitions—around Hanoi, and so on. Our pilots had to approach their targets by paths in the sky that were so well defined for the enemy (by our own actions) that his defense problem was simplified and our loss rate was increased.

There is no doubt whatsoever that all these political restrictions needlessly cost American lives, nullified the positive results the bombing campaign might have achieved, and notified the enemy that Washington was overcautious, uncertain, and hesitant. It is not adequate to reiterate the old shibboleth that Vietnam, or any guerrilla war (and Vietnam became far more than a guerrilla war), was a political war. Of course it was, but any war must have, first and foremost, a political objective or it is senseless slaughter. The problem of any war is to utilize military means effectively to achieve the political objective; in Vietnam senseless political restrictions hampered our military technology to such a degree that it became almost impossible to accomplish our political objectives.

Not that the military did not make mistakes; not that they are without some blame for the frustration and the unnecessary casualties. The Air Force wings in Thailand were controlled by a multiplicity of overlapping and unnecessary headquarters, cluttered with administrative red tape. The air war against the North was handicapped by our lack of technical preparation for it. The same weaknesses had been evident in Korea: the lack of a really effective all-weather fighter (the Navy's A-6 attack plane, which appeared midway in the war, was an exception); the inability to pinpoint gun or Sam sites and radar control stations; the lack of appreciation, at high levels, of what a sustained bombing campaign required. There had been too much dependence on nuclear weapons, and the "bomber generals" in the Air Force had long downgraded the tactical air arm.

Indeed, the Air Force has been unfortunate in much of its top-level leadership since World War II. Some of its leaders have been either "parochial" or political (in the narrow military sense), or both, and virtually all of them have come from the ranks of the bomber generals. Long before World War II, General C. L. Chennault, then a less senior officer, championed the role of the fighter in the achievement of air superiority at the Air Corps Tactical School. But he lost the argument, and tactical air power still found itself in Vietnam subordinated to the experiences and the prejudices of the SAC (Strategic Air Command) pilots and the bomber generals.

For the Navy, which had long emphasized tactical air power and which contributed so greatly to the air campaign against the North from heaving carrier decks in the Tonkin Gulf, this was not a problem. But what hurt many of the fighter-pilot "tigers" of the Air Force, flying from their bases in Thailand, was the feeling that their own service did not always understand their requirements and their problems and did not champion the men who were doing the fighting and dying.

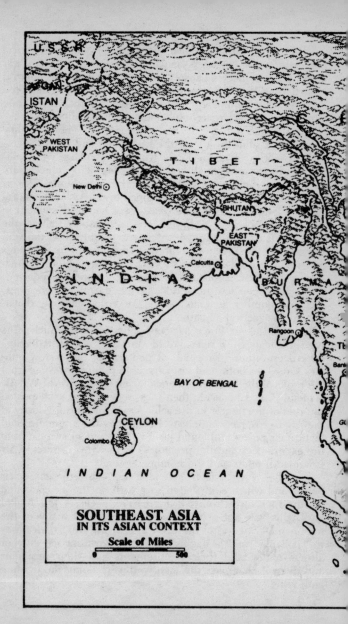

U.S.S.R.

GAN
ISTAN

WEST
PAKISTAN

New Delhi

T I B E T

BHUTAN

EAST
PAKISTAN

Calcutta

I N D I A

B U R M A

Rangoon

Th

Ban

BAY OF BENGAL

CEYLON

Colombo

G

I N D I A N   O C E A N

SOUTHEAST ASIA
IN ITS ASIAN CONTEXT

Scale of Miles

0   500

THUD RIDGE

Republic F-105 "Thunderchief"

1.

A BIT ABOUT WORDS

Much of what I have written in this book is flavored by the exclusive world of the fighter pilot, a man who assumes that everyone understands what he is doing and how he talks. (I have heard it said that if you tied a fighter pilot's hands behind his back, he could not talk coherently for more than sixty seconds.) So I have written this book in the language of the Thud drivers over Vietnam, and that language necessarily includes a good many words whose meaning you're not likely to know unless you've been there. Rather than break up the narrative with repeated explanations or end the book with something in the nature of a glossary, I have chosen instead to give you a capsule account of any government-issue throttle jockey's Thud combat tour. In the course of this summary, you will, I hope, form a clear picture of how our various air combat units were put together and how we worked together in them. And along the way you should get a better idea of the meanings of some of those odd-sounding special words.

The GI pilot stumbles onto a new base overladen with suitcases filled with worthless things that he will not need during his tour, plus a few pounds of personnel and pay records that the administrative folks will lose or maim but always make fatter while he is fighting the war. He is first assigned to a fighter squadron which becomes his basic anchor. The squadron consists of about three hundred enlisted airmen and forty officers (about thirty-five fliers and five supporters) and is commanded by a lieutenant colonel. The commander must be concerned with all facets of his squadron but our new pilot focuses on the operations section, supremely ruled by the major or lieutenant colonel known as the operations officer. The buck pilot is then assigned to one of the four flights in the squadron which are ideally run by four hard-nosed majors, each with eight pilots and five or six aircraft under his thumb. The details of when he eats, sleeps, flies, draws charts and maps for his buddies, or acts as squadron duty officer are controlled at this level.

There are three fighter squadrons within the parent unit on a base, which is called a wing. The wing commander has a staff made up of the commanders of all the support units, such as the supply squadron, civil engineering squadron, and medical unit, in addition to the fighter squadrons. The wing commander's prime assistants on this staff are the vice commander, the deputy for operations who oversees the operational employment of the three fighter squadrons; the deputy for materiel (which means both parts and equipment) who oversees the maintenance squadrons and the materiel squadrons; and the combat support commander who is the focal point for all the housekeeping units. Lumped together, these people become wing weenies to the fighter pilot, and when a full-time pilot shows talent indicating he can be plucked from the pure stick-and-rudder business of the squadron and assigned chores as a wing weenie, there is bound to be some degree of trauma. The term "weenie" appeared someplace way back when, but the first time I encountered it was in Korea when our commander, Gen. John Murphy, used to call us together at six o'clock every other Sunday evening. He would go through our boners of the past two weeks and regularly announce, "You are a bunch of dumb weenies." The sessions were dubbed "Weenie Roasts."

The deputy commander for operations (DO for short) is the executive who produces the airborne combat effort. His empire centers around a building called a combat operations center where all combat communications are received and dispatched. This is where those concerned with the action can find, at any minute of the night or day, who is flying which aircraft, when they left, when they are scheduled to return, and what they are accomplishing while in the air. The fragmentary portion of the headquarters instructions pertaining to a particular wing's effort for the next day (frag) arrives in this section at least daily, and upon receipt of the frag, the next section of the DO's people go to work—those known as mission planners or frag breakers.

The frag breakers must decipher page after page of times, coordinates, and numerical target designators to translate the frag into an understandable schedule of activity for the wing. When they have reduced the data to a simple form showing how many people start engines at what time to get from here to there, they assign responsibilities to each of the three fighter squadrons to provide the assets to get the job done. Full preparation must be accomplished in triplicate to cover the primary target assigned, plus first and second alternate targets. The man leading the entire show for the next day, the mission commander, must dictate his attack guidelines for each of the targets. Pilots selected by the squadrons then make out the maps, flight lineup cards, and detailed navigation cards to be used by the pilots within the strike force, and they must depend upon yet another section within the DO's shop—the intelligence section.

As soon as the intelligence people are alerted to the next day's requirements, they scurry through huge files and produce the applicable maps and photos to be used by the aircrews. They collect any information available on past attacks on the target, and they attempt to predict the defenses that will be encountered. This prediction can never be exact as the enemy refuses to leave his mobile defenses in one place, and a gun battery that is active, or up, one day may not fire—or may not even be there—the next day. Their prognosis must cover likely sectors of automatic ground weapons fire, such as machine guns. It must present the best estimate of action by antiaircraft guns varying in caliber from 37 millimeter to 100 millimeter, some firing visually and some firing under radar control. They must attempt to pinpoint the mobile Russian-built surface-to-air missile sites—Sam to us—and they must bring us up-to-date on how many interceptor aircraft—Migs—we might look for.

Some of the DO's people, such as the weapons officer, specialize in the use and delivery of bombs, missiles, and gunfire. They can advise on the best angle of dive and the best airspeed for any particular dive-bomb run. Others are constantly evaluating the tactics of the attack to determine the best approach to maximum efficiency, while still others constantly evaluate the performance of the pilots and the manner in which the bombs go to Hanoi.

At least two hours before the first start-engine time, the mission commander gathers all of his charges together and conducts a very detailed briefing on each of the three probable missions. Somewhere in this time frame the decision will be made in Saigon as to which target we will attack (we say we are executed on that target). The decision is flashed through the combat operations net to the mission commander, quite often too late to make for comfortable timing in the still necessary internal flight briefings, physical transit to the aircraft, and launch of the strike force. You can bet that if a subject addresses itself to the primary job of attacking the enemy, the wing weenies have worked it over long before our throttle jockey walks out to his Thud.

If we now have our driver matched with a machine, we need to talk about what we are going to do with him. He will normally be sent into action as one member of a flight of four aircraft. This flight will be sent against a target of its own, or will be part of a strike force or group of flights all tasked to strike the same target. Each flight of four will be given a phonetic designator to facilitate identification and radio conversation. If we assume a call sign of Wabash, the flight leader would be known as Wabash one or Wabash leader. Wabash two would fly on the leader's left wing, and together they would be the lead element of the flight. Wabash three is known as the element leader and is the second in command of the flight. He flies on the right side of the leader with Wabash four on his right wing.

We can utilize our combinations of men and machines in several ways. If we launch them to bomb a specific building or piece of real estate, they are on a strike mission. If we launch them with instructions to look up and down a certain road or to roam a narrow geographical area and attack the best target observed by the flight leader, they are on an armed reconnaissance, or armed recce. If their announced purpose is to participate in a rescue attempt, they are on Rescap. Anytime you are monitoring someone or something below, you are on Combat Air Patrol. If our aircraft are being used to help the ground forces achieve some specific objective, they are providing close support. This support can be directed by a forward air controller, or FAC, who flies a slower aircraft and drops marking devices on the target, or it may be directed by radio or visual signals from the ground. If we send fighters to protect other aircraft from attack by enemy aircraft, they are escorting. When the forces are available, escort by faster, more maneuverable aircraft is desirable for slower aircraft or aircraft involved in a mission that demands all of their attention or all of the capability available in their machine.

Our fighter-bomber pilot is concerned with putting the bombs and rockets that he carries onto the target. Just as he must have internal wing support to get into the air, he must have airborne support to achieve his goal. This support includes photographic and electronic reconnaissance aircraft whose mission differs from his own armed recce only in that their goal is to find, record, and identify, as opposed to destroy. It includes aerial refueling support from huge tankers whose only task is to pump fuel through a tube in their tail and into a receptable in the nose of the fighter. Overloaded fighters use a great deal of fuel when they accomplish maximum performance maneuvers. They must depend on ground radar stations, manned by a group known as controllers, to steer them and the tankers to a common piece of sky where they can accomplish the mandatory fuel transfer.

The helicopter has assumed a place in the direct combat support of the attackers. These choppers can stand still over a downed pilot and hoist him to safety, if the chopper can locate him and if the chopper can survive the two-way trip and the pickup. To find a downed pilot and steer the chopper to his position we use old propeller aircraft which are less vulnerable to small-arms fire from the ground, yet faster than the chopper. They have the ability to stay airborne for long periods and the heavy load of bombs, rockets, and guns they can carry allows them to harass the enemy on the ground near the downed pilot and thus protect both the pilot and the chopper.

But our GI pilot worries little about all these other folks at the start of his tour as he is more concerned with perfecting his own techniques. He knows that North Vietnam is split into six segments called Route Packages, and he knows the defenses are lighter in the southern-most package—Route Pack 1—and get tougher as the numbers increase to Route Pack 6—the northernmost segment. Although he will fly his first ten missions in the easiest of the areas, the first one is still bound to be an exciting event. When he starts to taxi out for that first takeoff, the bombs and missiles on his aircraft are inert due to the safety clips inserted in the fuzes. When he gets to the arming area at the end of the runway and the arming crew pulls those red-flagged clips out of the system, those munitions are armed and ready to go. He is carrying live ordnance and he is off to combat.

His first few missions will be scheduled in good weather where he can see the ground and the other aircraft around him—Visual Flight Rules, or VFR. After he has had a chance to respond properly to the numerous changes in radio chan- nels by following his leader's instructions to "go to button three"—a switch to channel three—without making the wrong move and losing contact with the rest of the flight, and after he has accepted fuel from the tanker in sequence with the rest of his flight—or cycled off the tanker—in the bright sunshine, he will no longer be scheduled selectively for good weather. He will get to perform under IFR, or Instrument Flight Rules, when the weather is bad and when he flies only by position on his leader if he is a wingman, or only by reference to his flight instruments if he is leading others.

On his first few missions he is almost sure to use more fuel than any of the other flight members. He knows that he must maintain flight integrity and that he must go where his leader goes. Except for a few seconds on the dive-bomb run itself, he must maintain tallyho, or visual contact with all his flightmates. This is not always easy to do with a big bombload, and until he learns the tricks, he will make up time and space by lots of burner. The afterburner, which gives additional power but on the Thud engine consumes fuel as fast as you could pass it through the necks of six milk bottles at once, is activated by simply pushing the hand-held throttle sideways.

The flight leader is responsible for steering properly, or maintaining the correct heading. and he is responsible for putting all of the flight in the right place at the proper airspeed. If the wingman fails to respond to his leader's actions properly, he can plug in, or stroke the burner, to cover up, but his fuel supply will tell the story. Each mission has an established minimum-fuel radio call to enable the leader to make fuel plans based on the man with the least fuel. It will be the new man who reaches this state first and calls bingo.

There is a good chance that during these early missions he will learn that what we call switch actions are not always as simple as they seem. There are nine separate switches that must be activated to insure that the bombs will leave the aircraft properly during the dive-bomb run, and the pilot sets them up when he crosses into enemy territory and the flight leader calls, "Clean 'em up, green 'em up, and start your music" (clean up your cockpit, maps and charts stowed, ready to attack; activate all your armament switches and check for the green lights indicating your munitions are ready to go; if you are carrying radar-jamming pods under your wing, turn them on). If he forgets one—and when things get rough this is possible—it may cost his life. He had better learn to jink properly during these missions. That is the art of weaving, bobbing, twisting, and turning to avoid enemy gunfire as you come off the dive-bomb run. They used to call me the Super Jinker, but I never got hit coming off a target.

As he approaches the end of the first ten missions he will find his flight leader priming him more and more on things like the performance envelope of the Mig. He will learn where the Mig is at its best and where it is weakest. He will find what his particular leader expects when he calls "break" and throws his flight into a hard turn or into violent evasive action to avoid being shot down by an enemy aircraft. There will be no doubt in his mind that he will jettison, or toggle, his bombload short of the target only as a last-ditch life-or-death alternative.

If a Mig or anything else makes him toggle short of his target, he has been defeated. Moreover, in this war that pits high-speed fighters against small, hard-to-see targets in the middle of politically sensitive areas, he doesn't want to give the enemy a chance to repeat his old song about bombing civilians. He must disregard the fact that "civilians" working in and around the big rail yards and those manning the supply dumps and the vehicle repair shops are the backbone of what he is fighting against. They don't wear uniforms—they just haul ammunition. The first time he goes to Viet Tri he will be shot at from the "hospital," but that will not come as a surprise. He must be accurate. Even if he gets in the life-or-death spot, the Thud driver will avoid the population. I cannot guarantee the precise detonation point of every bomb that has left every one of our aircraft over the North, but I can guarantee that I have never seen a Thud driver guilty of wanton bombing. We had several who should have toggled their loads but did not because the bombs would not have gone on their target. They got killed for their trouble.

By the time he learns enough Thai to know that *nit noy* means "a little thing" and *C H I Dooey* means "sorry about that," he will be through the first ten and ready to go against the North. The first time he pulls into the arming area as a member of a big strike force and watches the modified two-place F-105 Fs take off with their Wild Weasel crews intent on killing the Sams, who will be trying to kill him, his mouth will be unbelievably dry. Perhaps Sam will seek him out, or perhaps a Mig will put on a little air show for him and send a heat-seeking Atol missile his way. Perhaps a comrade will fall, and if the comrade is fortunate enough to get his parachute open, the automatically activated electronic emergency beeper will etch its screech on his memory forever. For sure the guns will fire on him, and for sure he will be impressed as he moves along Thud Ridge and uses North Vietnam's own terrain to mask or block the view of the radar operators on the other side.

He will feel like a big man when he gets back from that first one up North, and that he is.

2.

THE THUD

To the men who fought there, the string of small mountains that stretches like a long bony finger to the north and west of Hanoi is known as Thud Ridge. From Hanoi's view the ridge must have been a geographical indicator that pointed out the direction from which the attacking fighter-bombers would approach the heartland of North Vietnam. For me, as an attacking fighter pilot, Thud Ridge was one of the few easily identifiable landmarks in the hostile North, marking the route to the modern fighter pilot's private corner of hell—the fierce defenses and the targets of downtown Hanoi.

Thud Ridge sometimes poked its scrubby peaks through the mist and clouds that hung almost incessantly over the area to tell me the weather would never let me get to my target that day. Sometimes Thud Ridge provided shelter from some of the piercing radar eyes of the enemy as I streaked past its sides, leading my companions as low and as fast as I dared to go. To those of us engaged in this most demanding facet of this most peculiar of all wars, Thud Ridge, once we saw it, always served as a reminder that we were among the privileged few to take part in the grimmest contest yet conceived between sophisticated air and ground machinery

and people. This singular piece of real estate is the locale of
the statistics that have appeared in many a newspaper, and its
slopes and peaks now hold the carcasses of the majority of our
aircraft classified as "missing in action." The F-105, affectionately
known to her pilots as the "Thud," carried the bulk of the
load against Hanoi from the very start, and these machines
and their pilots daily rechristened Thud Ridge.

Someone must tell the story of Thud Ridge and as there are
so few of us who have had the opportunity to tell it from the
firsthand vantage point of the seat of a Thud over Hanoi, I
feel something resembling a duty to set the story down as I
see it. It is more than a duty. It is a desire to give perma-
nence to some of the briefing room jazz that flows so wonder-
fully from pilot to pilot, never to be registered again except
over a cool one in the stag bar or through the medium of a
less vivid conversation when two comrades in arms meet
again after months or years. It is never quite the same the
second or third time around. Those of us who were in this
thing all went different ways within a short time after our
most personal involvement in fighting and surviving. The
rapid changes in surroundings and people either dim or
brighten the remembrance of the events. And, oh so often,
there is just no time to spend in re-creating the feelings when
you meet that old wingman again years later. He is rushing
past your life, you are rushing past his, and the chance
meeting is never satisfactory. It is sure good to see old
so-and-so but—got to run—see you again soon—if you are
ever in town, give me a call and the wife and I will have you
out to dinner; it just isn't the same.

I have lived this story day and night for what now seems
like most of my conscious life. I entered West Point shortly
after I turned seventeen, and after an accelerated course that
crammed the normal curriculum plus flying training into an
unbelievably compact three years, I pinned my wings and
bars on my tunic and found myself in the middle of the
fascinating world of fighter aircraft and fighter people. I have
flown every operational fighter plane the Air Corps, and later
the Air Force, has owned, from the P-47 to the F-106—with
one exception: I never got to fly the F-94, and by the time I
recognized that fact, it was a museum piece. (I understand I
did not miss too much.) I have about as many fighter hours as
anyone, and as I was fortunate enough to break into the jet

set early in 1949, my jet fighter time and experience puts me
right on top of that heap too. It all adds up to 216 fighter
combat missions, but the sense of accomplishment is tempered by the humility you learn from leading your people
and equipment into the caldron of aerial combat.

I have also had a part in helping develop the skills and
techniques that have made the jet fighter a formidable weapons system. We started the process in Nevada with the
Lockheed F-80 "Shooting Star," when we reopened the des-
ert gunnery school in 1948. I learned a great deal about
precision and about extracting the maximum from man and
machine as I led the Air Force acrobatic team, the Thunderbirds,
from 1954 through 1957. Every time I was due to move on
from that job I managed to wangle a new and faster aircraft
from the inventory and accept new challenges that culminated
in 1956 with the world's first supersonic precision acrobatic
unit. I reveled in the challenges of making the electronically
complex F-106 and her pilots perform with distinction through
three windswept, subzero winters in Minot, North Dakota,
and I wept when I lost superior people because I had not yet
fought hard enough to rid the Air Force of the F-106's
bugaboos, among them the killer ejection seat. (My Air Force
career almost terminated during a few emotional shouting
matches about this ejection seat in 1964, but we did clean up
the F-106 and for the moment reliability and pilot survival
triumphed over sterile and unduly complicated engineering
and manufacturing techniques.) I even found minuscule areas
of satisfaction in the professional education programs that
have led me to a master's degree in the various military and
civilian halls of knowledge, but when I completed the National War College in 1965, I knew that the thing I wanted most
was to get back with my fighter guys in the real big league of
the air war over North Vietnam.

Surprisingly, this was not the easiest thing to accomplish.
There always seems to be someone around who wants to
manage your career for you, and while I had been relatively
successful in the past in dodging the snares of the personnel
specialists intent on saddling me with innocuous jobs, I found
it much harder to do as a colonel. There are many, many
positions, especially in the Washington area, that are filled by
virtue of the colonel rank and with little attention to experience.
If you engage in a few casual conversations around Washington,

Convair F-106 "Delta Dart"

you will find that the productive output from these positions is quite often inversely proportional to the amount of assembled rank and the length of the job title. The Air Force has established a section known as the Colonels' Assignments Branch and their unrewarding task is to select round colonels to fit all the square boxes on all the organizational charts hung throughout the world. The high-level service schools, such as the National War College, are most lucrative hunting grounds for these personnel specialists, and while many prospective selectees succumb to the headquarters pressure, there are some who fight it. There is, however, no guarantee that the fighter will avoid the assignment that he considers less than an honor, and the career implications demand that the fighter use deftness in the attack lest he offend the one he may wind up being assigned to.

The rationale behind the decision to fight or not is quite simple. Once you have a few years under your belt as a colonel you have to make a basic decision. If your prime goal in life is to become a general officer, your best odds, by far, come from going the big staff route. If you fight to stay with operational command in the action areas of the world you will find yourself less liable for promotion, and recent selections give credence to the thought that the farther you are removed from the battle, the better off you are, at least in terms of your career. Even in an organization designed around airplanes and people, the support expert and the politician regularly outdistance the combat leader in striding toward the highest-level positions. In my case, while I was still at the National War College, I was interviewed for two positions that were clearly oriented toward the easy, nonoperational route to promotion. Early in the school year I managed to wriggle out of an assignment to an administrative position in charge of the General Officers' Assignment Section. (The incumbent was promoted to brigadier general a few months later.) Two months after that it looked like I was hooked for sure on the second interview, and I received a set of printed orders that told me I was designated as Chief of Plans, Office of Legislative Liaison, Headquarters, United States Air Force. It just did not seem to me that the assignment was the best place for a forty-year-old colonel with a wealth of jet fighter experience and a burning desire to go and fight another war. My maneuver in personnel banditry took some discreet handling and still almost blew up in my face. But although I came close enough to the new and unwanted assignment to attend a welcoming cocktail party, I managed to pull off a last-minute switch and the day I graduated from the National War College I headed for Southeast Asia.

I spent my first year there assigned to a fighter wing whose home base was in Japan. Normally a fighter wing can best be described as a unit of up to five thousand people who are all responsive to some need of the three fighter squadrons assigned within that wing. The squadrons are the small, semi-independent units—each owning about twenty fighter aircraft—which actually accomplish the job involving the pilot and the aircraft. With the complexities of current equipment, the squadrons would not survive very long without the direct support of all the specialists within the wing structure. Usually the wing commander, his assistant or vice-commander, and selected members of the wing staff are seasoned fighter pilots who inherit an administrative command by virtue of their position, and who sometimes earn an operational responsibility and respect through their airborne accomplishments.

The basic operating unit in the fighter business is a flight made up of four individual aircraft. The flight leader is the eyes, ears and brain of his three charges and maintains absolute authority in flight. Each of the two-ship elements making up the flight maneuvers in close proximity to the other so as to provide the mutual support and protection that are essential when the shooting starts. The man who taught

me this game, Gen. C. T. (Curley) Edwinson, impressed me
from the start with flight discipline. I went where he went,
and I fully accepted his edict that if he flew into the ground
there would be three holes alongside his.

Fighters may attack in a single flight of four, or several
flights of four may be committed to a single attack in what is
termed a strike. In attacking the Hanoi area we usually used
about five of these four-ship flights to make up a twenty-ship
strike effort. The individual flights in a strike maintain their
integrity and their leadership, but—as in the flight structure—
they support and respond to the lead man in the lead flight.
The wing draws the outline of the mission and the squadrons
fill out the strike force with aircraft and pilots. The wing
designates the strike force commander, and while this is not
necessarily pegged to rank or job position, in our wing the
leaders on the ground were the leaders in the air. The man in
the number one aircraft assumes complete control of and
responsibility for the wing effort, and from the time when,
two to three hours before the first engine turns, he gathers
his people together to brief them as to what he will do and
what he expects, until the last engine is shut down after the
mission, those men and machines are his and his alone.

When you are on the wing staff, as I was, you are assigned
to a particular squadron for the purpose of flying your missions.
We always tried to balance the assignments so that each of
these squadrons had about the same number of wing weenies
assigned since we did cut down the number of missions
available to the primary duty squadron pilots. I am sure that
often they felt they were carrying a load, but in our case, all
of our staff people were highly qualified, not only in the
aircraft, but in the overall business of fighter combat. This
function of flying with the squadrons was a most vital portion
of the operation of a good wing. To do the job properly, you
had to lead by example. This is true in most fields of endeavor,
but it is of greater importance when you are directing a
life-or-death effort. You had to put your leaders out in front
and show your people how you wanted the job done, then
insist that they do it your way. If you did not lead well, or if
you did not have your people following you to the letter,
pilots got hurt and aircraft were lost. Nowhere was this
truism more valid than in the Hanoi area. There was simply
no room for error. Those who made mistakes—and even

many who did everything properly—ended up dead or as guests at the Hanoi Hilton.

To lead well in this environment, you had to be a perfect combination of automatic responses and flexibility. Automatic because you had to develop a precise plan and lock the details inside you so as to spill out without conscious demand. Much of this was accomplished through target study and through the premission briefing that you, as the leader of the strike, gave all of your pilots. It was like getting yourself ready for a final exam every time you went North. All of the detailed information needed to chart the course to the target and put the aircraft in the precise position to put the bombs on the target was catalogued and stored by intelligence specialists assigned to the wing, and the specifics for a particular mission were sorted out a half day in advance by the pilots who would fly that mission. Because you had to be capable of switching your effort to alternate targets in the event that weather or some other factor caused you to divert, the mass of papers and maps that we lugged to the pilots' briefing was terrific. You could almost fill the cockpit with the paperwork, yet it was all necessary because you had to have specific alternate places to put those bombs if necessary. North Vietnamese noise about wanton bombings is sheer nonsense.

Once the maps and charts were in order, it was no small task to digest the information in front of you. I found it helpful to go over the general plan of attack in conjunction with the leaders of the other flights within my strike force and also the members of my particular lead flight. Then I found it mandatory to withdraw after this initial planning phase and study alone. You simply had to drill on details. I considered myself prepared to lead a strike only when I could recite my complete route from takeoff to the target and back, with the compass headings, airspeeds, altitudes, call signs of other units and a dozen other details. As I recited this to myself, I also had to be able to visualize a map presentation of the route I was to follow. After a few mental trips through the area, I would insist that my mind's eye be able to conjure up a picture of the exact terrain features that I would see.

I had a map hung on the wall in my office that was 10 feet high and 20 feet wide and covered the entire Hanoi-Thud Ridge area. It was a 1 to 50,000 scale and thus showed each

peak and valley on Thud Ridge, each bend and turn in the
canals and roads and the outline of towns and villages. I
paced back and forth in front of this map, flying the mission
with my hands. I entered the area, turned down Thud Ridge,
cleared the Russian-built, Russian-installed and Russian-advised
surface-to-air missile sites—known to us as Sam—avoided the
heaviest flak concentrations, streaked past the Russian- and
Chinese-built Migs at Phuc Yen, spotted my lead-in indicators,
whether they were roads, rivers or towns, made last-minute
adjustments in my airspeed, rechecked my armament settings,
started my pull-up to gain altitude and better see my target,
rolled in on the target (even in the dry runs I visualized the
areas I had better avoid, knowing that they would be black
with flak), examined the target in detail, rolled my beast into
a breathtaking 45-degree dive, picked my aiming point based
on the winds I had been given, went through the activation of
switches required to drop the bombs, and pulled my guts
through the bottom of the seat to avoid the ground and the
guns, relighting the burner and following my specific landmarks as I egressed, jinking, rolling, climbing and diving to
present the worst possible target to the enemy. When I was
mentally back out of the target area, I paced some more and
started all over again. I found that about two hours of this
preparation put me in pretty good shape for any one target.
With this degree of prestudy, I could concentrate on looking
and reacting, and the details automatically fell into place.

Yet I had to be flexible as well as automatic because it was
not too often that everything fell neatly into place. Somebody,
often me, was always nursing a sick aircraft. Some of the
complex systems were always out of their advertised best
form and any strike can well be affected by one sick bird. The
weather was a terrific factor and could cause you to alter your
route or your entire plan. The Thud was not a straight and
level bomber like the B-17s and B-24s of World War II, nor
was it optimized for all-weather, night harassment. These
facts often seemed to escape some of our high level leaders.
But if you are going to employ a tactical weapon like the
F-105 in a strategic bombing role, which was what we were
doing, then you have to use a little imagination in order to
survive and still complete a meaningful strike effort. If you
dragged your force in too low, the ground fire got them. If you
brought them in too high, where the Mig was in his preferred

envelope, he could force you to lighten your aircraft for better performance by jettisoning your bombs, lest he outmaneuver you and shoot you down. If you flew straight and level, without terrain masking, either in clouds or in the clear, the Sam could get you if the enemy wanted you badly enough to fire. If you flew on the top of an undercast, you couldn't see Sam when he launched, and if he accelerated and came bursting out of the clouds unannounced, he most probably would gobble you up.

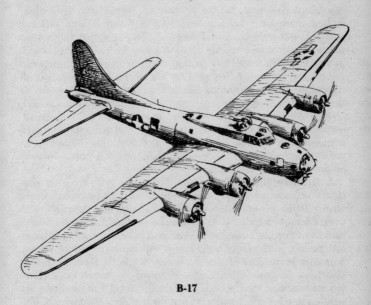

B-17

When I was there, we flew taking advantage of these truisms and our know-how. They now have standard rules and standard tactics directed from a headquarters thousands of miles away. But in that environment, the true payoff depends on the airborne smarts and tactical flying skill of the mission leader and his team. Nothing else will get the job done right with minimum losses, but unfortunately the only ones who

know this are those who have been there, or those who will
listen to those who have been there. I am constantly amazed
at the number of instant experts who have lost the ability to
listen. The North Vietnamese don't read the academic studies
done in Washington or Honolulu and they don't understand
or respect the great straight and level strategic bombing
prowess that many of our current leaders acquired in the
1940s; they don't know they are not supposed to shoot down
standardized, headquarters-directed and stereotyped flights.
I shudder when I think of the worthless loss of people and
machines this ironclad party line of stupid and inflexible
tactical ignorance has caused. I understand fighter tactics,
and I've been there, and I feel very strongly that the astro-
nomical and unacceptable fighter losses, which skyrocketed
in the latter part of 1967 to double their previous numbers,
were largely due to ineptness, dictatorial enforcement of
minuscule and incorrect details of tactical mission accomplishment, and lack of good sense and understanding of the actual
air-war situation in the North on the part of command
leadership at a high military level. I could well pursue this
subject in detail and may do so later. For now, I note it in
passing and return to the healthy and stimulating atmosphere
of the air war at wing level.

It is important that you know the people you fly with and
that you know what they are doing. This does not come from
sitting in an air-conditioned office and clucking sternly over
unimportant details. It comes from getting hot and sweaty
and from getting your fanny shot at. There is no way to shake
out people and procedures except by being a part of them.
You only learn part of the game when you fly the easy ones;
you have to take at least your share of the tough ones. The
troops watched that schedule pretty closely. They knew who
was leading for effect and who was for real, and they responded
accordingly.

The best way to get this togetherness was to work generally
with the same group of pilots and definitely in the same
squadron. It can be argued that we all should know the same
basic job and we are all the same black box that is plugged
into the rest of the machinery and thus it should make no
difference who flies with whom on any specific mission. I
suppose this theory might have some validity in some sections of the flying forces, the realm from which it originated,

CHINA

CHINA

Nanning

Red River

Black River

Hanoi

Haiphong

GULF OF TONKIN

NORTH VIETNAM

HAINAN (CHINA)

Vinh

SOUTH CHINA SEA

Vientiane

L A O S

Udorn

T H A I L A N D

Mekong River

Hue

Da Nang

Takhli (Col. Broughton's Wing Base)

Korat (Avis Wing Base)

Bankok

C A M B O D I A

GULF OF SIAM

SOUTH VIETNAM

Phnom Penh

Saigon

Tan Son Nhut Airbase

MEKONG DELTA

SOUTHEAST ASIA

Scale of Miles
0   50   100

and probably any big airplane driver can move his monster from point A to B and back as well as another; it isn't so in the fighter business. Anyone who has played ball knows that there are combinations based on talent and the experience of working together that get the job done better. It was even more so in this big league.

Any specific fighter wing can be assigned many tasks outside its basic mission of launching a combat effort. My first year in Southeast Asia centered around our wing's role as mother hen for a new fighter base emerging from the green jungle of Thailand. Our task was to maintain our basic combat posture, and at the same time to provide the pilots, aircraft, support equipment and support people to conduct combat strikes out of Takhli, Thailand, until we could physically establish a wing that could stand on its own down there. While this was being accomplished, I shuttled back and forth from Japan to Thailand, and when the job was finished I moved into the new wing for full-time duty.

I had not been the only one involved in building a new wing or a new base. From the time of the Gulf of Tonkin incident, it became clear that America was committed to an extensive air effort in North Vietnam and that facilities had to be expanded rapidly to accommodate this effort. South Vietnam was about to sink into the sea from the sheer weight of the American effort there, and was not the place for new airfield construction or expansion. While we stewed under the wraps of security, the news media of the world had little difficulty pinpointing our effort in Thailand. It was well into 1967 before formal press visits to the Thai bases were sanctioned, and even then the clearance was not universal, but the world was informed that we were operating Republic-built F-105 fighter-bombers out of our location at Takhli, Thailand, while the Avis wing was operating the same type of aircraft further to the east at Korat, Thailand. The McDonnell RF-101 recon-naissance aircraft and newer additions to the lineup (the fighter and reconnaissance versions of the McDonnell F-4C) were visible to the press from Udorn, Thailand, to Da Nang and Saigon in South Vietnam. The rescue helicopters and their slow but sturdy propeller-driven escorts, the Douglas A1E, were dispersed wherever they would stand the best chance of dashing into hostile territory to recover a downed airman. The giant airborne command and control aircraft, which could help you with a radar vector when they were in flight, and the huge Boeing KC-135 tanker aircraft were very obviously in place when the press entered the scene, and in case there was any doubt in anyone's mind, their presence confirmed the fact that current fighter-bomber aircraft needed to refuel in flight when they were committed to the North with their heavy bombloads. This the North Vietnamese already knew since their radar watched us daily as we refueled in flight and headed their way without the benefit of surprise.

Thus our force was in place to operate from Thailand to North Vietnam. We had Thuds to strike the enemy and we had either bombing or Mig escort help from the F-4C "Phantoms." We had tankers to help us keep the fighters full of gas. Our reconnaissance aircraft could take target photographs before and after raids and our choppers, which needed their A1E escorts (we called them Spads, because the A1E's age and performance approached that of the World War I machine with the same nickname), could sometimes get in and out of enemy territory to accomplish a rescue. Except for occasional equipment modification, the buildup of the force that was to fight in the North was complete and we were ready to probe the Hanoi area.

Fighter pilots call their aircraft birds, and each of our birds has had a name that has sought to point toward some potentially great feature of the machine. The "Thunderbolt," the "Lightning," the "Sabre," were perfect matches of name and appearance. Yet there we were, striking the toughest targets in history, and what were we calling our number one aerial machine of the day? The Thud. Without a doubt, that is the single most unattractive moniker ever attached to a winged craft.

Actually the F-105's given name was the "Thunderchief." It came from the publicity office of its manufacturer, Republic Aviation Corporation, and the name stuck for a while during the long struggle that any machine must go through from the drawing board to the flight line. The Thud came from a long line of good aircraft. They have always been comparatively big, heavy, sturdy and most capable of doing the job they were designed for. They have never been the lightweight, turn-on-a-dime delight of the acrobatic champion, but then they were never built to be. The P-47, nicknamed the Jug, with its big radial engine out front, did its job in World War

Republic P-47 "Thunderbolt"

II and the first time I strapped a Jug to me I thought it was
the biggest thing I had ever seen. I saw a restored Jug at
Wright-Patterson Air Force Base a couple of years ago, and
by then it looked like a little bird. The Jug was as true as they
come and after some eight hundred hours of flying time in it I
had learned my first lesson in respect for Republic products.

After the Jug came the Republic F-84 series of jet fighter
aircraft, some of which were good, some not so good. Some
of them earned names like Super Hog and Lieutenant Eater
and none of the pilots felt at all bad when one series of the
F-84 was hauled away on flatbed railroad cars and used as
targets for fire-power demonstrations. Other models were
superb, such as the ones I used in Korea to test a new
air-to-ground rocket after I had finished my Korean tour in
F-80s and the ones we used as our first aircraft in the
acrobatic demonstration team.

The Thud did not do too well at the start as the birds were

plagued with problems in both the airframe and the engine. It is a complicated machine and in many supply and mainte- nance areas we were not prepared to handle this degree of sophistication. The constant struggle to keep the early models in the air did not go without notice and the unromantic Ultra Hog was a natural name which stuck for some time. One of the saddest days in the Thud's history followed the Air Force's efforts to modernize the aerial demonstration team— the Thunderbirds—and enhance the sagging reputation of the Thud at the same time. Unfortunately, there was a lack of proper homework in the selection and assignment of specific aircraft to the demonstration team and the venture was unknowingly doomed from the start. My old command, the Thunderbirds—with my old acrobatic wingman and dearest friend, Lucky Palmgren, at the helm—worked their hearts out getting the show and the people ready. The stripped- down bird performed beautifully and the tremendous engine power and the skill of the pilots resulted in a demonstration that amazed almost everybody. The Thud turned, looped and rolled with the utmost grace, and everything looked rosy. On the first trip, Gene Devlin, one of the team members, streaked in over the runway at Hamilton Air Force Base. As he pitched out of formation to land, the aircraft suffered a major structural failure that should have been detected beforehand. One of our best men was killed, shocking many spectators and fellow pilots throughout the world. That was the end of the Thud as far as the Thunderbirds were con- cerned and the Ultra Hog was a tough item to defend.

But for the challenge of the air war in the North, I guess the Thud would show in most people's books as a loser. Struggling under a bombload that was huge for a fighter, the Thud waded into the thick of the fray and those not in the know coined the name Thud—with all its derogatory connota- tions. But gradually a startling fact became apparent—the Thud was getting to North Vietnam as nothing else could. Nobody could keep up with the Thud as it flew at high speed on the deck, at treetop level. Nobody could carry that load and penetrate those defenses except the Thud. Sure we lost a bundle of them and lost oh so many superior people along with the machines, but we were the only people doing the job, and we had been doing it from the start. There were other aircraft carrying other loads and performing other functions, pushing a lesser portion of explosives to the North, but it was the old Thud that day after day, every day, lunged into that mess, outdueled the opposition, put the bombs on the target and dashed back to strike again. Any other vehicle in anybody's Air Force simply could not have done the job.

The record of the Thud versus the Mig bears additional comment. It can be a bit difficult to knock down a clear-weather, air-to-air fighter, such as the Mig, with a heavy, complex fighter-bomber, and that's not the primary job of a fighter-bomber anyway. Thuds have knocked down more Migs than any other aircraft in Southeast Asia but only a few Thuds have fallen before Mig attack. The Thud has made an impression on even those flying for North Vietnam—whoever they may be. Yes, the Thud has justified herself, and the name that was originally spoken with a sneer has become one of utmost respect throughout the air fraternity.

I want to tell you about the Thud drivers. I want you to feel and see some of what they felt and saw. I want you to see some of the things this highly experienced group of combat pilots, whose average age was thirty-five, fought for and fought against. I want to give you a feel for the way those of us who devoted our careers to fighter aircraft and their tactical employment wanted to do the job and I want to expose you to the oversupervision and the costly, restrictive attitudes imposed by our strategically or administratively oriented supervisors.

How do the Thud drivers and their charges fit in with what's going on in Southeast Asia? To begin with, there were at least four separate and completely different air wars (if you disregard the spooky stuff, which we will not talk about). There was a war in the South; a support war; a war in the easy part of the North; and the tough air war of the far North. First of all, there was the war down South, the bitter and ill-defined struggle that made all the magazines and papers day after day, the war in support of the crunchies slogging back and forth in the practice of the second oldest profession. It was the war of air strikes against specific positions in conjunction with ground force attacks. It was an all-day and all-night air war conducted close to the home airport of the fighter and in a quite permissive atmosphere—permissive in the sense that you could make mistakes and talk about them

later. For instance, if you got zingoed on your ninth strafing
pass on the same target by some guy with a pistol, you had a
good chance of riding home in a chopper—in one piece. Your
air discipline could bend and you could still get the job done
with only a slight chance of really grim results. While intense
supervision and countless restrictions made the pilots' jobs
demanding, they didn't have any Sams or Migs to trouble
them. They lived sort of dirty—but they didn't have to fight
too dirty. Their aircraft and pilot loss rate was less than the
loss rate in the training program in the States.

Another war in the air of Southeast Asia that you should be
exposed to is what I refer to as the support war. This was a
vast operation, and the tonnages hauled and the sick and
healthy people shuttled back and forth were quite impressive.
The formal military airlift program expanded to monstrous
proportions and seemed to be getting the job done. The
heavy reliance on civilian carriers must have made lots of
people happy, but many of the military people got just as
unhappy with this government-sponsored civilian airlift scheme,
especially when they stood on one foot and then the other,
wanting to get somewhere and then saw a civilian superjet
going to their desired destination devoid of anything but crew
and stews; they couldn't get on board because they were not
on "funded" orders.

In other words, the U. S. paid for the aircraft and the crew,
and the military airlift people controlled the booking, but the
same military people would not fill an empty seat with a
military man from Thailand who had a few days off unless he
was on official ("funded") business. Seems sort of silly to hire
a vehicle and run it at less than the maximum capacity. The
crew couldn't have cared less, but the rules were the rules. It
was definitely half a war in many commonsense areas like
this. The people in Thailand had none of the goodies such as
Rest and Recreation—R and R, that is—so the combat crews
who fought the air war over Hanoi were *personae non gratae*
with the Military Airlift Command people.

Local unit support fits into this picture and a great mass of
people not assigned to the formal military airlift effort were
involved in flying the original C-47 gooney bird or some more
sophisticated model thereof. Each unit and headquarters had
many runs that just had to be made, rather like running the

family car to the drugstore, the post office, and so on. We
needed them, and there were many highly dedicated people
in this endeavor, but there were some there who never
seemed to make the combat team and who adhered closely to
the business-as-usual approach, no matter what the operation—
and even they managed an air medal now and then. I don't
envy them and I think that support flying is not so pretty
good. I wouldn't change places for anything.

C-47

Next in this tour is the third air war, the easy route
packages—the Thud driver's definition of the southern parts
of North Vietnam. North Vietnam was divided into six
numbered areas, from 1 in the south to 6 in the north. This
was a matter of administrative convenience, but the intensity
of the defenses went up with the Route Package number. The
easy southern Route Packages have cost many a man and
many a machine, but although they could be most deceptive,
those who fought their war there did not face the ever-
present pressure for split-second timing, and the exposure
rate allowed more ease of maneuver without the Sam and
Mig threat. We used that area as check-out grounds for our
new F-105 sports. A pilot needs a few rides to get in shape,

just like an athlete, and this was the place for our warm-ups. You can get into real trouble on the simplest of combat missions (I guess even our B-52 crews faced some problems, like stepping on each other's fingers reaching for the coffeepot and things like that). The BUF's have been this far north a few times, while the world stood still, the monkeys trembled and the toothpick manufacturers cursed their ill-chosen, old-fashioned production methods. (BUF stands for big ugly fellows in polite conversation, but is suitably amplified in true fighter conversation. This terminology irritated the big load drivers, and the Strategic Air Command general in charge of their operation issued an edict that the B-52 "Stratofortress" was not to be referred to as a BUF. His edict received amazingly little attention outside the strategic empire.) It is great sport to barb our fellow aviators on their operational areas, and there are many who would respond eagerly should the bell ring for something better, but face it we must, the toughest area for the BUFs and for many fighters other than the F-105 was our training ground. It was where we went when operational conditions were unacceptable in the big league.

And the fourth air war was the big league. The true air war in the North. The desperate assault and parry over the frighteningly beautiful, green-carpeted mountains leading down into the flat delta of the Red River. The center of hell with Hanoi as its hub. The area that was defended with three times the force and vigor that protected Berlin during World War II. The home of the Sam and the Mig, the filthy orange-black barking 100-millimeter and 85-millimeter guns, the 57- and 37-millimeter gun batteries that spit like a snake and could rip you to shreds before you knew it, the staccato red-balled automatic weapons that stalked the straggler who strayed too low on pullout from a bomb run, and the backyard of the holders of rifles and pistols who lay on their backs and fired straight up at anyone foolish or unfortunate enough to stumble into view. This was the locale of Thud Ridge.

For those of us who fought there, geography was a basic fact of life. On the west, the Red River meanders out of the mountains and valleys that form the northern extremity of North Vietnam and the southern flank of Communist China. Nine-thousand-foot mountain peaks that are cut in places like the teeth of a giant saw lie to the southwest of the Red and separate it from its parallel traveling companion, the Black River. The stark peaks, deep river gorges and green unrelenting jungle were something to see from the air at 500 knots plus—that's the only way. Our area of concern started along the Red River slightly north of a place we called the Brassiere, a well-defined pair of hooks in the river surrounding the viscous little town of Yen Bai. As a fighter pilot, you couldn't work too far north of there without taking the chance of stepping on your necktie along the Chinese-border buffer zone, an unpardonable sin. I guess we are not giving away too much in operable infantry-type ground in our self-imposed buffer zone, a big fat 30-mile-wide strip of mountain territory that follows the Chinese border all the way across North Vietnam to the Gulf of Tonkin, but it does include many heavily traveled roads and rail lines stretching to the border of China and it provides a sizable hunk of free airspace for Mig sanctuary when things are not going the Migs' way.

Yen Bai was one of the Thud drivers' pet dislikes. It has the reputation of being Ho Chi Minh's hometown and the way they shot from there you'd think it was manned by the Turkish brigade protecting Ataturk's tomb. Maybe they had a statue of Ho down there—they sure seemed to be protecting something. I have been there many times and from the air it seemed that all you were battling was the guns. The rail line was dumpy and beaten up and the roads were dirt, as they are most everywhere in North Vietnam (don't let those lines on the map representing roads fool you). Regardless of what they were protecting, Yen Bai was not the spot to wander over, or even near. If you came within a few miles, they would shoot and shoot hard, whether they had the slightest chance of hitting you or not. I swung about 3 miles north of there while inbound to a target one day and they opened up with everything they had despite the fact that we were far out of their range. The situation gave me the opportunity to study the ground defense pattern with relative impunity and I believe they were simply shooting straight up in the air. They unleashed volley after volley and the muzzle blasts of the big guns sparkled clearly from all sides of the town and from the center. The smaller-caliber guns spat from around every house in town and the place looked like a giant short circuit, yet all the bursts were directly over the top of Yen Bai

and far from us. They were still shooting as they faded behind
us and I often wondered how much of that jagged metal fell
back on top of their heads. Maybe that was why they were
always so mad up there—they shot straight up and clobbered
themselves.

From Yen Bai the Red swings south and nuzzles up to the
karst—a geologist's word meaning sharp, rough hills—and
breaks away to take the big dip past Phu Tho. Phu Tho was
pretty much the start of the big circle that surrounded the
hot area—the area that was always dangerous. You could fly
near it one day and not see a puff while the next day the sky
would blacken at your approach. You could never relax for an
instant from there into Hanoi, and you always had to be
prepared for drastic action. Continuing to the southeast, the
Black swings up from Hoa Binh, a dandy little center of
activity for people and supplies located on busy Route 6;
passes the airfield at Hoa Lac; and then flows past the
reservoir and joins the Red just before the series of curves,
bends, and twists that identify Viet Tri from 20 miles out on a
clear day. There were not too many clear days, but those
river junctions were a welcome crutch in solving tough
navigational problems. Once past Viet Tri the hot area spreads
southward following the karst to about Nam Dinh and thence
due east to the Gulf of Tonkin. You couldn't be very comfortable along the coast up past Haiphong to the edge of the
buffer zone around Ile Ba Mun, unless you could take solace
in all the big, fat boats of many nations rolling contentedly as
they awaited their turn to unload in the harbor. It was
amazing how familiar some of those flags looked. That must
have been a lucrative shipping business.

Starting inland from the Gulf of Tonkin side of the buffer
zone, the truest outline of the hot area runs past the Mig air
base at Kep, thence past Thai Nguyen and back to Yen Bai.
The long mountain ridge that originates about halfway between Thai Nguyen and Yen Bai and stretches out like a
finger pointed to the southeast and aimed at Hanoi is Thud
Ridge. Thud Ridge because so many of our trusty mounts
have flown their last into its side? Thud Ridge because it
pretty well split the delta and pointed to Hanoi? Thud Ridge
because it stood out clearly in that hostile land where high-
speed, low-level fighter pilots needed an anchor, and where

that corner of the war was reserved almost exclusively for the Thud driver? Take your choice. I am sure the North Vietnamese have their name for it, but Thud Ridge it shall ever be in the annals of the fighter pilots.

3.

VETERANS DAY

On Veterans Day my amigo Art drew a target way up there
and we all knew it could be rough. Mine was south of his and
we led separate flights. From the forecast we knew the
weather would be sour, and he drew the roughest weather to
match his rough target. It was the long way around and the
best that could be expected was a grueling trip both ways
with the stiffest of opposition at the midpoint. You can hear
almost everybody in the world on the aircraft radio, and even
though you are intent on your own job the old mental
computer subconsciously keeps track of the entire effort; this
day it all sounded bad. All elements of the defenses were up
and there was sheer panic in many of the voices issuing from
the area of Thud Ridge. When you are in the middle of the
action you don't notice how tense everyone sounds, but they
always sound bad when you are not quite there or when you
have left and it is someone else's turn in the barrel. As Art's
section turned inbound from the coast, it became brutally
clear that things were very tense. Any place where there
wasn't a cloud, there was gunfire.

* * *

B-52

Art and his wife Pat are two of my favorite people. They
are the kind of people that I only need to meet once to know
that they are my kind of folks. Art and I were assigned to the
wing in Japan together for a while and Art was assigned to
almost every unit within our wing at one time or another.
Whenever things were in a state of change, which was most
of the time, he was one of those I would move from hot spot
to hot spot and he always did the job the way I wanted it
done. I guess he and I shared many of the same likes and
dislikes and had lots of the same prejudices during that time
period, so we got along just great. Both families are Episcopa-
lians and that tie also brought us together on several occasions.

Pat, a nurse prior to their marriage, had the formal handle
of Mary Ann and there is a lusty fighter-pilot ballad, by way
of England and the Royal Air Force, called "Mary Ann,
Queen of All the Acrobats." It happens to be one of my
favorites, goes well with the uke and is known and sung by
most of the fighter troops throughout the world. It is always
interesting to introduce her as Mary Ann and watch the sly
smiles of the singing fighter troops and it was only natural
that this lovely gal found the name Pat more to her liking.
She and AJ (my wife) became the best of friends. They both
had the talent for minding their own business and staying
clear of the politics of the Officers' Wives Club, which was no
small accomplishment on an Air Force Base.

Art had been down south in Thailand before on some
temporary duty stints and had a fair number of missions
under his belt when I left for reassignment down there. He
was trying as hard as I was to get back to the action and get

his full tour in before rotating back to the States. He was
most happy for me when I got my orders and, I am sure,
twice as determined to break loose and join me. Art and Pat
were most helpful as we packed up and went once again
through the normal idiot act that accompanies any military
move.

Just before we left Japan, AJ and the kids heading for
Hawaii to sweat it out for a year and I heading back to
Thailand, we spent the evening with Art and Pat in their
home. We had a few cocktails, and as Art and I were both
stereo fiends we examined his newest equipment and bickered
about the best combinations of speakers, tape decks and the
like. After a great meal AJ and I left for home amid the
familiar farewells exchanged between pilots' families. Art
handed me an envelope with two sheets of paper in it. One
had the addresses of the wives of several of our mutual
buddies who had been zapped into an unknown status while
flying missions down south; the other sheet is one of the most
valued treasures that I own. Written in his own hand was his
token to me, his true friend launching into a new effort. It is
an old prayer of the Church of England, from the Middle
Ages. As we stood in the dim yellow light of their front
porch, Art bowed from the waist in the most polite oriental
fashion and wished AJ well. AJ was a bit misty-eyed as we
walked home. She has not seen Art since.

The clouds increased and all flights except Art's were
forced to turn back. He thought he could make it and he
thought it was his duty to try, try, try. He pressed, despite
almost insurmountable obstacles, and he got to his target—
only to find it obscured by cloud. He still wouldn't quit and
arched his flight up through the high cloud above to gain the
altitude he would need to establish a steep and fast dive that
would assure maximum accuracy. Then over and down at 500
knots plus into the gray murk, and the big question was,
where is the bottom of the clouds and where is the ground
and where are the guns. They broke out of the clouds and
there was the target. But there also were the gunners with a
perfect altitude reference provided by the base of the clouds,
should some stupid American be brave enough to try them
that day. The gray murk of overcast cleared long enough to

get the desired sight picture by alligning the pipper in the center of the gunsight in proper reference to the target, then gave way to the black and orange overcast of the predicted 85-millimeter barrage, but the hurtling beasts were delivered of their bombs, which sought, found, and detonated squarely on target as the flight relit the burners, picked their way between the clouds and the mountains to avoid the still-pursuing guns, and dashed for the coast.

The perfectionist with the indomitable will had done it again, but something was wrong. The egress was too low. The clouds were too close to the hills and the aircraft were too close to the guns, too close to the small-arms fire. Suddenly Art commanded, "Take it down." Why? That is a reaction you would expect from a Sam launch against you. Nobody else had a Sam indication and there were no Sam calls at that moment. Did his equipment indicate a launch? Did he see something on the ground that indicated Sam launch to him and automatically triggered the response to seek the cover of the hills to protect his charges? Who knows, but down he went, into a hail of automatic weapons that ripped the belly of his aircraft to shreds. The fuel gushed, torched and covered the aircraft from cockpit to tail pipe; warning lights in the cockpit raced each other to call attention to each system's plight; the idiot panel turned amber; the fire panel glowed its sickening shade of red; control lines burst releasing their hydraulic lifeblood and one by one the systems began their methodical bleeding countdown to imminent control seizure and explosion.

But the old pro was not done for yet. He lit the burner and—clouds, Sams and Migs be damned—scratched for every ounce of altitude and speed he could get. Now the coast was only 30 miles away—the coast with the possibility of water bailout, Navy rescue craft and another chance. He got to 18,000 feet and 600 knots, and he could glide from there. He must have thought, if only the engine can outlast the fire for another minute—if only the last hydraulic system can scavenge enough fluid to let me steer for two minutes—if only. But the systems wouldn't hold. Violently she rolled to inverted position and the nose snapped through toward the hills far below. The safety of the water moved from under the nose and in front to under the belly and to the rear. She was all done.

* * *

I had not been in position at Takhli too long when Art got a chance to come down on temporary duty from my old fighter wing in Japan and finish up his one hundred missions. We were desperately short on flight leaders and the personnel pipeline just couldn't hack the course. He had previously flown with the same squadron I was assigned to, and I managed to engineer the assignments so that he rejoined the same unit. It took him no time whatsoever to get back in the swing of things and he and I flew together often—in fact, we got my first Distinguished Flying Cross of this war together. (Don't ever let anybody tell you that you get those things by yourself in this facet of the air-war business.) He was most precise in all that he did, and I liked to fly with him because we would alternate the lead position from day to day and he would always be the best critic in the business.

There is always room to improve combat techniques and when you stop trying to learn ways to do it better, you are asking for trouble. While this truism would appear obvious, it was generally ignored or lost within the multiple layers of command superimposed upon the operational units. The fighter pilots who were putting their lives on the line each day constantly found better ways to get the job done, but were seldom able to force their ideas up the line for acceptance. If you returned full of holes to criticize a concept as being impractical, and tried to offer a new approach, you could well wind up with a swat on the knuckles from a desk driver somewhere above you. Most of us learned quickly that change was not a welcome subject and we innovated as we felt necessary within our own realm of authority.

Art and I nit-picked each other until we were two of the best in the business. We generally did it over an exhausted cold beer in the sweaty squadron lounge. Sometimes we could not wait for that and I can clearly recall Art's rebuke on the radio one day as we moved and sought targets at 600 knots; "Get your butt back up—you're five hundred feet low." He was a perfectionist, and a good one.

As he headed into the stretch for the magic one hundred missions that would send him back to the States, Art took a five-day R and R and caught a ride back to Japan to spend a few days with the family. It seemed most appropriate, espe-

cially since a typhoon had ripped the roof off his house while
Pat and the children huddled in the corner. Nobody was hurt
and repair and replacement were not too difficult, but I am
sure the entire thing was scary for a gal in a strange land with
her guy in an even stranger one.

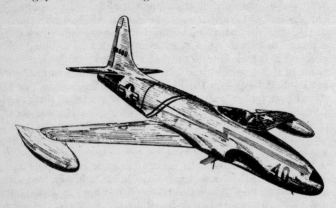

Lockheed F-80 "Shooting Star"

When I was up there in gayer times my fetish for parsley
was usually good for a giggle at squadron and wing parties. I
just like the stuff, and I have ever since we used to get beef
blood and parsley soup on the training table during football
season. It became apparent that I was one of the few who
gobbled up the parsley from the shrimp cocktail or the steak
and soon I was receiving donations at each dinner. It became
a monster, and there have been times when I had more parsley ceremoniously passed to me than I had steak. I tried to
keep up the front for a while but finally had to admit that
there was more parsley served in the officers' club than I
could possibly eat. Art came back from that R and R all full of
pep and ready for the stretch dash. The rest had been good
for him, but the big stimulus was the fact that he had
received the assignment he had requested and was was going
to Nellis Air Force Base in Las Vegas, Nevada, to work for an
old friend, John Black. He was overjoyed, and as each
mission ticked off he would rerun the plans—when he would

finish, when he would pick up the family, how long it would take to clear the quarters in Japan.

Pat had sent me a present—a carefully wrapped tin container with some number one cookies and, for her old parsley-eatin' buddy, fresh parsley sealed against the trip in waterproof bags. I don't think I have ever been more touched by a present, whatever its magnitude. But the timing was wrong, the elements were too strong, the flower had wilted, the parsley was rotten, and everything turned sour.

Off came the canopy and he got out with a good chute and a good beeper, the screeching electronic emergency signal that is activated when the chute opens. The guys followed him down and stayed as long as they could without losing another one to fuel starvation or enemy fire, and the Navy rescue guys gave it their usual superior college try, but we couldn't get him.

This was the curse of the Thud. She would go like a dingbat on the deck and she would haul a huge load, but she was prone to loss of control when the hydraulic system took even the smallest of hits. There is just no way to steer her once the fluid goes out, and I can tell you from bitter experience that you can lose two of the three hydraulic systems that run all of your flight controls by the time you realize you have been hit. Once they have a vent they are gone. We had been agitating like mad for a simple backup control, just something that would lock the controls in some intermediate area and give you a chance to keep her in the air by changing engine power. We didn't care about precision flying at this stage of an emergency, we just wanted something that would sustain flight to a safer bailout area. We finally got just such a system but too late in the game. If we had had such a modification at the start of this war we would most probably have at least one hundred fine pilots still with us who are now statistics. The modification came through too late for Art, and for want of a few thousand dollars worth of gear and some combat engineering and planning forethought, another prince was lost.

All the notification details are cumbersome and irritating at best. They are sheer torture when you truly know who you are advising and who you are advising about, but they have to be done. I even managed to badger a phone call through the multimillion-dollar communications confusion we own to talk to Pat. When we got to the other end of the 3,000-mile line, the last phone drop did us in and we couldn't hear each other. We relayed our sentiments through an airman on the switch-board who could hear both ends, and she was beautiful as always. Many letters have passed since, but one stands out. She wrote the squadron to tell them how proud Art was to have served with them, that he would serve again, and that she wanted to know what she could do for them when she got back to the States. I found out later that the big boss in Japan had not even bothered to call her on the telephone, much less go by and say hello. They didn't get along socially and besides, it was some sort of big holiday.

We brag of our concern for the families of those under stress. I don't believe it. I've seen the system stumble time after time, and I have seen letters to these gals addressed "Dear Next of Kin." This fine woman has received close to zero assistance or information since she returned to the States and she is not the only one in that situation. She received a telephone call recently advising her to watch television the following Saturday as there would be some films on prisoners, and to let them know if she thought one of the prisoners might be her husband. The poor woman stewed through Saturday and until Monday when the film finally appeared, then strained over the television picture through some of the most gruesome seconds of her life.

We could not go to her home with projection equipment or take her to a government facility with projection equipment and stop-frame that film and blow it up and give her a decent look. We could not even use our intelligence sources to tell her what to look for. We told the world why in a statement from Washington. The film was Communist tainted and we would not touch it. I wonder if the film is as tainted as the slop our guys have been living on the past few years. Absurd. I'm afraid she made a mistake in a letter she wrote to me when I returned to the States. She said in part, "It's just wonderful that Colonel Broughton is back and safe. I know that you won't forget those of us for whom the war will continue. . . ."

I still have the prayer Art gave me in Japan and I read it

nightly. Quite often it is all the emotional stimulus that I can
stand.

Lord of all power and might, Who art the Author and
Giver of all good things, mercifully grant us grace valiantly
to fight in Thy cause. Give us the sure conviction that Thou
art ever by our side. Grant us in battle unflinching courage
and an unconquerable spirit, so that no hurt nor obstacle
may ever deter us from our duty. And in victory, O Lord,
Grant us to be worthy of Thine everlasting love and to
continue Thy Faithful Soldiers and Servants unto our life's
end: and this we beg for Jesus Christ, His sake. *Amen*.

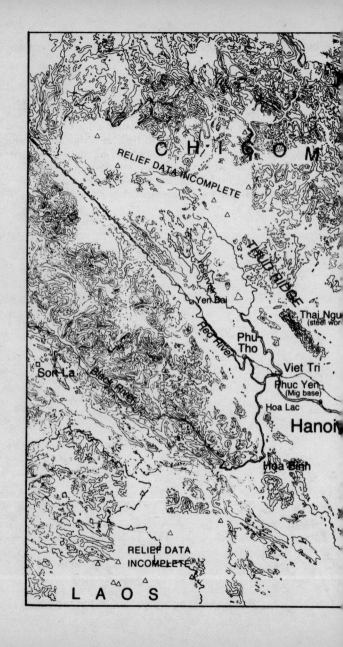

CHINA

Kep (Mig base)

Ile Ba Mun

Haiphong

GULF OF TONKIN

Nam Dinh

**THUD RIDGE AND
THE HANOI AREA**
Contour interval 100 feet
Scale of Miles
0 5 10 15 20 25

4.

KINGPIN THREE

The calendar rolled for a month and a basic change in our overall policy became apparent to us at the operating level when we were assigned a new series of targets. The United States was stepping up the pressure, even if only a little, and we knew it as we started studying maps and photos that told us we would probably get to attack closer to Hanoi sometime soon.

Each day Saigon would issue the many hundreds of tele-type pages that made up an Operations Order. Each contained the minutest of detail on times, headings, airspeeds, target coordinates and every conceivable nit for every aircraft that was to make a move in Southeast Asia. While we had to know what the other units were doing, we made our specific plans based upon the small fragment of this immense document that pertained to our wing operations. Thus, in our terminology, from within this fragment of the overall operations order, we were "fragged" to do thus and so each day. In other areas of the war fragging meant rolling a hand grenade into the boss' foxhole because you didn't like him. Sometimes, when we got a dumb target with directed approaches that dragged us through the toughest defenses, we thought Saigon was rolling the grenade our way.

While we knew we had a bundle of hot target information that we had to digest in intimate detail, we also knew that any number of considerations, not the least of which was weather, could preclude our being fragged on the selected targets for an indeterminate time period. We also knew that those of us doing the job at wing level would have nothing to say about when or how we did the job or what we would use to do it with.

We knew that we would be required to prepare ourselves fully for several alternate missions each day, and that at the last minute we would, in our terminology, be executed against one of the targets we had studied; that is, we would be sent on one of them. We almost never got canceled out completely. We knew that we would use every ounce of power in our engines, plus our afterburners, and water from an internal tank mounted in the aircraft sprayed into the flame pattern of our tail pipes to gain every possible ounce of push to launch our bomb-laden birds off the concrete and into the murky air of Asia. Shortly after takeoff we knew that the people who ran the ground radar stations would direct us to the spot of sky where our tankers would be waiting, knowing that we had already used a sizable portion of our fuel just to generate the power necessary to coax our charges to altitude. We would nuzzle up to them and they would nurse us northward as far as they dared go, and then with our bellies stuffed with fuel we would fall off the refueling boom extending from the rear of the flying gas stations and charge to the north. We also hoped that they would be there waiting for us later to nurse us south again, and we hoped that we would be there and in condition to accept the homeward-bound present of fuel.

One day, when it seemed that we had been on this particular merry-go-round for at least a year, it was Don's turn to lead and I was flying number three for him. He and I generally agreed on tactics and techniques, but everyone has his pet areas of emphasis. Don, one of our squadron commanders, was a speed man. He believed in jettisoning the drop tanks when they fed out and going just as fast as he could, regardless of fuel and regardless of defenses. He was also of the school holding that if you ran into Migs, the only course was straightaway speed. I preferred not to drop my tanks unless absolutely necessary as it was one more variable that could goof you up, and a tank that does not go properly can knock you flat out of the sky. (We have at least two of our troops in the Hanoi Hilton for this very reason, and probably others we don't know about.) Also, without the tanks you were not good for rescue cover, should it be needed; you went to the tanker and filled up and by the time you were back in the hot area you were so low on fuel that you had to leave again. All of us wanted lots of speed with the Migs, but I preferred high speed and maneuvering in my favorable performance envelope, at low altitude, with the chance of getting a shot at the Mig.

Although there was no disregarding our orders from Saigon, we were pretty sure that we would get skunked on weather on the mission for this day, and, even worse, we would leave little doubt in the enemy's mind as to what we were after.

The weather beat us time after time and forced us to the nonsatisfying alternate targets, but the word for this particular day was try again. We went through the normal routine, and as we departed the tankers we got our force nicely lined up in their appointed positions and headed once again into the delta area. As we switched over to the radio frequency we would operate on during this strike, we found the radio channel already full of noise and active from all the others in the air. It was so noisy on this particular day that I activated the miniature Japanese tape recorder I had stuffed in the back of my cockpit and connected through my headset. I knew that this would be a noisy one and I wanted to have it all on tape to restudy after we returned.

"This is Nash four five here, ah, weather looks pretty sloppy. We're in position at this time."

The simple "Rog, copy" indicated that his mate understood and was ready to go to work.

His boss was obviously not pleased with the weather outlook and the protective blanket that it provided for the Sams working underneath it. "Rog, I'm just crossing by the little islands. Pintail is the force leader and, ah, let's stay pretty close together today. It doesn't look very good."

Adequate time had passed since the command to change radio channels and our flight leads were mechanically checking to insure that their charges were on the right channel and ready for action. Don started the parade with "Pintail check."

He was greeted with a sharp "Two."

"Three."

"Four."

"Elmo check."

"Two."

"Three."

"Four."

To be absolutely sure of exactly where we were, we were forced to depend heavily on the Doppler inertial navigation system that provided each pilot with constantly updated positional information. Before the rest of the flights checked in, Don announced an aircraft problem with "Pintail three— lead here. I've just lost my Doppler." That was about average. The Doppler is a precise piece of navigation gear that is a beauty when it works. Initially you had to tell the rig where you were by setting some knobs and gadgets over a fixed geographical point, and from then on, it will tell you all sorts of good things like where you are, how to get where you want to go, and how fast you are really getting there. When you are moving at a pretty fast clip in an area where there are no aids to navigation other than what you can see, it is an important gadget. When you can't see anything, as we couldn't on this day because of the cloud cover, it becomes very close to vital. The only problem with the mechanism was that it was about as temperamental as a batch of black boxes could get, and believe it or not, it seemed to have the uncanny ability always to go ape when you needed it most. Our maintainers had a barrelful of statistics to prove how great the system was and nobody other than the participating pilots took the repeated complaints too seriously. There are superior navigation systems that have been available for some time, but they never computed out as cost effective, so we wound up with an old, second class system.

Don's call on the Doppler failure was old hat, and simply meant in this case that he was on top of an undercast over hostile territory and that the machine was feeding him false information that made it most difficult to maintain his position accurately, and made it impossible for him to move the force in the precise manner that was necessary if he was to hit an exact spot and avoid all other spots. Anything less than the exactly correct solution can cost you people, aircraft, and bombs other than on the precise target. One of number three's duties was to know as much about the flight's location and progress as the lead did and to fill the gap by steering the flight when the lead ran into the Doppler problem. I answered, "OK, ah, swing about, ah, five degrees to the right," and the navigational problem had become mine.

"Mallard check."

"Two."

"Three."

"Four."

"Harpoon check."

"Two."

"Three."

"Four."

"Harpoon three, take the left," indicated that Harpoon three had not done his homework or had not assimilated the instructions at the briefing, thus causing his leader to clutter up the airways with a useless call in order to get his chicks in the proper fighting position.

"Waco check."

"Two."

"Three."

"Four."

When someone else is forced to do the steering, the lead usually gets nervous. He knows that the element lead is perfectly competent, providing his gear is working properly, but it is sort of like letting your wife drive the car in traffic. She is OK, but— The sweat factor is increased by the fact that the leader always knows he has bought the entire show, and that if anything goofs, it is still his baby doll regardless of who is steering. If all the cockpit indications would just go away when the gadget breaks, you could ignore the problem to a degree, but they don't. They feed you all sorts of crazy readouts, and you can't ignore the tapes, dials and pointers that whir improperly in your face.

"Pintail three," Don called to me, "how does this heading look?" Don knew we were approaching the critical point where we had to turn to intercept Thud Ridge at the right point for the run on the heartland.

I gave him, "Swing another five degrees left, Pintail," as I lined him up on the turnpoint with a last-minute correction. Then as my indicators looked through the murk for me and told me that the time was right, I headed the force in on the run. "OK, we're swinging our turn point now, Pintail. Go ahead and turn." If we had wandered too far upriver on this heading, we would have been advised of our error by a volley from all the big guns that guard Ho Chi Minh's hometown. They were just like a combination stoplight and turn indicator. I know they didn't mean to help, but they were bound to get your attention.

The squadron was down in the dumps, there was no doubt about that, and one of my first challenges as a commander was to get to know them and try to strike the chord that would get them up again, but without the loss rate that they had suffered before. Strangely, the boss never told me that I had that for my first job. Nobody even mentioned it. It was just something you knew if you had the touch.

The new squadron commander had taken the reins shortly before my arrival, and I was amazed to find a rapidly balding, rather slight Ph.D. at the helm. I have a master's degree myself and I sometimes wonder if that was really necessary, but this guy was a doctor. A forty-plus doctor driving the Thud and leading his people up North and, like the rest of us, receiving a $2.16-a-day combat bonus. I confess to a bit of wonderment as to whether or not he was the desired solution, but that was short-lived. Don made one of the best and nicest—which to me is strangely important—fighter commanders I have ever met. There was no doubt that he had been exposed to the higher education routine and he looked the part, but like me he had had enough of the school kick and wanted only to be the best possible leader and airman. Much later when he received an assignment forecast that pointed him back into the Ph.D. area, he was most disturbed. You could tell upon occasion that he had been away from the business for a while and that the challenge of running his maintenance complex was new to him. You could tell that he had been at school during that portion of his career when many of his rank were learning the intricacies of administration and control of airmen, but you could also tell that he was very smart and it seldom took more than a casual

suggestion to steer him. It is fun to be able to command that
way.

Once I got started, I flew with Don a goodly portion of the
time as he and I, perhaps subconsciously, picked each other's
brains. We each wanted to see how the other operated and
flying combat will show you that in a hurry. He wanted to
satisfy himself that this new colonel in the wing really knew
how to handle the squadron troops in the air; he also wanted
to be sure that nobody allowed said colonel to fracture his
rear end while getting started in this war. I flew behind him
on at least one of every type mission before I would assume
the lead for that particular type. I think we spent the most
time together when "they" finally released the stranglehold
enough to let us nip at the outskirts of Hanoi itself. Nobody
kidded himself that it would be an easy series of targets, but
everybody wanted to be on the schedule, and our theme song
for the months of December and January was "Downtown,
Tonight, I'm Gonna Go Downtown."

One thing that Don did have to put up with was the fact
that I liked to fly and I was in a position to outrank him on
the hot missions. I tried to be fair about that, and I even let
him lead his own squadron once in a while. Actually, we got
along great on that score, and when I would bump him on a
particular go that I wanted to be in on, he would simply
move down to number three in our lead flight and become
deputy lead for the wing force. That way we had two qualified
wing leaders up front and either could take over should the
other be unable to continue. When this particular batch of
targets came out, we went even further and tried to keep the
same four-ship flight scheduled daily for the specific big
targets. That had a good side effect and it was no small badge
of honor to be selected as the colonel's wingman or the
squadron commander's wingman for the hottest targets yet
uncovered in this war, and admittedly the most fiercely
defended targets ever faced by any pilot in history. The
adrenaline count was high throughout the wing. We were
primed and ready to go. We got visits from generals telling us
the import of our tasks—as if we needed any extra pumping
up—and we got lousy weather.

*   *   *

Don and I were on the morning kick for this particular series. A two o'clock wakeup makes for short nights and, coupled with the other duties that kept us going until about eight in the evening, everything sort of all ran together and we just kept charging. Our little breakfast club was made up of the same group every day and after a while it got sort of tough to work up a hearty smile or a strong appetite for greased eggs at two thirty. Normally, you were not on the same schedule for too many days in a row and you could make up, to an extent, for lost sleep. But on this one, the weather in the target area would not break and the schedule would not change. We sat on this package for almost forty days before we got the job done properly. Some mornings you would get all the way through briefing before the words would come in. One day the words would be to divert to a lesser target, the next, to slip the schedule two hours—and everybody fall down someplace and catch some extra sleep. Some days we would let the newer troops go if we got a lesser target, other times we would go to keep in practice. Many times we would get the frustration of a long weather reconnaissance. If just maybe there was some slight chance that we could get to the target, we would launch and go all the way, through all the buildup, only to have to break off at the base of Thud Ridge when we knew for sure that we were over the top and the target was blanketed with low clouds and rain.

The decision on a mission like that lies with the mission commander, the guy up front. It is a tough one to make and each one excites different sensations. Basically, you don't want to take your people into an area where you cannot see the target well enough to bomb the way you should. You do not want to limit your attack by committing them with a cloud ceiling above them that will either cut down their available dive-bomb run or throw all your flights into the murk at those speeds. But most of all, you want to get the job done and strike a telling blow at those who have hurt you and your people with relative impunity for so long.

Laredo flight was doing our dirty work on the Sams for us that day and according to our plan for this one, they had swung off in an arc from the main force and were probing the sites we anticipated trouble from. "Hello, Pintail—Laredo," indicated he probably had some news for us on something other than Sams, as he seldom bothered with the introductory formalities when the missiles were flying.

"Laredo—Pintail. Go ahead."

"Ah, Roger, we crossed the Red and I'm almost to the Ridge, and I'm on the tops of it, and I'm about five thousand, and it's solid as far as I can see." Laredo was doing good work, but he was not in a very healthy position at that time, and he was quite on his own. That would put him about in the backyard of the Mig-21s at Phuc Yen. I wondered how thick the clouds were and if the 21s had enough room to get off the ground underneath the overcast. Maybe they would try, and crash on takeoff. That was a comforting thought.

Don did not have to deliberate on his reply and came back with "Roger, we'll press on down the Ridge anyway." The reply took no thought as he had no freedom at this point. The normal fighter pilot determination would take him to the point where he could see his target area and be sure that there was not some freak hole that would allow him to sneak the force in and get the job done. His good sense and good eyes could tell him that from several miles out, but under the current rules this was not good enough. We were under direct order to fly over the target itself before making the determination. Aside from being a tactical blunder, this was more than somewhat of an insult to those of us who were leading. The thought that the bosses would take a highly experienced senior officer who had volunteered to come over here and fight this mess, would put him in charge of two fighter wings and all the supporting effort, and then would insist that he drag the entire force through exposure that was unnecessary, just to be able to report that the leader had flown over a specific point, always galled me no end. I never hit a target that I would otherwise have aborted by flying my troops through worthless exposure periods, nor did I ever abort a target run where I had not made up my mind in advance of entering the area of maximum exposure. Oh well, as I said, the pressure was on.

Everyone knew we were going for a ride over the defenses, but just hearing the lead announce the fact again was calculated to raise the breathing rate and make the eyeballs a bit more efficient. "Five degrees right, Pintail," lined us up quite nicely.

Immediately, a curt call announced, "I've got four bogies, ten o'clock low." Another impetus to the eyeballs.

As Don rolled out from his correction, he seemed to track nicely down the desired path and for the moment at least we had solved the drift problem and were on course. I figured this knowledge would please him and verified our track with "Steady on, Pintail." A quick "zip, zip" acknowledged that things were progressing satisfactorily. That zip was accomplished by a quick repeated depression of the mike button and it saved a transmission and kept the air clear for other calls. It shows how simply and efficiently you can communicate with those who understand a common mission. It is a sharp and brittle little sound that to me reeks of confidence and competence.

"Saturn check."

"Two."

"Three."

"Four."

We were no longer the only effort in the area; we could expect the radio chatter to get more intense. "Otter, we've got another Sam, three, four miles out at eleven o'clock." Whoever they were, they were getting a rousing welcome. Nice guys, I was sure, but you couldn't help but hope they soaked up all the Sam activity. Fat chance of that happening, as this was the time period when the Russian general accused the North Vietnamese of shooting their zillion-ruble missiles, which the Russians were paying for, "like they were firecrackers." The Thud drivers shared his concern if not his intent.

"Rog, Otter, check your gear for interference."

"You're OK. We're going to climb a little higher here." As busy as you may be, it is impossible to keep the mind's artist from painting a picture of the game of hide-and-seek you know so well is going on in some other quadrant.

Our hunters were doing the same thing, and while they were not Sam-saturated, it was apparent that they had plenty of action. "Laredo, you got any guns at twelve o'clock?"

"Rog, ah, four's got guns. Four o'clock along the Ridge."

"Three same."

"Laredo's got guns at nine, Phu Tho area." That pretty well sealed the area from both sides and dispelled any doubt that they were looking at us from both sides of our ingress route.

Anybody's problem becomes everybody's problem about this time and the announcement "Three, it's siphoning again" alerted us to the fact that a balky tank or a set of fuel control valves was giving one of our troops a problem. No sweat on that for right now. It was not the kind of problem that would break up a flight and leave us out of balance. Even one set of eyes or one unprotected flank of a flight would have been bad news at this point, to say nothing of the problems to be faced by the stragglers who might have to drop from the mutual protection of the force in the event of mechanical abort.

"OK, let me know when it stops." Good comment. Worrying won't fix it anyway.

"Wonder—this is Stewart. Clear down and behind." Amazing how it all fits into the puzzle and how the calls tell you of actions you don't see. The escorts and the support guys were together and were clearing each other from Migs and Sams as they patrolled on the fringes of the action.

The mind was brought quickly from the fringe to the center with "And—Laredo has a contact—we'll be staying low. Sams up."

When Sam or the large guns came up, or either started looking right at you with their radar prior to launching or firing at you, their radar contact on you would activate a cockpit warning panel. It was a sophisticated version of the radar warning device you can buy for your car should you choose to duel with speed cops on the highway. Among other things ours would tell you if it were Sam or the guns or both of them that were looking at you. It also had a visual screen and an aural tone that buzzed just like a rattlesnake. If Sam or the big guns had a weak contact on you, a small, dim and intermittent green circle would glow in the middle of the screen (one ringer) and the snake would rattle mildly to get your attention. If the contact was pretty good you would get a larger circle glowing steadily (two ringer) and the rattle would become irritating. If Sam or the big guns locked on with a good contact and were ready to launch or fire at you, you would get a still larger green ring that would shine brightly (three ringer) and it would sound like that big rattler was coiled in your flying-suit pocket. Definitely an attention getter.

"Pintail two has a three-ringer at about two o'clock," brought it about as close to home as it could get. They were looking right down our horn, but Don wasn't sure he had heard correctly.

"Say again."

"Pintail two has a three-ringer at two o'clock." He heard right the first time.

"Roger. Pintail—Laredo. You under the stuff or on top?"

"Roger, we're on top."

The Sam activity caused all the leaders to recheck their charges and their position and the support boss called to his escort, "Stewart—this is Nash. How many chickens you got?" He couldn't afford to get those sweptwing escorts mixed up with any Soviet-built types who might have wandered into the sky he was covering.

"I got four."

"OK, we're going to try and stay nice and close today." What a beautiful way to say, Get up here where you belong and sharpen up that formation, without being nasty to the escort you must depend upon.

"Pintail, lead steer eight degrees left." I had to keep Don on course. "Steady on, the readout is three zero." He was headed for the spot we wanted, and now had only 30 miles to go. You could already tell that the target weather was stinking.

"OK, Elmo one has negative Doppler."

At least Don's gear had quit far enough out so that I had plenty of time to recheck all the indications and establish a smooth entry, but Elmo, coming up behind us, found himself without the proper steering gear and had to switch responsibility in a hurry. It would be sheer ecstasy to have a navigational support manager who resists progress riding along in one of the two-seater F-105 Fs that our Wild Weasels used on our Sam suppression missions at a time like that so he could bite holes in the seat and see how important the little things that make a fighter go can become.

"Rog, Elmo three here, thirty right." Good thing he had recognized the failure and called when he did as the size of the correction indicated that he had already passed his turn point.

As we thundered down the Ridge, we accelerated even with that big ugly bombload under us, moving and looking, and the support guy announced, "Stewart is at thirty-six thousand." I thought that must be a comfortable place to be, especially with another flight covering your rear end.

Then Laredo updated the Sam picture with "Laredo's got a high indication," and I changed my mind and decided I would not care to be sitting up there waiting to see if Sam could accelerate all the way out to the point that I could not see him as he reached for me. Those guys earned their money.

"Four o'clock" pointed to the Sam's location and then the friendly supporters got the talking disease and began to garbage up the air just when we needed it clear.

"Rog, I'm at thirty-three."

"Laredo's got another high one at eleven o'clock." This was vital information that needed to get through.

"Six two, are we bothering you, Bill?" I didn't know who in hell Bill was, but they were sure bothering me, and we were at the point where the steering had to be perfect.

"Pintail, steer four degrees right." Don responded with a precise 4-degree correction which at 600 knots is no small feat, and I knew he was receiving my calls.

"High threat indication—and he's going down—four five say again."

Shut up, you idiot, is all I could think, but the old mouth worked better than the brain for a change, and I confirmed Don's turn with "Steady on."

We were quite close in and there was nothing resembling a break in the clouds. I would rather face the guns I can see than cruise along in anticipation of what I can't see underneath me. The clouds up there are sort of a dirty gray color at best. They looked downright ominous that day, and each Sam call made each of us sit a bit lighter in the seat.

"And Laredo's proceeding south of the Red down towards the Black. It's still solid."

"Roger." We didn't have much further to go now.

"Stewart, you on?"

I guess he was; I hadn't heard much other than support chatter. "Stewart going north, twenty degrees."

"Stewart, got a two and a half ringer at two o'clock."

"Laredo, keep it down. Sam activity at eleven o'clock. OK, Laredo, let's go right here. Keep him on the nose."

"Four five, you call a turn?"

"Ah, Rog, zero one, two. You make the calls and I'll turn with you."

"Contact is back up, Laredo." Those two had a running battle for the air and I so wanted Laredo to win that I would have gladly throttled our supporters if I could have reached them.

"Pintail, one zero to the right." That was the final correction, and if we had been able to do so, that was the time we would have gone to work in earnest and would have been rolling over the top to face the guns and put the bombs on target.

"Rog, Pintail's following your Doppler. I'm over the edge of the area and it's definitely not open." Don had filled the square necessary to announce his decision.

I helped him with "Yeah, I agree, it looks like a loser to me. I concur and would say negative on the whole works for Pintail and all the rest of the flights."

Don executed the abort with "Pintail here, we're coming out, coming out. Left one eighty." Back down the line of flight leaders the call was echoed and each of the four-shippers swung to a preplanned divergent course to establish the necessary separation between the low-flying, fast-moving flights as everyone reacted without delay to get someplace other than on top of that gray blanket covering the active defenses.

Laredo did his best to keep us advised, but continued to have trouble getting through. "Contact is back up, eleven o'clock, high indication."

"Ahh, Pintail, ah—this is Nash four five. What are your intentions?"

A proper reply would have been to tell him that I was going to talk to him about radio discipline when we got back on the ground, but Don confined himself to "Roger, withdrawing."

"Pintail—this is Harpoon. Understand you are withdrawing."

"Pintail, that's Roger." That third flight of ours had been having trouble ever since they got their wingman on the wrong side way back by the river.

Laredo finally got through with "Pintail, suggest you exit back up the Ridge. We've got lots of two and three ring Sam indications down here in the Phu Tho area." He really did good work for us and was most interested in seeing that we did not get down into the little box he had worked himself into as he baited the defenders.

"Roger, we'll cut back north," and the exit was in progress. "OK, Harpoons, we're withdrawing." He talked almost as much as the support guys.

Sam was not ready to quit and Laredo passed on, "OK, contacts at your four o'clock—high indication."

"Nash one one, four five returning to orbit." Good, I thought, maybe he'll be quiet out there.

While Nash faded, Harpoon made up for him with "Pintail— this is Harpoon. Understand you are calling it off." What was the matter with him?

"Rog."

"Ozark."

"Two."

"Three."

"Four."

This exchange told us that the first flight from the next strike wing was entering the area, and from the briefing, we knew that flight to be their Sam chasers who would be contacting our boys before long for a rundown on what was hot in the area.

Meanwhile, Otter flight, whom I had thought so unkindly of before, was still soaking up the Sams in the other quadrant and I felt much better toward them now that I was headed out of the area. "Contact is at one o'clock—high indication only. Otter, you hear me? Launch at one going to six." It sounded like they were having quite a day.

It looked like Ozark was going to inherit the same voice problems that Laredo had endured as he attempted to make initial contact with "Laredo—this is Oz—"

"Nash zero one, the target is three six zero now."

A patient retransmission of "Laredo—this is Ozark" showed he was still fresh and unfrazzled.

"Nash flight going to three six zero at this time" was all he got for his trouble and he wisely decided to wait awhile before trying again.

Our strike flights had the problem of finding an alternate area that was suitable to work and having flown all the way in on top of the clouds, we knew that would not be easy, yet we did not want to haul those bombs all the way home.

"Pintail—Elmo."

"Go ahead, Elmo—Pintail."

"Rog. Boy, you see anything north of the Red worth working on?" There was nothing really worthwhile and the only faint hope might have been back past the area of the initial turn-in.

"Ah, it looks like there might possibly be some slight breaks back to the northwest, but this—it's really solid."

"Nash, Nash, go three six zero at this time."

"Harpoon is up by the lake and there's nothing up here."

The radio was just too much for Mallard lead and he made the smart move with "Mallard, let's go flight manual, flight manual, Mallard." He had switched his radio to a preselected discreet frequency and would no longer know what everyone else was up to, but he felt he would rather look a bit harder to keep track of the rest of the flights and at least be able to direct his own people without being cut out on every transmission.

"Laredo, contact and guns, Phu Tho."

"Laredo—Ozark."

"Lead, Ozark's calling you."

"And the contact is down."

"Ah, Pintail—this is Nash four five. Ah, what—"

"Calling Pintail, say again?"

"All flights, the gap is open, the gap is open" was a reasonably good assurance that the way back out was no worse than it had been on the way in.

"OK, Laredo, we'll be heading back out now." The game was not over by a long shot and I had constantly drilled into all our guys the examples of the Thud driver who was relaxing straight and level at 18,000 feet on the way out, thinking he had it made, only to be blown from the sky by a wild but accurate Sam, and the flight lead who got complacent and low and slow with 50 miles of the homeward trip under his belt, only to run across the top of a stray gun that knocked him out of the sky. We lost them both.

Elmo gave up on the radio. "Elmo lead, let's go to another channel."

"Rog, Elmo's, let's go to flight manual, flight manual."

But the supporters and their escort took up the vacated ether. "Three, I'll take the top."

"Three, Roger, OK."

"Hello, Pintail—this is Nash four five. Do you read?"

McDonnell RF-101 "Voodoo"

Patient Don showed not the slightest annoyance as he launched into the same discourse again. "Roger, Nash four five—this is Pintail. Go ahead."

"Roger, Pintail, what are your inten—"

"This is Royal, this is Royal. Time is four three, Mig scramble, sector sierra sierra, time four three, Royal out." That was the single most irritating call of the bunch, and it came from the heavy-voiced controller far from the battle, viewing the area on his radarscope, who seemed overjoyed to blast everyone off the air with his powerful transmitter. One of his scope heads had plotted a launch and, following the rules, he felt obliged to let the world know.

In the first place, the coordinates were worthless, and the information was old and contained nothing resembling direction, altitude or speed. Secondly, nobody cared what time it was by his clock, and we didn't need to be told twice who it was, as we could recognize his voice anytime and anywhere. Those of us with some knowledge of the state of the art in the recognition and defense business could not fathom the complete lack of accurate and timely information that would have done us some good, and which could have been presented in a far more acceptable manner. I complained repeatedly and bitterly about this completely unsatisfactory system, but my complaints either fell on deaf ears or else got me chewed out, as I supposedly did not have all the facts. I was able to see a very slight improvement toward the tail end of my tour over there, but the warning and control systems we use today are unsatisfactory and antiquated, run by insufficient numbers of inadequately trained people. Should you agree, don't bother taking up the sword for the cause. The real lack of aptness in the system is buried under mountains of phony statistics and denied by those in a position to demand improvement in the system. You have to go up there and get exposed to it from the driver's side, under stress, and nobody with enough horsepower to do anything about it is going to be caught in that position.

Royal's reverberating tones faded, and the chatter and the withdrawal progressed. "Pintail—Harpoon."

"OK, Laredo, keep your eyes open. We got two up there at eleven o'clock."

"That's a four-ship flight."

"OK, got them just below those clouds." Their external fuel tanks were empty and now could only slow them down when they needed speed, so he said, "Let's get rid of the tanks," and they jettisoned them. Laredo had found the Migs, no thanks to the warning system.

"Laredo—this is Pintail. We're clearing the area. Get moving. You're all by yourself."

Laredo knew that he was low on fuel and the last one in the box. This was not the time to attempt to become a Mig hero. The Migs had not spotted him and he had pickled his empty tanks to reduce drag and speed his exit to fight another day. "Rog, Pintail, Laredo's OK. We're heading for the Red."

"Laredo—Ozark."

"Roger, Ozark."

"What's the good word?"

"Roger, you can forget it. It's solid, about five thousand feet, solid as far as you can see."

"Where did you work?"

"I, ah, came up to the Ridge. Couldn't get across the Ridge. It's mostly enshrouded so I came south to Phu Tho and Viet Tri and it's still solid all the way." The entire series of transmissions had been clear and without interruption, and we were now satisfied that the commander of the second part of the strike force, who was still on the way in behind us, knew what the situation looked like. A small task—but then the radio exploded again.

"Rolleyes, go manual. Rolleyes, go manual."

"Rolleyes three—"

"One o'clock low—"

"Muskrat, flight manual—"

"—I'll be turning to zero two."

"Pintail three, can you contact the other force?"

"Pintail, why don't you try and get contact through Royal?"

"Say again."

Don had finally had all the noise he could use. "Pintail three, go to channel seven and see if you can pass the word to somebody. I'm going to manual frequency."

I was most happy to accept this little chore and came back with "OK, will do, I'll go to seven. Meet you on manual." The channel changer clicked through its paces and the silence was golden. Now if I could only get Lincoln to talk to me. "Lincoln—Pintail. Hello, Lincoln—this is Pintail."

"Pintail—Lincoln. Go ahead."

"Roger, Lincoln—Pintail. It's negative, negative, negative. No dice. We're on the way out." He rogered and we went home. It had been a crummy day and a crummy mission, and I had a headache when I crawled out of that beauty back at the base.

We sure telegraphed our punches. There were not all that many targets in that area, and it did not take too many smarts to figure out about where the force was headed, especially when we headed them there day after day, made them fly up to the target before making the go or no-go decision on weather we knew was not acceptable, turned over the target and then came back the next day to try again. The pressure was on to get this complex, and when we got into that configuration, it was amazing how the simple basic portents of warfare slipped by the boards to be replaced by determination to accomplish what we had been directed to accomplish.

In the situation over there, the bosses were fighting several problems. The first has been discussed around many a table and is simply the target restriction problem. There are places that, in my opinion, should have been hit long ago. Some were more sensitive than others, but the hard-core targets were like little prizes dangled on a string in our face. When one of the fringe targets would be released, the eagerness to get to it immediately approached a panic at each intermediate level of command. Even though the operating units had no control over things like the weather and the fortunes of war, operational commanders took a lot of unwarranted heat from distant staff commanders if a target was not destroyed within hours of approval to attack.

Common sense and in fact military sense, often fell by the wayside, and the fact that Hanoi was not going to move during the next few days seemed lost to decision-making view as did the fact that we had waited a long time for these targets and could afford to wait a few more minutes to do the job right. Those doing the job felt that it would have paid better dividends to mix up the signals a bit and that if we had to feint and battle impossible weather parameters, it would at least have been wise to mix up the feints. We were all for making a dry run if it looked like we had a chance, but if faced with the same weather odds the next day, we wanted to feint in a different direction or go someplace else completely and come back a day or two later. In our restricted and oversupervised environment, the pressure would not allow that approach to the problem.

Additional pressure was generated by the fact that there were different services and different command elements participating in a limited geographical area and competing for a limited number of worthwhile targets. There is bound to be a degree of competition under these circumstances, and I believe this competition is both healthy and productive as long as common sense prevails. There was plenty of action for everyone who could fly an airplane up there, and there were more than enough defenses to go around. I have never reached the level of command in this business to gain the unhealthy degree of competitiveness that generates bitterness and drives out good sense. Such attitudes do exist and they are most harmful, but fortunately, they are above the operating level, and most Navy and Air Force crew members of my ilk benefit from the exchange of tactical knowledge and doctrine that goes on at the aircraft operating level. It seems that the poor attitudes are directly proportional to the distance from the cockpit control stick, multiplied by the number of years, if ever, since the individual has been shot at in real anger.

We had a good program going wherein we would run

monthly exchange visits with our Navy buddies. They would gather a group of four or five aviators in positions like group or squadron commander and pile them into their Cod, which carries the impressive title of Carrier Onboard Delivery, Grumman C-1A, Trader, and launch from the ship to recover at one of our fighter bases. We would then spend a number of days or hours yakking about what we were doing and how we were doing it and the exchange would be both enjoyable and refreshing. A couple of weeks later, a group of our people would visit the ship and have a similar interchange of ideas. These sessions helped all of us. One of my favorite Navy fliers, Dutch, was so enthusiastic when he visited us that he was reluctant to leave at the appointed time. He was torn between more discussion and the once-in-six-months opportunity to take a day off and enjoy a much needed rest in Bangkok. We agreed that you can only push yourself so hard before you become less than productive, and that a day's air-conditioned sleep in a posh Bangkok hotel could be followed by a continuation of our discussion on the ship on the next trip. His exec brought the Cod back on the next cycle, and I met him when he landed. "Dutch got bagged," he announced with deflating certainty. "He was leading the outfit, and they fired two Sams at them as they approached the beach. He took them down and told the guys to watch out, there would probably be more on the way. There were, and the next one was a direct hit on Dutch." That hurt as badly as if it had been one of my own squadron or flight mates. He and I both admitted freely that there was no corner on ideas and that neither one of us had all the answers. There is no friction at the operating level.

The day after that particular dry run to Hanoi, I noticed that Don was getting nervous; we all were. There are many things that eat at you when you sit on a series of hot ones as long as we had been on this package. But by nature, Don was jumpy at times and he was jumpy as we were directed to the primary target again. I can still recall his statement as we entered the small squadron briefing room for our flight huddle after the big wing briefing: "Anyone who is not completely terrified doesn't understand the problem." We called our signals in the normal tense atmosphere, and you could feel the tension within yourself, you could see the tension in the other guys, and so many things became unimportant.

Everybody knew the flight briefing by heart, and you talked about things you would rather forget. Like, "If one of us gets shot down, the other guy in the element try and cover him as well as you can and see if you can spot the chute impact. The other element go high and start screaming for the Rescap people (Rescue aircraft and fighters who fly Combat Air Patrol to cover a downed pilot). High element conserve fuel and we will cycle off the tankers as necessary. Let's not leave singles Capping (covering a downed pilot) alone in rough country. That's the plan for the way in and the way out. If one of us gets knocked down in the Hanoi area—forget it. We all agree there is nothing we can do for each other then, and there is no sense losing more machines and people. Agree? OK, see you in the personal equipment room in ten minutes."

While maps, charts and target photos were folded and rammed into kneepads to form some semblance of order, there was a dash for a quick cup of coffee or a soda pop and a swing by the john. It was a long trip at best. Leaving the john, I became painfully aware that someone was violently ill in one of the closed stalls. That horrible retching choke set my bravado back a few steps. My second impulse was to shout out and see if any of my guys was having trouble. But who goes around sticking his head into john stalls asking who's throwing up and why? I dismissed the thought and strode to the personal equipment room. I have often wondered who it was.

The personal equipment room was air-conditioned. All the pilots' gear was carefully stored, checked and cared for there. We wore a cotton flying suit and boots that came pretty close to hunting boots. The first step as you entered the room was to remove anything identifying or personal such as rings, wallets and the like. Once you were clean, you started lashing yourself into the fifty pounds of gear that you hung on yourself. First came the anti-G suit that resembled a pair of zippered chaps and also served as backup flotation gear should you want to blow it up in the water. It was covered with pockets, all of which were stuffed with survival items, and flares, knives and the like were sewn on all areas not served with a pocket. I personally wore my pistol and ammo on a holster belt, and this was strapped on next and lashed to my right leg with rawhide to be sure it stayed out of the way. The mesh survival vest came next, and it was loaded with myriad goodies should they be needed. We found out from our people who had gone down and been recovered that the adrenaline exercise created an almost uncontrollable thirst and people had been known to leave good cover in a wild search for water. We found the best water containers were plastic baby bottles and carried two full ones in the vest. The big item for our war was the survival radio, and it was also in the vest. Like the parachute, it had a beeper capability. The beeper is the most ghastly-sounding little device known to man. It broadcasts a signal of distress like nothing else you have ever heard, a harsh, high-pitched "A-RAAAH, A-RAAAH" that keeps on and on until it about drives you out of your skull. Many of the guys checked them in the personal equipment room before each flight. I didn't. It didn't fit into my emotional scheme at that particular stage and I couldn't stand the sound of it. All you needed then was a back parachute, a cumbersome hard helmet, a kneeboard full of flight-planning cards, a book bag full of standardized normal and emergency procedures and a crane to lift you into the personal equipment truck that took you to the aircraft. You didn't really need all the standardized checklists too badly, but if you ever busted an aircraft without having them on board, the really big guys would hang you.

We got to the machines plenty early so we could look them over and strap in at leisure. I personally spent minimum time with this operation as generally anything my crew chief had not found was not likely to expose itself to me. I asked him if it was ready to go and if he said yes, I assumed he was right. I walked around the bird, kicked the bombs and the tires and shook the tanks, just because it seemed to be the thing to do. I could manage this with five minutes to spare and that was the time I liked to walk back to the blast deflectors and have a cigarette, all by myself. By that time I was tired of talking to humans and I knew I was about to embark on several tough hours. I liked to take my head out of gear and talk to the really big man, and watch the flight line and the sky go by for a few seconds. Then it was grind out the butt, zip the survival vest and stride up to the ladder. It was time to go to work. The hardest part of the mission was already over.

The next thirty minutes was just plain hot. You sweated so badly that sometimes you could hardly see. The flight line was organized confusion as one flight after the other hit the starter button and filled the air with the stench and smoke of the black-powder cartridge starter that spun the engine through its initial starting revolutions. The noise was deafening and one of our problems was protecting the ears of our pilots and ground crews. Most of the pilots ignored the problem, especially after they had been around for a few years, and that is why most of us have some degree of hearing loss.

The ritual of properly adjusting the helmet and personal gear takes a few minutes and each pilot has his own idiosyncrasies about strapping in. It took me a few moments to adjust the skullcap that I wore under my custom-built Lombard helmet, but this guaranteed me no hot spots or pressure points, which can drive you to distraction and can, in fact, cause lack of proper attention to the job, and even accidents. A sweatband across the forehead partially blocks the sweat from your eyes, but the sweat can still fill up your ears and make you feel like you're underwater. Next came my super sunglasses which a doctor friend of mine built for me to take me down past twenty-twenty to perfect vision and depth perception. (My buddy, Sam, could have used a pair of these. It got to be a joke to see who would steer the number three colonel in the wing to his tanker rendezvous, since Sam was just not seeing the tankers as fast as some of the young sports. Sam decided to shake the young troops and called the tanker outfit prior to one mission and cross-checked the voice call sign of his tanker against the painted Air Force serial numbers of the craft. As they approached rendezvous, one of the flight members gaily called out a tanker at eleven o'clock and prepared to steer the colonel to the tanker. Sam rogered with "Yeah, I see him. His tail number looks like 72534," while still some 20 miles distant from letters 10 inches high. Several minutes later when they pulled up alongside tanker number 72534, Sam was one up on his young sports.)

Once the helmet was on, the roar of the other starting machines was cut out, replaced by the high sidetone from the crew chief's plug-in face mike connected to the belly of the aircraft so he could talk to you during the start and pretaxi checks. We had quite a ritual, and ran through a number of checks that sent him scurrying from one end of the machine

to the other. It took ten minutes from engine crank until you
actually started to move. When you had checked all flight
members and the spare on the radio and had received tower
instructions, you flung your arms out of the cockpit and the
chief's helpers pulled the chocks as the chief used hand
signals to move you out of the cramped parking area and turn
you toward the taxiway. Once he had you around the corner,
he stepped smartly back and threw you the sharpest salute
you have ever seen. There was no baloney in the way that
highball was rendered and returned. Those troopers knew
the score and they knew full well that this might be the last
time they would see you or their personal machine that
they had sweated over so long and hard. One of the many
sad aspects of losing a guy was the look of complete
bewilderment on the face of the chief whose bird didn't
return. They really sweat out their work and their vehicle
and this salute said, "Go get 'em, boss—and bring my bird
back."

Once we dropped off the tankers and headed into the hot
area, Don, who was Kingpin three, and I, as Kingpin lead,
knew that the weather was still not looking so hot; in fact, it
looked rotten, but you had to go all the way—no easy outs.
We had a little radio problem getting Don onto the strike
frequency as we set up the bombs and got ready to go to
work, but this in itself did not seem unusual and when he
came up on frequency, I assumed all was OK. As the attack
progressed, you could feel tension and you could hear tension
in each curt voice and each crisp command. As we crossed
the Red, Sam warnings already garbaged up the radio. I
wondered if they were for the Navy guys and thought they
must be since we were the first Air Force ones in for the day.
Mig warnings came on top of Sam warnings and I mused,
What's it going to be—a Sam day or a Mig day? It sounded
like a little of both. There was nothing I could do about that,
anyway, so I paid attention to leading, and there was Thud
Ridge, but just barely. Only one point of the northernmost
peak showed, and it was three-quarters covered with those
rotten clouds.

Sam was not to be our big problem that day, although he
was active. Trouble was spelled Mig, and the first ones to
verify that were our Sam hunters as they swung off to the
side of the main force and started searching.

"Two bogies one o'clock Flamingo," announced the number three man in the specialized flight.

"Rog, got 'em," came from the leader.

As I turned the force around the northern corner of Thud Ridge, I knew the stinking weather was about to beat us again, and I knew that at least one of my flights was already being forced to divide their attention between their main job and the harassing Migs.

"You got bogies at nine o'clock now."

It sounded like Flamingo might be in the market for some help now that he had them on both sides of his flight, but he had disappeared into the murk and cloud underneath, and we were not really in position to do much for him at the instant. He would call soon if he really needed help.

Both Thud wings were scheduled into the area, running pretty close together today, and that was OK by me, as it doubled the Sam hunters; and it already sounded like they had plenty of action in store for them. It looked like my boys would be less than fully effective with the Migs already on board. "Laredo's got a weak Sam, one thirty," sounded good and told me that another flight of F-105 F Wild Weasel Sam hunters was on the job.

While things were not off to a joyous start, we had everyone in good position and I was particularly pleased with the structure within my own lead flight. Don had the element with Bing on his wing and that was a good combination. I had Rod, my old next-door neighbor from Japan, on my wing, and they didn't come any better than Rod. This was a funny business. Not too long ago Rod and I had been out in the backyard complaining about the noisy Japanese street that ran behind our houses, clogged with the 24-hour rush traffic of Tokyo that screamed and smelled and would about knock you off the government furniture in those little ancient and uncomfortable government shacks. It was quite different at the moment, and the noises and smells that counted now were capable of doing a lot more than knocking you off your chair. They could knock you clean down into that hazy obscured little valley below that told me we were almost halfway down Thud Ridge with no weather break in sight. In addition to being a superior pilot, Rod has one of those sets of eagle eyes that seem capable of picking up the bogies wherever they may be.

"Kingpin, there's a flight of four fives back there at five o'clock." My seeing-eye captain was doing good work for me today.

Then Hot Dog flight started to get in on the action. They were picking up a fair amount of Sam activity, and the leader had decided to dump his now-empty external tanks to allow a bit more freedom of movement, but number two's tank refused to cooperate. When you have a single bird in a flight carrying the additional drag of a 20-foot-long tank, you have a problem. If he tries to stay up with the rest of the flight as he must do in a danger zone like this, he is at full power all the time and his fuel goes much too fast. If you drag everyone back on the power to give him a break, you compromise the entire flight position and defeat the purpose of tank jettison. It is such a simple matter to punch off a tank, you would think it could never be a problem, but it was. Many of the more agonizing aspects of fighter combat are the direct results of the failure of the simplest systems. It's hard to figure how we can go to the moon, yet we can't build a simple, foolproof system that will allow you to let go of a big blob of a tank when you want to.

"Hot Dog, you know of any other way to get this thing off of here?"

"Say again," from the leader indicated that he had not yet recognized his problem or was involved in something else.

"Yeah, you know of any smart ideas on how I can get this tank off?"

"Negative."

"Rog," and now two was stuck with the problem all by himself.

The lead had a problem of his own. "OK, Hot Dog, we've got a valid launch, valid launch, at two. Keep your eyes open." They were stuck on top of that overcast and they knew there was at least one Sam headed their way from underneath the clouds. The question is two-fold—where will it come poking through the murk, and will you have time to do anything about it when and if you see it? It is a spooky feeling. I supposed that Hot Dog two had at least temporarily forgotten about that hung tank of his, and I just hoped he didn't have to go through some wild gyration to avoid the unseen Sam that would result in that dizzy tank pulling off and wrapping around the wing, as they had a nasty habit of doing.

"Flamingo has guns at twelve." Now the array was complete as the big radar-directed guns were probing for us.

"Junetime, Junetime," blurted out from the big birds surveying the area and told us that they too had seen the launch at Hot Dog. That is about the most useless warning you can get, as all it tells you is that the white telephone poles are flying. About all you could do was assume that they saw the same one Hot Dog was looking for and working against, and go on with your own job.

"Flamingo three has multiple guns."

"Hot Dog, ease it down, multiple guns, Hot Dog." Those two flights were really getting in among them. "Hot Dog's got another Sam, two o'clock."

We had enough going on now to know that they were ready for us again today, and I figured it was about time to let my troops know what it looked like from the lead seat. "Kingpin lead here. I'm about halfway down the Ridge and it doesn't look like it's going to be any good, but we'll press on a ways." About the time you make a call like that you can visualize at least twenty guys muttering under their breath, wondering what's the matter with that idiot up front—of course it looks lousy—can't he make up his mind?

"Hot Dog, take it down."

"How's it look, Kingpin?" Somebody didn't get the message, but I didn't have time to repeat it as the only patch of undercast that looked even hopeful was sliding by underneath me and it just would not open up for me. We were going fast now, just as fast as those little beauties would go with that big ugly rack of bombs jiggling and shaking under the belly. How fast is fast? Whatever the slowest machine in the flight can do at full power. You just keep easing it up until it looks like one of your guys is about to have trouble staying with you, then you back off just a tad.

"Flamingo's got a launch light."

"MIGS!"

"Flamingo, break left—NOW!"

The Migs were all over us. They had a perfect setup and had listened to their ground controllers guiding them into attack position under the clouds. Now as we came into the heart of the target area, they cobbed their light maneuverable craft and spit up from our blind bellies. We really needed all the speed we had and they could wrap us up in any turns we made if we let that speed drop off. If we could hold that speed, they could give us fits, but they probably couldn't hurt us too badly. I have gone thundering down that Ridge with them right in formation with us. They could match speed with us at that altitude, but unless they got a lucky break or unless your tactics or your people were so weak that they put you in an impossible box, they could seldom get enough advantage to attack the way they wanted to. They could hose a missile at you, but if you keep thundering, they couldn't quite get the edge they wanted. It must have been frustrating to them, and I had one Mig-21 who got so wrapped up in trying to shoot me down that he made us a flight of five and even stuck in there as I pulled up and rolled in on the bomb run. It was not until the massive ground fire from his compatriots engulfed us that he realized he was in sort of a stupid spot and got out. It seems like every hassle we get wrapped up in pits us against lightweight and highly maneuverable interceptors who always have the ability to outturn us and disengage at will. Perhaps someday we will produce a machine capable of turning with them on even terms. If we ever do, our Mig score should go sky-high. In the meantime, while we insist on building large supersonic flatirons whose pilots must avoid the basic aerial maneuver of trying to outturn the enemy, I would strongly suggest serious thought toward a rearward firing missile as that seems to be where the Migs show up most of the time—on our behinds. That would be a real kick, to have a Mig jump you at six o'clock and promptly dispatch him with a missile right in the snoot.

My buddy Geeno had the flight right behind me and the Migs broke through the cloud in just about perfect position on him.

"Magnum, Migs. Drop your tanks, Magnum."

Time was of the essence to Magnum flight. The Migs were well within air-to-air missile range and they had a perfect angle on him. He had to clean up his aircraft and use everything he had working for him to the utmost. It was also vital that everyone in the flight got their birds cleaned up together and that the mutual support of the four men and machines not be compromised even for an instant.

"Magnum, drop tanks."

"Kingpin, two Migs at seven—correction—five o'clock." Bing in the number four position on my far left had spotted the second element as they popped up in almost identical position on me. Those guys were getting pretty sharp, but why not? After all, they had no shortage of practice and had probably dry-run this attack on any one of the many dry runs we were making into the target area. They just waited for the ideal setup and implemented plan alpha. I couldn't see them right away and the two different clock calls were a bit confusing as they forced me to try and look backwards on both sides. "That five o'clock for Kingpin?" Before he could answer, I found out for myself. They were indeed at five o'clock and closing nicely on a well-charted intercept. "OK, let's get rid of the tanks. Kingpin, tanks." Now I was the one who had to move in a hurry or lose somebody, but I was not about to get rid of the bombs. Not yet. I had lugged those damn things all the way up there and still had hopes of putting them on something better than the open rice paddies. A quick glance showed my guys to be in good shape and tanks were tumbling earthward, but the Migs were still in excellent position, and I didn't want anyone loosening up the formation or surrendering that mutual support capability we had.

"Watch it, Kingpin, they're behind us, right behind us." Rod flew such a beautiful wing position, I could almost feel him out there.

"Magnum four, Mig Twenty-one about six thousand out." Magnum four was in trouble. We were right over the target now and there was no hope of attacking it. It was solid. I needed to get out of there, and I needed to do it without letting those Migs on my tail get enough turning advantage to do us in.

"OK, move it around, Kingpins, keep it moving." I had enough of a head of steam that I could afford to wiggle even if I couldn't afford to turn. No sense in making yourself a steady target. "This is Kingpin. The target's no good. I'm starting a one eighty turn to the right. Keep your eyes open and let's see if we can work these guys back up the Ridge." That might be tricky, but we had to turn, as straight ahead there was nothing but Hanoi and more of the same problems we were already facing.

I was working my Migs pretty well and they had not closed on me quite as well as they had on Magnum. His were in so close that he could not turn until he managed to get some spacing on them or they would have cut him off in the turn and gained the ideal position to shoot him down. As I worked around in my turn, he flew straight through and passed to the south of me.

"Let's push it up, Magnum. He's closing." As the Mig closed inside that 6,000-foot range, he was really getting in there and Geeno would be needing some help pretty soon. By flying past me and on to the south, he had actually put me behind his pursuers and if I could just dump these little tormentors on my tail, I would be in a good spot to move in and assist Geeno.

"Roger, Magnum here. Light the burner."

"Kingpin, you coming out?"

"Rog, Kingpin is coming out now. The target stinks and we've got lots of company up here."

"Which way you breaking, Kingpin?"

"To the right."

As my own transmission faded from the headset, I knew that Bob, who had the flight bringing up the rear, had found himself a piece of that action and also that he had his usual favorite seeing-eye lieutenant, Baby Huey, on his wing. "Where's he at, Huey?"

Bob and I had played football together back at West Point some twenty-four years ago. Funny how you always recognize certain voices. That football had been fun, good clean fun. But this was fun in a way also, real dirty fun, with your life or your buddy's life as the price for losing.

Geeno was going to have to make a move pretty soon, and it sounded like he was about ready. "Kingpin, you turn left?"

"Kingpin's turning RIGHT."

"Roger, Magnum's turning left with two Mig Twenty-ones— ah—" Sometimes it gets a bit difficult to talk while you are trying to look out of the back of your head, and you could hear Geeno straining to see what his antagonists were up to.

I had worked my attackers about halfway around the turn and had my plan pretty well formulated on how I was going to support Magnum, but I wanted to be sure I knew what he was up to, since we could ill afford crossed signals at this point. "Say again, Magnum."

"Rog, Magnum's turning left and I've got Migs straight and level with me."

"You're clear, Bass four." That was one of those irritating little calls that always seem to clutter up the air at the wrong time. I had no idea who Bass four was except that I knew he was not one of mine, and while I was glad that he was clear of whatever he was concerned about, I wished that his radio would quit.

Geeno had started to work back to his left while I continued my turn to bring me around on his tail and thus on the tail of those tailgating him.

"OK, Kingpins, he's moving past our nine o'clock."

Bing still had the best angle on our Migs from his perch on the far left and announced, "OK, Kingpin, they're still at four o'clock level, but they're starting to break away." They either realized that they were gaining nothing on us while we worked them back toward the outbound course we were looking for, or they had frustrated themselves on fuel, or most probably, they assumed that I was trying to move to a spot where I could close in on Magnum. Perhaps they felt they could double up on Magnum since he was in the worst shape and, by strength of numbers, do him in. They slowly slid further right and when I figured I had them beat, I moved toward Magnum. That pair would never recover a position to bother me now. They started off strong, but they just couldn't hack the course and for the first and only time that day, things started going right for a few minutes, except you suddenly couldn't hear yourself think. The flights had become a series of units operating separately and everybody had something important to say, so important that they all cut each other out and nobody could say anything.

"Flamingo—" Was Flamingo still down on the deck dodging Sams?

"Clean 'em up—" Who in hell clean what up?

"OK, you're clear, Nick—" I wondered if Nick was in the same flight as Bass four.

I had turned Kingpin, and Geeno had turned Magnum so that I was now directly behind him. I could see the entire show as his wingman called, "OK, Magnum, we've got a Mig Twenty-one at five o'clock now." The Mig slid back, out of Magnum's field of view, and the wingman wrongly assumed that the Mig had faded off to the right as had the two that were on me.

"Roger, you're clear—"

I couldn't wait for him to finish, as the Mig had only momentarily moved back to the side. He must have been getting low on fuel and decided to give it one more college try and go home, or he moved back to change some switch setting, because he pulled directly astern of Magnum and sprinted to a perfect spot high and to the rear between Magnum lead and Magnum two. They couldn't see him and he was in an ideal spot for a double kill.

"Negative, Magnum, negative. He's still on you, Magnum— six o'clock, Magnum, a little high. He's sliding around on you."

Magnum two slid to the side a bit and dipped his wing enough to catch the awesome sight of a Soviet interceptor boresighting himself and his leader for a heat-seeking missile launch. "OK, Magnum two's bombs coming off now, watch it."

"Flamingo's got a Sam on the southeast edge of the Ridge." Man, I was glad that good old Flamingo was soaking up all those Sams.

While Magnum lead and two unloaded their bombs and pulled for their lives, one of my original pursuers got in on the act.

"OK, Magnum, Mig at three o'clock." As I watched, yet another unwanted visitor slid in on Magnum's right side. I decided the bombs had to go. We had already used so much fuel that we would have little time, if any, to look for a good target once we managed to haul our fannies out of there. We had covered a fair amount of sky at 600 knots and, lo and behold, there was a slight break in the clouds and, wonder of wonders, one of the forbidden sanctuaries sprawled beneath us. This one came off the protected list some time later, but I claim the first load of bombs into the middle of that baby doll.

"Kingpin, let's get rid of these bombs and go help them. Kingpins, bomb now."

You could almost feel the Thuds leap with joy as the

cumbersome iron blivets left. We stroked the burners and
waded into the tail cone of the leeches clinging to Magnum
and the frame of reference changed. Now we were lighter
and faster than we had been and we were closing from their
six o'clock. It was probably none too soon, as you could hear
the strain within Magnum flight.

"Where's he at, three—er—four—er—three, Magnum."

It's a tough way to make a living.

"Rog, one behind and another at three o'clock." But now
we were closing from the rear and Geeno had his flight lined
up on the heading he wanted back to the north.

"Hot Dog two, hit the burner."

"OK, Magnum, let's take it back out the Ridge." I hoped
Geeno wouldn't get overconfident now, and I wanted him to
know he was not home-free yet. "You still got 'em, Magnum."
He saw that he still had them on him, and he knew his
element could no longer hold their bombs.

"Clean 'em off. Clean 'em off. Heads up, Magnum." The
bombs fell and we charged in from the rear, but not without
duress.

"OK, we got flak from the Ridge, keep it moving, Kingpins." That was about all the Migs needed to convince them
that their afternoon was ruined. They had bombs falling in
their faces, they had a flight closing on their tail, and the
crunchies from the ground were shooting at the entire gaggle, now knowing, and probably not caring, who was who. So
the Migs disengaged. Just like that. They plugged in their
burners, racked their sleek charges up on a wing, and were
gone as rapidly as they had appeared.

"Cactus, Mig up ahead going left to right."

"Where's he at now?"

"Cactus lead, Cactus three can't get rid of the right tank."
Beautiful system. I was sure Cactus was hoping that his Mig
would keep going from left to right.

"OK, Kingpins, back to the left. Let's move up the Ridge."

I thought that perhaps the drama had ended for the day,
but I was wrong. The strangest little drama that I have ever
been exposed to occurred during the next few moments. I
have gone back over it time after time. I have listened to the
magnetic tape from the miniature Japanese tape recorder so
that I could reconstruct these wild minutes back on the
ground. I don't know what happened to Don. I don't know

what he did or why. All I can do is relate what I saw and
heard and try to fit the pieces together from what I can
remember of my somewhat nervous, horribly intelligent little
doctor friend. My friend who should have been teaching
young men in the classroom, but who instead felt that he
should be herding a 49,000-pound monster around the skies
of North Vietnam at 600 knots in this crummiest of all
so-called wars.

When we figured that we had Geeno out of the bag, we
headed back up the Ridge, planning to turn west at the north
end and beat a track for the Red River and thence south to a
tanker and home. Rod was still on my wing like glue and as
we rolled clear of the flak from the Ridge, Don and Bing
were on the right side and together, and everything should
have been OK. We were still moving around; that flak from
the Ridge could still reach us, and we all knew that there
were plenty of Migs still capable of giving us trouble. I rolled
about 20 degrees to the left and gained a few hundred feet,
then dropped the nose and let it fall back to the right as I
kicked in a little rudder to make the bird slide slightly
sideways in an uncoordinated maneuver calculated to hamper
the tracking activities of any gunners looking at me. Rod
moved in the same general plane, but crossed his controls
with a different degree of emphasis and timing so that while
we moved together, we presented different, uncoordinated
targets. If you fly smoothly or play the show formation game,
you help the gunners solve their problem.

As I came back to the approximate track I had left only
seconds before, I automatically looked to the right to check
the element, and I saw Don's nose start gradually down while
Bing held his wing spacing. As Don's nose dropped, his
speed increased and he pulled abreast and then slightly
ahead of me. It was a strange move, and he made no radio
transmission. (I did not realize it at the time, but replaying
the tape later, I found that in all that melee of voices, Don
had not spoken once since we had started down the Ridge. A
good wingman or element lead doesn't have to talk to get the
job done, and it is ideal if he keeps quiet unless he has
something important to pass to the other members of the
flight, but there had been an awful lot of calls made in the
hassle and the odds were that some of them should have been

Don's calls.) Suddenly, the multiple ejector rack, better known as the MER, a big piece of metal to which the bombs are attached, left the belly of his aircraft smoothly and cleanly, indicating that he had jettisoned it from the cockpit. This was weird in that his bombs were already gone, and his tanks were gone, and while the MER is a slight additional drag factor, there are only a couple of reasons why you would drop it. The first would be a situation where the bombs were hung up and refused to release from the MER. If everything else fails, you can get rid of the load by pickling the MER and all, and the entire load of bombs plus the rack goes in one big, inaccurate blob. This was obviously not the reason for his action. The other reason for getting rid of the MER would be to insure that the aircraft was absolutely clean of all outside garbage in the event you wanted every bit of maximum speed you could get, and Don was a speed man. It wasn't a logical move, as the speed difference is not that significant, and the MER's were a critical supply item. (We were even bringing bombs back when they were hung up or we couldn't get them where we wanted to put them, to say nothing of the racks. The official line that there was no bomb shortage forced us to use various subterfuges to keep visitors from finding out the truth. At the same time, some of our high-level commanders were in a race with the Navy to see which could record the most flying hours. The result of all this was that we were at one time sending kids out to attack a cement and steel bridge with nothing but 20-millimeter cannon, which is like trying to knock down the Golden Gate Bridge with a slingshot. Stupid missions like that cost us aircraft and people.)

Even as I was trying to figure out what was going on with Don, I instinctively rechecked my left side. You learn early in this game that you can't afford to keep your head still in the cockpit and you can't depend on even the best wingman in the world to do all of your looking for you. Almost without brain command, the head moves constantly, the eyes searching. As mine swung left, I saw the prettiest aircraft I have ever seen, and I have never seen another one like it. It was a Mig-21 in about a 40-degree dive approaching me from above in my eight o'clock position. He looked like he had rolled over from far above me, perhaps 25,000 or 30,000 feet, and pointed his charge earthward in a graceful screaming dive, and he was really moving. He went by me so fast I could have imagined that my engine had quit and that it was time to eject. As he streaked past, just off my wing tip and in complete control of this beautiful piece of machinery, I saw the most unusual paint job I have ever seen. The craft was painted several shades of gray in a scalloped pattern with the peaks of the scallops pointing upward toward the top of the aircraft. The paint blended beautifully with the sky and clouds, and was one of the most effective camouflage jobs I have ever seen. I know of nobody who paints their machines like this, but it would be an excellent idea. This guy was different; he was no run-of-the-mill North Vietnamese trainee. I couldn't see his eyeballs, but I'm willing to bet that they were both round and blue. It was a bit reminiscent of Korea many years before when you could pick out the master attempting to herd his charges through their combat upgrading. When they failed to respond properly, you could almost hear him scream "Idiots!" and launch into a masterful pass of his own. I certainly hope that our management of statistics and stories does not delude us into believing that we have met and conquered the best of the world's airmen. It just is not so, and the 10 to 1 kill ratio racked up by the Mig-21's a bit later ought to make somebody do a bit of thinking. I am not talking about a bunch of clods in old beat-up Mig-17's and Mig-15's; I'm talking about good pilots in good machines. We have many very competent adversaries, lying in the weeds, but that is another one of those unpleasant things that as an Air Force and as a Department of Defense we have cultivated a deaf ear for. We don't like to hear anything that does not please us.

He never batted an eye at me and I had already instinctively plugged in my burner and started a swing toward his tail as he passed me. He was so far ahead, it was hopeless, but you try anyway. My head swung back to the right, and what I saw horrified me. In just the few seconds since I had last looked at him, Don had fired up his burner and accelerated to a position several thousand feet below and in front of me. Our mutual protection was gone, and what was worse, I could tell that he was still accelerating and pulling further away. Bing was fighting madly to stay on his wing, but Don was pulling away from him. What was he thinking? He was heading for a break in the lower layer of the undercast, but it was only a

Mig-15

small hole and there were only a few feet of clear sky between those clouds and the ground. Suddenly I knew what that pretty Mig was after. He had Don and Bing spotted and with his speed and maneuverability, he was gracefully floating into a position to blast them.

"OK, Kingpin three and four, you got one on your tail." I got no acknowledgment. The interval between them and the Mig shortened. "Keep going to the left, Kingpins." They were almost to the edge of the hole now, and he wouldn't talk and he wouldn't change course. "Kingpin three and four, go full burner, he's closing on your tail."

"Cactus three, break out and fall back there with Cactus four. He's got a tank hung and can't keep up."

Magnum had headed for the deck, but he was not yet free. "Back up, Magnum, we got Migs coming in again."

Probably the most confused man of all was Bing, and as they ducked under the cloud ledge, he knew things were very wrong. He was obliged to stay on his element leader's wing, and his job was to protect his boss, but his boss was taking him down into an almost certain trap, and his boss was eluding the protection Bing was offering. Bing had long since gone to full burner and had gone through the speed of sound in his chase. He was now at Mach 1.1 and still not closing when he thought that perhaps Don had lost the continuity of events and thought that he, Bing, was a Mig in pursuit.

"Kingpin three, this is four back here on your wing—"

"Magnum, a pair high at ten."

The thought flashed through my mind that perhaps Don had somehow become confused on his call sign, but that just doesn't happen very often. "OK, the pair of Thuds that just went under the clouds—Mig on your tail—get back up here." If the call sign had been a problem, there was no answer to prove it.

"Magnum two, light your burner. Light your burner."

"Kingpin lead—Chicago lead. Has the mission been aborted?"

All I needed was some confused radio chatter. "Chicago, it's aborted." Our fancy Mig was still visible as he approached the cloud deck, and I was after him in hopes that he would maneuver enough to allow me to get on him before he got three and four. I rolled a little left and dropped my nose to let my beast pick up all the speed I could get. I was sure glad I didn't have to worry about Rod, he was right there. "OK, Kingpin two, there's our Mig right down there. Let's go twenty degrees to the left—he's right at the base of the clouds—full burner now."

"Kingpin—Chicago. Say again, has the mission been aborted?" What in hell was the matter with that clod?

"A–BORT—A–BORT—A–BORT!" And shut up.

"Roger, understand the mission is aborted?" Unbelievable. "That's affirmative."

Our Mig blended with the clouds like he was invisible and then he disappeared under them. I knew I couldn't catch him or get on him underneath that deck if I didn't have him when he dropped through that hole. I had to bet that he would not find it to his liking down there in the haze and among his own gunners and would pop right back up through the layer and allow me to tap him as he emerged.

"OK, Kingpin, out of burner. Let's stay on top and see if we can pick him up."

"Magnum, take it to the right. Go hard left, Magnum, hard left now. Magnum two, rock your wings." Magnum was slightly scrambled; little wonder.

"Flapper heading zero two zero. Sam at ten o'clock."

"Cactus one, go left. Go left, burner now." I was glad to see that Cactus was still in good shape as I was concerned over the straggler with the hung tank. This was no place to be a loner, and with Don in some obvious trouble, we couldn't afford any further complications.

"Kingpin one, how about tapping burner? I'm a bit steep and slow." I was abusing my competent wingman and practically had him standing on his head. His only complaint was that he needed that after-burner power to stay there.

"Kingpin two, you got lead, OK?" I was sort of standing on my head also and wanted to be sure he was with me.

"Roger." He was there.

"OK, good boy."

We had picked up some altitude and then had let our birds fall off on a wing and drop back toward the clouds. This way we could keep our speed up and cover the entire area where I expected our Mig to pop back on top. "Let's go back up again, Kingpin. He's still down underneath it."

"Say again?"

"He's right down here underneath us, but he won't come back up again." Then up he came, right where we wanted him. We had plenty of speed, and we had a couple of thousand feet altitude on him. It was only about a 20-degree turn for me, and I was on him and closing fast from his eight o'clock. He didn't see me at first and I don't know if his ground controllers gave him the word or if he saw me when he made a little 20-degree check turn to the left. Regardless, he was plenty smart and realized that a pair of Thuds hurtling down on him was less than desirable. It was time for him to disengage and get out of there, and he wrapped his little beauty into a vertical 180-degree turn to the left and was gone. Just like that. I couldn't come close to staying with him, and he was gone. It must be great to call the shots like that.

As Bing had passed the top of the clouds, he had been doing Mach 1.2 and he caught a glimpse of Don through the wispy cloud and knew that he was finally closing on him. When you get one of these bombs going that speed, the process of slowing down could be as painful as the process of accelerating to that speed, and he yanked the power back to avoid overshooting his mysterious leader. He needed to get close to him and herd him out of there before they both bought a piece of the local real estate. As he raced through the bottom of the layer, he was blinded. The sun was down low in the west and it was ricocheting off the flooded rice paddies like an orange and yellow searchlight focused on a mirror. It was worse than Bing had expected. They were low, dangerously low, and down in the range of even hand-held guns. The nose was still pointed down toward the paddies, and they were much too fast to be in a nose-down attitude and still pointed toward the ground. Collision with the ground was imminent and he couldn't see where he was going. Bing did a great job in maintaining control of his craft, and anyone with lesser skill and determination could well have been finished right then and there. Where was Don?

"A-RAAAH, A-RAAH, A-RAAH!" A stinking beeper, the loneliest and most pitiful cry in the world. A call for help that you most often can't answer. A wail from men and women you don't even know telling you their world has just been torn asunder. You can't cry back, you can't help, you can't do a damn thing but save your own behind.

"Kingpin three—this is four. Kingpin three, you still this frequency? Kingpin three, you read four? Kingpin three, you read four? Kingpin lead, do you read four?"

"Five by. Kingpin three, do you read lead?"

"This is Kingpin four, how do you read lead?"

"Loud and clear, how me?"

Bing got his numbers and voices mixed up for a few seconds and let himself believe what he so much wanted to believe, what he knew he couldn't believe. Had he found his squadron commander? Was that Don on the radio? Had this all been some horrible mistake that he had imagined? He almost jumped through the radio. "Rog, this three?"

"Lead."

"Three, how do you read?"

Rod was still flying the perfect wing, protecting me as I hoped against hope that I could find Don and knowing that I had to get Bing back in the fold before we had another beeper. "Kingpin lead, we got bogies, far out at ten o'clock." I didn't have to tell him to keep track of them. He knew that I was down too low over nasty territory, and he knew that I had to try and put the pieces back together. Those bogies were his worry for the next few minutes.

"Kingpin three, you on your way out?"

Damn it. I knew I was too low, and I knew I wasn't positive of our exact location and I had dragged us right over the river and that rotten Yen Bai. Flak, bad flak, they almost got us—too close—trouble.

"Shooting, Kingpin." When you stumble into a trap like that and your wingman tells you what you already know, you almost feel like saying something real stupid like, "Oh, really?" but you know it is serious. That was the kind of spot where you could lose one or two so fast you wouldn't know what happened. When those red streaks reach up from the ground and the black puffs spit at you and shake the aircraft and when you can hear the stuff cracking and shrieking all around you, you know that you screwed it up by being there and you know that the next few seconds could be your last.

"OK, let's go over hard, burner, keep it moving. Watch it down there on my left. Ten o'clock. WATCH IT!"

"Still shooting, Kingpin."

"Rog, keep her moving." Sometimes it's hard to believe it when it stops. "Kingpin three, how do you read lead?"

"Kingpin four here, read you loud and clear." By now Bing should be past the worst of the shooting and at least we still had three of us in operation. We should have put a special strike effort on Yen Bai a long time ago and cleaned that dump out. There's nothing there but flak, and we have known that for years. Yet we have to piddle our people away on dry runs instead of spending a couple of days eliminating that thorn.

"Rog, four, you lose three?"

"Kingpin lead, two's bingo."

"And four's bingo."

I was bingo myself and then some, and I knew that there was no time to waste in getting us to that tanker. You can't imagine how fast that fuel gauge falls when things get hectic.

"Kingpin four, you with three?

"Negative, I lost him."

"Kingpin four, do you read three—correction—three do you read four?" It had been a hard afternoon and you could tell by the chatter that we were all pretty well beat out.

"Kingpin, we got a couple of bogies out front, low. Take a look at them."

"Kingpin three, do you read four? Kingpin three, do you read four? Lead, four is going to emergency frequency for a minute."

I rogered with "We'll stay this frequency until you get back," and Bing switched his radio equipment over so that it

would transmit on our operating channel and on the emergency channel at the same time, making another attempt that
we knew would not work.

"Hello, Kingpin three, do you read four? This is Kingpin
four on emergency, three, do you read?"

The next wing was well on the way into the area and their
leader, Baltic, wanted to know what was up. He switched his
flight to our frequency and they sounded fresh and crisp as
they checked in. "Baltic."

"Two."

"Three."

"Four."

"Kingpin—this is Baltic."

"Go ahead, Baltic—Kingpin."

"Rog, how's it look?"

"No good, there's a—it's broken, ah, broken coming down
the Ridge, but in the target area itself, it's solid. There's no
chance on it and, ah, it's loaded with, ah, Migs." I was
amazed at how tired I sounded on the radio.

"OK, have y'all called it off?"

"Yeah, we called it off. We went in with a couple and came
back out. We called it off. Abort."

"OK, ah, Kingpin, ah, what's your position now?"

"Ah, I'm headed back out now. The first three flights are
pretty well spread out."

"OK, we'll come up there in case you need our help, and
we're almost up there now."

I appreciated it, but I sure hoped we didn't need any more
help today. Part of my job was to give him any ideas I had on
where he might be able to do some good. "Rog, there's a
little open area between the rivers, and it's stretching out
toward the west and the northwest—there's an open area and
you might find something in there, but it's down low and
pretty solid over the target itself."

"OK, no chance of getting in."

"Nah, I wouldn't even mess with it."

"OK, is this Bob?"

"No, this is Jack." At least the Avis wing knew who the
leaders were in our wing.

"Rog."

"Kingpin—this is four back on. No contact with three."

"Rog."

5.

PEOPLE

If Don could have lasted a couple more weeks he could have been there when we started getting through on those targets that we had been sweating for so long. It was not that the weather turned good, it just got a little less horrible and allowed us to sneak in and do the job. We played the same old game and fought our way down Thud Ridge and found just enough room to work, and we did good work. We did good work under some grim conditions and we worked right on the edges of the sanctuaries that gave our adversaries all the breaks possible in working against us. We knew we were doing good work, not only from our own assessment of the raids but from the fact that Hanoi screamed like a bunch of wounded eagles every time we got a good lick in. The teamwork and dedication displayed by the pilots on that particular series of raids was truly marvelous. I had the privilege of being the big leader on a majority of these and I could not have dragged a lesser bunch of men through some of the things I dragged them through.

* * *

One of the first times we got through must have been one
of the most challenging rides down Thud Ridge anyone has
ever had. As we turned the northern corner we knew that the
Migs were up and nipping at our heels. There was a solid
layer of cloud underneath us but something of the Irish
intuition my mother, Elizabeth McGinley Broughton, passed
on to me from her ancestors led me to believe that it was not
too thick and that there might be enough of a hole down by
the river to let us work. I was hungry for the larger military
and commercial transshipment targets on the edges of Hanoi
and if there was a chance I was determined to get my guys in
after we had come this far.

As I headed south, the Migs moved into view and it
appeared that the time was ripe both to confuse the Migs and
to see what it looked like under the cloud. I started us all
down through the murk with the target only minutes ahead.
As I broke out underneath the clouds, I found Thud Ridge on
my left covered with rain clouds that boiled under the main
cloud blanket and went right down to the valley floor. The
cloud deck and the rain sloped downhill away from me toward
the river where it looked downright ominous. Maybe that
hole wouldn't be there after all, but I had committed the
forces and we were going to give it a try. I also found what an
excellent job the gunners had done in estimating the height
of the clouds as everything north and west of Phuc Yen let fly
at once. It was obvious that I could not hold the troops down
at this level, so I eased my twenty charges back up into the
rain. We were bouncing along close to 600 in the slop when
my trusty Doppler navigational gear, as usual, decided that
things were too rough and it went ape. I knew pretty well
how I had to steer from here for the next few minutes, but I
obviously had nothing in the aircraft to check my progress
and I could not see the ground to look for landmarks. My
buddy Geeno had the element and I gave him a quick call,
"Lost my Doppler. Steer me, Geeno."

The Migs, already in the air, had elected to stay on top of
the cloud layer when I descended and were pacing us and
waiting for us to reemerge. They climbed on board immediately and the show was now in a precarious spot. Because of
the Migs, I couldn't stay up here either, and at the speeds we
were moving I hoped that we had passed the heavy area of
ground fire that I had encountered several seconds ago, so I

took us back down. This time I broke out in heavy rain just north of the Mig sanctuary at Phuc Yen and the traffic pattern was full of Migs taking off to go after my trailing flights and after the next wing due to follow me into the area. I flew almost down the runway itself and made what amounted to a head-on pass at several pairs of Migs turning out of traffic and preparing to attack. If I had not had that bombload on board and had not been herding my troops into the target I could have had a couple of them about the time they reached for the handle to pull their landing gear up. I could also have glide-bombed their airfield and torn it all to hell, but that was forbidden as were the Migs unless their wheels were off the ground.

I knew that the Migs I was now passing would only have to turn on their armament switches and make another 180-degree turn to be on the attack but there was not too much I could do about it except wonder why we had not cleaned their clock about a year ago. I ducked down another couple of hundred feet to avoid a heavy rainstorm, but this one held some of the promise I was looking for. The entire valley was a nasty shade of gray approaching black in spots, but this storm was a dirty brown color and as I sped toward it the brown got lighter and blended into an almost amber tone. That meant that there was good light on the other side and perhaps sunshine and the clearing we needed. It had to be, or we were out of business because the seconds were ticking away and the target had to be right there. Geeno called a few quick steers and we broke through the wall of rain and the river was under us. I had broken out on the right side of the target rather than the left as we had planned, but the hole was there and the target was there and we worked it. As I arched up into the long pull and turn to get in bombing position, one of the Migs we thought we had left in the murk behind us arched right along with me and the heat-seeking rocket he fired at me went streaking underneath my nose to detonate in my face and convince me of two things. First, that particular Mig-21 driver was either determined or stupid to press right into the mass of flak that now nipped at us from the target itself; and second, that I had better pull a little harder if I intended to complete this run. I completed the run and the egress across the delta was exceptionally noisy that day and involved a series of vertical gyrations, as every time I dropped

down, the ground gunners reached up, and every time I
went up a Sam burst at or close to my altitude and course,
but I got out.

The number three man in the last of our flights was not
quite so fortunate, since the Migs I had been forced to pass
up as they took off from Phuc Yen had now settled on my last
flight as their prime target. They waited for them until they
came up off their run in the clear air to the south. They
picked their target wisely, they maneuvered properly, they
tracked and fired properly and they hit.

The first time Spade knew he had been hit was when he
wound up crammed up against what was left of the front
windscreen, with nothing left but the throttle grip, which he
clutched in his left hand, and the seat on which he was
sitting. His flight had been fighting the Migs off all the way
down the Ridge but had made it to the target, bombed and
were on the way out, but still in trouble. His wingman,
number four, had been fragged to carry a cumbersome camera pod that takes nice color pictures for the documentary
program but increases the drag on the machine considerably
and thus slows you down. The number four man just could
not keep up as the bombs came off and the Thuds headed out
of the area. As a result of this incident, we were finally able
to convince our headquarters that while the documentary
program was nice, we could not afford to lug external camera
pods to Hanoi. The fact that number four was dragging did
not go unnoticed by one of the previously thwarted Migs, and
he pushed in between and under the two separated Thuds
and let fly with his air-to-air missiles, which had Spade's
name all over them. Spade never saw them coming and when
he found nothing under him or around him but air, he
dropped the 6-inch-long throttle which represented all that
was left of his multimillion-dollar steed and pulled the handles. His chute worked, though unknown to him at that
instant his back was already broken, and he hit the ground 30
miles south of Hanoi.

We carry a parachute in the tail of the aircraft which we
deploy on the runway when we land to slow up our landing
roll. His number four man saw the drag chute billow as the
tail of Spade's aircraft disintegrated, and shortly after saw
Spade's chute and promptly assumed and announced, on the
radio, that there were two pilots on the way down. It was not

until we were back on the ground that we were able to count
noses and figure the basis for this call.

Considering the area that he had jumped into, we figured
that we had lost Spade. The condition of his aircraft when he
jumped had been bad enough, but he had jumped almost
into the outskirts of town and we had never recovered anyone
that far up. But the Spads (officially known as Douglas AE-1
Skyraiders) and the choppers were to write a new chapter in
rescue history that day. Spade's beeper and the calls from the
other flight members triggered the rescue effort and the
rescue troops were more than ready when he landed on the
crest of a little knoll with a few rock piles on it. In that he had
landed in the immediate target area when the strike was only
half completed, the noise of the guns and bombs was loud in
his ears, and the bad guys of the local guard unit were
already on their way up the sides of the hill to pick him up.
To his amazement, he was able to establish contact with the
rescue forces and they were on him in no time. The Spad
flight leader instructed him to crawl into one of the rock piles
and sit tight, which he managed to do despite his broken
back and other injuries suffered in the shootdown and the
ejection.

The rescue pilots fly the slower Spads and they can get
right down in the bushes and look for people on the ground.
They can also take quite a beating and with their less
sophisticated systems they have a better chance of keeping
the mill going. They get some rotten jobs because of their
unique capabilities and one of their assignments is working
with the choppers on rescue cover missions, or Rescaps in
our terminology. Not only can they find a downed crew, they
can turn and maneuver tightly enough to keep the rescue
scene in view and suppress ground movement with their
rockets and guns. Their birds are so much older than ours are
that the moniker Spad, borrowed from World War I, is a
natural.

The Spad leader called the choppers in from nameless
places to the back door of Hanoi, and Spade viewed the most
effective close-support demonstration he had ever seen. The
Spads set up a gunnery pattern around his rocky hilltop
fortress and proceeded to hold the North Vietnamese ground
forces at bay while the choppers lumbered onto the scene for
the pickup. The Spads strafed and rocketed in every direction

from treetop level, and forced back every advance of the ground troops. Their firing passes were so low that as they went past Spade they would go below him and down into the valleys surrounding his knoll. Needless to say, both he and the Spads were targets for all the gunfire the locals could bring to bear on this quintet of invaders in their backyard. One small squad of North Vietnamese almost did him in when they escaped initial observation by the Spads. They were within 50 feet of his rock pile when they lost the cover of the brush and as Spade frantically called out their position on his emergency radio, it looked for a minute like the valiant game was about over. One of the Spads spotted them at the last possible instant, but how to stop them was the problem. He called Spade on the rescue radio and said, "Now just sit tight, this will be a little close, but I've got them clearly in sight." He roared in and fired a full pod of rockets at them, some scant eight body lengths away from Spade in his hastily acquired rock fort. The earth trembled and the fire, noise, and smoke were severe, but when it cleared and the Spad dipped into the valley and back up, the pursuers were done in, and Spade was still secure.

The choppers made it into this inferno and, I am sure to the consternation of the local guard commander, hauled Spade out of Hanoi and back to safety.

We had him back at Takhli a day later and, although he didn't look or feel too great, it was wonderful to see him all propped up in that hospital bed. It was just a temporary stop on the way back to the States and and the full-time medical care he would need to get back into shape. I managed to make the right contacts and we got him to the Stateside hospital he wanted, and we also got him the assignment he wanted while he waited for his back to recover fully. I got a kick out of him as he lay there apologizing for not being able to get back in the cockpit and fly some more. He was also concerned about me. "Colonel, why do you fly all those rough ones up there? We have lots of guys like me that can find the target and take the knocks. We need you running the show." I couldn't agree with his analysis of the duties of a combat leader but the thought that my guys were devoted to the point that they considered their behinds less valuable than mine made me try even harder. The last I heard, he was

still fighting to get back to Southeast Asia and into the fray
again. He has to go high on my list of people with spunk.

A few days later and a few miles further north, Joe didn't
make out as well as Spade, but he has to go way up at the top
of the list as one who probably displayed the utmost calm and
presence of mind that I have seen. This particular strike had
been an uncomfortable mission for him from the start, as it
had been for all concerned. The target was one that had
never failed to cause us problems and this day was no
exception, as it cost us three birds and three pilots on this
mission alone. The weather was stinking en route and the
flights had trouble on the tankers. That weather over there is
the thickest I have ever seen and when you get inside of one
of those big thunder-bumpers you are in for a good ride.
Most clouds you fly through have their share of bumps but
the visibility inside is usually good enough so that you can sit
on the wing of another aircraft and fly formation off him. You
just maintain the position you want and when he turns or
rolls his aircraft, you roll right along with him. You have no
idea where you are if you are on the wing, but that is up to
the leader. The only time you get into trouble on the wing is
when you try to fly position and also try to outguess the
leader. This usually winds up in a case of spatial disorientation
called vertigo. If this happens you can be sitting straight and
level and swear that you are cocked up in a 60-degree bank
going sideways. It is a most distressing sensation and sometimes almost impossible to get rid of. You can shake your
head and holler at yourself and sometimes it won't go away,
and it can be fatal. In most clouds if all aircraft have their
external lights on, you can at least see the wing-tip light of
the aircraft next to you and when things get rough you can
just fly off that light. The clouds we flew in over there were
different and, I am sure, the most dense in the world. You
could sit in perfect position and watch the leader's machine
just fade away until you could not even see his tip light or
your own nose. This is bad enough when you are on the
gauges yourself, but quite desperate when you are on the
wing. There were always lots of bumps along with the
visibility problems and with the speed and weight of our

machines, it all made for some real precision work. For a real thrill, I recommend you try this type of flying on a black night.

Joe had bounced through the refueling sessions and managed to stick with his leader, but his wingman, who was number four, was not so fortunate. He got bounced off the tanker boom by a particularly rough piece of air and was never able to find the flight again in the murk, so number three had come all the way into the target without the benefit of that wingman for mutual support. The Migs were there, but they made it in and number three beat the big guns over the target. Coming off the target at about 7,000 feet, Sam got him. Nobody saw a Sam and nobody called one, but we already had two guys down at the time and the beepers were squealing and things were moving fast. The first sign of trouble was a large rust-colored ball that enveloped his aircraft. Coming out of the ball, his aircraft appeared intact but he started a stable descent with his left wing dipped slightly low. His only transmission was "I gotta get out. I'll see you guys." With that, he pulled the handles and we saw a chute and heard the beeper as he headed for Hanoi via nylon.

The Sam site that got him didn't have to be there. We let it be there. Why? As fighter pilots, none of us could understand or accept the decision to allow the Sams to move in and construct at will, but then fighter pilots must be different.

Yes, fighter pilots are a different breed of cat. The true fighter must have that balls-out attitude that immediately makes him somewhat suspect to his superiors. You can't push for the maximum from your troops, yourself and your equipment and win any popularity contests. You are bound to tangle with nonfighter supervisors and with the support people up the line who wouldn't have a job if it were not for the airplane drivers. This they don't understand in many cases, and fighter pilots don't know why they don't understand it. Good figher pilots move fast, and they do what looks like the thing to do to get the job done. They are prone to ignore the printed word when it conflicts with something real and human and physical. This does not always make them the darlings of all those involved in the defense business, but take a look at the history of aerial warfare and see who is always in there slugging—the fighter guys. War is our profession.

I'll give you a "for instance" of how they get into trouble. This fine gent was one of our strongest and he could handle the full spectrum of jobs within the fighter field. He had gone the staff route when appropriate and had the well-balanced background needed to get to the spot where he could run a squadron in combat. He was a fierce competitor and a fearless airman who always put himself where flying leaders belong—right up in the number one spot, flying combat. Restrictions and regulations have been heavy upon us for many years and you learn to live with or around them. Only a small portion of the total force physically puts the instruments to test in a shooting situation, and those who do, attempt to comply with the rules as best they can. The rule book tends to fade a bit at times but we are all aware of the basic constrictions under which we live.

One of the most difficult restrictions to understand was the one put upon our troops when the Sam sites started rearing their ugly heads in North Vietnam. The sites look like nothing else in this world, and it did not take a great deal of smarts to figure what they were up to. In that the fighter

Sam

pilots felt most personally involved with these budding sites,
and in that they knew the end product was meant for them
alone, they were most anxious to dispatch them the moment
they started to appear up North. What could be more logical
to a stupid fighter pilot than to knock these potentially
dangerous developments off the face of the earth as soon as
they appeared? But we obviously did not understand the big
picture. We did not visualize the merit of allowing the free
movement of construction equipment and people as they
scratched out the sites and stockpiled the equipment and
missiles. We failed to see the logic of allowing them complete
freedom until the first six sites were finished and firable
before they became targets. We also failed to see why the
next sites entering the construction phase got the same
immunity as the first six even after the first six were firing.
Perhaps I should be more impressed with the importance of
protecting blond-haired, blue-eyed missile experts shooting
at me. Sorry—I'm not. But, protected they were, and the
direct order was out that you would not attack these sites.
Period. That's it. No questions please.

The man I am discussing accepted these dictates with the
same degree of distaste as many others, but they were the
rule. He was on a late afternoon mission way up North and
things got hot and heavy as usual during his bomb run. As he
pulled off the run, he came under exceptionally heavy fire
and as he horsed his Thud to avoid this unexpected fury, he
found himself looking into the middle of one of the six
partially completed sites. The thing was full of construction
equipment and people and they were scurrying about their
task of getting the defense position ready to shoot at him with
the least possible delay. The delay would probably not be too
great, as the site had missiles already on hand. The supporting
guns were well ahead of schedule and they were already in
good positions that had allowed them to cover him as he came
off the target, and they were still in fact giving him fits. Those
following him would get the same welcome and the chances
of losing people were high.

This was the time for action and he plugged in the burner,
pulled his Thud up and over the top and attacked the site
with his cannon, the only armament he had left. He shot up a
storm. He blew up construction gear that burst into flame.
He ripped open Sam fire-control gear that would never be

recovered to fire at us. He ignited Sams that raced about the area like fiery snakes gone wild and chasing their masters, and he shot the guns and the gunners who were shooting at him.

When he got back to the base and went through his debriefing chores, he was asked the routine question—did you see anything unusual? "You bet your ass I did," he replied, and gave them the full scoop on his destruction of the Sam site, which promptly entered the mechanized reporting system that takes the information to everyone in the government who makes more than forty cents an hour. The difference between debriefing on the late mission and briefing on the early, early mission is only a few hours and he had himself set to go on the first one in the morning as the target was hot and he was the natural one to lead. He had a quick bite of food, a couple of hours of sleep and went back to work.

He got off on schedule the next morning, long before the sun popped into view. He was over the target area of Hanoi before the frenzied telephone calls came cascading down the line of command. Instructions were that he was to be immediately grounded, and court-martial charges were to be prepared against him for striking an unauthorized target. It was academic. By the time the telephone was hung up and confused and bewildered supervisors at wing level tried to figure out what to do, he had been shot down. Ironic? It's more than that, it's sick.

It's sick because we handcuff ourselves on tactical details. First, we oversupervise and seem to feel that four-star generals have to be flight leaders and dictate the details of handling a type of machinery they have never known. Second, we have lost all sense of flexibility, and we ignore tactical surprise by insisting on repeated attacks without imagination. Third, our intelligence, and the interpretation and communication of that intelligence, is back in the Stone Age. Fourth, our conventional munitions are little improved over 1941 and those who insist on dictating the ultimate detail of their selection, fuzing and delivery do not understand or appreciate their own dictates. (This, of course, assumes that they have adequate quantities and varieties on hand to be selective.) Fifth, we have not advanced far enough in the field of meteorology to tell what we will have over the homedrome an hour from now. Our degree of accuracy on vital details like bombing winds over the target is abominable. Sixth, many of our high-level people refuse to listen to constructive criticism from people doing the job. The refusal to listen to anything that is not complimentary to our system is costing us people and machines. In defense of my tirade. I hasten to add that pilots do miss, but when they do, it is usually because there is too much stacked up against them. They certainly don't miss from lack of desire, because when it is your head that is on the block, you spare no physical effort to do the job properly, knowing that if you don't, you will be back to try again.

Unfortunately, hit or miss, we often find ourselves repeatedly fragged against targets that have already been bombed into insignificance except for the defenses that are left, and reinforced, to capitalize on our pattern of beating regular paths to each new target released from the "Restricted" list.

They figure if the Americans want to keep coming back here again and again, they might as well move in all the guns they can and get as many of us as possible. This is not a new approach to the battle between aircraft and ground defenses, and it usually resolves in favor of the defenses. The big advantage of fighter aircraft involved in an air-to-ground struggle is the element of surprise, and the ability of the aircraft to be flexible in the attack. When you take these factors away from the airman, you put him in a position of dueling a fixed and stable platform from a rapidly moving and unstable platform, and most of the odds go to the guns. A good gun defense is made up of several mutually supporting guns or groups of guns. It is not like being able to roll in and pick one specific, well-defined spot on the ground and saying, "If I can hit that spot, I can silence the guns." You have to look for the optimum spot to cover all the guns in the complex and hope that your ordnance will get maximum coverage for you, or else you have to pick the most formidable single gun or group of guns and go after them while their buddies have at you. Even if you are able to cover a fair number of guns, all the guns for miles around can rapidly identify your intended routes of attack and they are quick to respond to cover your ingress and egress.

The ideal way to beat these forces is to hit each defense only once, get the job done and get out. If we were perfect all the way, as regards ordnance available, fuzing utilized, intelligence, weather, tactics, targeting and delivery, this would be possible. It does not happen too often, and when we get a strike that works out like that, the joy level is high. If you do not put all the bombs exactly where they belong—and there are many who have never been there who do not accept the fact that there are reasons why this can happen—you have to go back. If the bomb damage assessment by one of the many reconnaissance vehicles available does not satisfy all concerned as to what you saw or claimed, back you go. Perhaps the greatest source of irritation along this line is the interpretation of the photos the reconnaissance aircraft bring back. You can have as many assessments of damage as you have viewers of the pictures. Unfortunately, the groups known as photo interpreters are not always of the highest level of skill or experience, and their evaluation quite often does not agree with that of the men doing the work. I have bombed, and seen my troops bomb, on specific targets where I have watched the bombs pour in and seen the target blow up, with walls or structures flying across the area, only to be fragged right back into the same place because the film didn't look like that to the lieutenant who read it way back up the line. I have gone back on these targets and lost good people and machines while doing so, and found them just as I expected, smashed. But who listens to a stupid fighter pilot?

But the photo guys are sometimes quite correct. If the complex is large enough, they can sometimes tell what percentage of the structures are still standing and how effective the complex may still be. The problem then is with those overzealous to the point that they want each and every outhouse flattened. This you can do, eventually, but what is it worth, if the complex is already broken, to get that last little 20-foot by 20-foot outhouse? I don't think it's worth an aircraft or a guy, yet how many of each have the outhouses cost us? This is where the defenses take us apart little by little. They know where we can bomb and where we can't. Thus, the forbidden areas can be less heavily defended, as long as the enemy can recall their deployed defenses at will. When they look at the areas we hit, their problem then becomes only one of where to put the most emphasis. Their answer is quite simple. Put them where the Americans struck yesterday. They know we will be back, and they know we will be back again, probably from the same direction at the same time of day and with the same number of aircraft. They move the guns in, and we oblige by providing more gunnery practice and the game compounds while we assume they must be protecting something very valuable, yet our pilots return and say there is nothing there but guns. We back ourselves right into the corner we abhor and wind up dueling fixed gun positions, and then we wonder how we lost so many people and machines on little targets or little pieces of larger targets.

We started this game around Pyongyang in Korea and were amazed at how rough that little rail yard became. Of course, we went the same route everyday and even had canned routes where we would hook around the tracks to the north and come thundering down the tracks like the Kimpo express, at the exact same time each day. We lost our fanny regularly. It would even have been fun to go around the course backward, or at least an hour earlier or later. In North Vietnam we fell into the same trap in a much rougher league, and on a larger scale. The flexibility is just not being utilized and it is costing us.

And what of fuzing on our bombs? This, plus the size of bombs used, is worthy of some consideration. Fuzes accomplish one of three basic things. They set a bomb off just before it hits the ground and the resultant fragmentation and blast destroys targets such as guns sitting on the ground. Another type sets the bombs off the instant they touch the ground and this is effective against personnel or against something relatively light that you want to blow over or collapse. The third type will delay the detonation of the bombs until they have penetrated the surface of the targets and this approach is most effective for blowing up or cratering hard surfaces. The size of the bomb is another factor that weighs heavily on the outcome of a particular mission. In the simplest of terms you can carry several small bombs or a few large bombs. If you are trying to hit a big target hard, the big blast is the answer. If you want coverage, take more of the smaller bombs. Even from this most basic armament discussion, it should be clear that several small bombs that go off the instant they touch a big strong bridge are going to do little more than scar the surface. By the same token, if you drop an instant load on a dirt road, for example, you will sure dust off the area, but there are no postholes afterward. By the time the dust settles, it is apparent that you might as well have stayed home. Our command mismatching in this segment of our operation has been gross. We have not done our homework properly, and this makes for useless return trips and needless exposure of our resources.

The weatherman can force you to go back to a target several times. The most obvious way is a bum area forecast. When you get one of these and are sent North, only to get within a few miles of the target and then have to return, the frustration index is immense. Perhaps one of the most damaging aspects of this is that you have telegraphed your punch, and the enemy knows what you are after. We get so full of pressure on getting some crumb that might have been released to us that we don't quit once we get lined up on a course. Needless to say, the enemy is well prepared when we break through those last few miles of marginal weather after we have had him going through dry runs for days ahead of time. But a more subtle weather factor is the prediction of wind direction and velocity in the target area. In a closed-circuit operation like Vietnam, the pilot is not overly concerned with winds en route to the target or winds at 30,000 feet. These winds play a part in the game, but we know where we have to go and about how much of everything it will take to do it. The wind we need is the wind from the point in our dive-bomb run where we punch the release button to the point where the bombs hit the ground. This is the payoff for the whole effort. If you tell that stupid bomb that the wind is going to be 10 knots at his back and that is why you are releasing him pointed toward a place short of his target, the bomb can't do doodle-doo about it. He falls the same way each time that you release him at a specific speed and in a specific dive angle. Now, if that wind is correct and if the pilot established the proper aiming point, that bomb has no choice but to crash directly into the target, to be triggered by his fuze. If you dispatch him into a wind that is not what you told him—if it is 10 knots in his face—he can't possibly do the job for you. Imagine the effect this can have when you are aiming at a 20-foot square building. Wind errors like this are not uncommon, nor are they due to a lack of desire to do the job right on the part of the weathermen. They simply are not prepared to give accurate winds over a strange spot on the ground. Each hill produces its own eddies and under our present degree of understanding our bombing winds are just not good enough.

We went to the big steel mill one day with a wind that was forecast out of the south at 20 knots, and that is a fairly tough wind to compete with in the solution of the bombing problem. My assigned portion of the complex was the northernmost of three large buildings whose long axis faced almost due east and west. To hit my target, with the reported winds, I had to displace my aiming point to the south of the building, or into the wind. My run was a good one and the sight picture as I aimed and pressed the bomb release button was just what I wanted. We found out from pilot reports that the bombs got a surprise. The wind was 20 knots all right, but it was from due north, not from due south. Fortunately for my ego, Ho Chi Minh had the foresight to slide the southernmost of those three buildings right under my two 3,000-pound bombs and I clobbered it, preserving my accuracy record—no thanks to the weatherman.

It was such a target, refragged through a combination of these factors, that set the stage for a story about one of our older warhorses. As one of our more venerated heads, he was flying in the number three spot on one of our nastier assignments when we returned for about our tenth strike on a hot little railroad and bridge area. The place had claimed many of our Thuds and people, and the claims were valid. The place was hot to start with, and as we returned time after time, the North Vietnamese figured they could make the best of a good thing by moving more guns into the area, which they promptly did. Someone figured it was worthy of another strike. We hadn't thought so when it gobbled up five Thuds over a couple of days from the Avis wing, and we hadn't thought so a few days ago when we had been there, but we were on the way back. On the most recent one, I had been leading the wing and our warhorse had been leading one of the other flights. We had split just before the target and as I came off target, Sam appeared in two flights of two. The first two went between my flight and his and turned his number two man, one of our fine young captains, into three long stringy globs of flame and junk that seemed to stop and hang over the target like a grotesque oriental lantern. The second two Sams goofed and hugged the deck. They went out of sight, in perfect formation only a few hundred feet above the ground accelerating to full speed in a wild chase to the northeast and the Chicom (Chinese Communist) border—but none of us were there. I've got that picture locked in my memory and would love to be able to paint it.

I could tell from the transmissions within his flight that the old warhorse would much rather have been up there in the number one spot. We entered, did the job, faced the problems, and suddenly were on the egress route. Everyone was so tense that anything different that had happened would have been welcome. Halfway back to the water, he blurted out in his unmistakable tones, "Lead, if you would kindly slow down a bit, it might be possible for some of us back here to catch up with you and rejoin."

Lead came back with "I don't want to hurt your feelings, but we're behind you."

There was a short pause while the veteran contemplated a suitable reply to fling at the fledgling flight lead he had obviously not followed properly. "Well, in that case we are in good shape," he retorted.

But he couldn't win. Number four piped up with "Now that we have that straightened out, three, how about slowing down so I can catch up with you."

6.

THE ALL-AMERICAN BOY

Every night except Sunday at five o'clock, we had what we called a stand-up briefing. The reason we omitted Sunday was that we liked to have some indicator of time passing, do something different once in a while. So Sunday no stand-up, but every other day at precisely 1700 we launched into a routine that took thirty to forty-five minutes depending on how formal you wanted to make it. When I first got to the wing, I personally felt that the stand-up was a little too much of a show affair and that we could save some time and effort and still get the job done. Our deputy commander for operations at the time was Col. Aaron J. Bowman, and Bo shared my views. Whenever the boss was not on the scene, Bo or I would run the show, depending on who was available, and we would compete to see who could cut the affair down the most. I managed to get it down to seventeen minutes, by urging everybody on and not tolerating the wandering self-effacing approach. One night when I was still airborne, and the boss was gone, Bo took it and pared it down to fourteen minutes, then, in one super push after that, I got it down to twelve minutes. But it didn't work. Because the boss was there much of the time and liked a very thorough briefing, both Bo and I gave up the capsule idea and went along with the program.

We spent thirty to forty-five minutes each day going through, first of all, our schedule for the next day, how many of what aircraft hauled in how much freight and mail for the past day, our statistical results for the present day showing how many missions we were fragged for versus how many we flew; then we compared our statistics with those of our sister F-105 wing at Korat, the Avis wing. (Nobody can afford to be second statistically these days and if the figures aren't right, you figure them a different way.) We then went into the intelligence portion that covered, in quite some detail, the accomplishments of each flight launched during the past twenty-four hours, and then came a few appropriate comments from our intelligence officer on trends in the air war up North or pertinent points from the overall world situation. We next looked at some visual presentations plotting the primary targets for the next day and then the weather officer would get up on the platform and give us his WAG (wild ass guess) on the probabilities of getting into the target the following day. He covered the outlook in all target areas, in the refueling areas, and of course, gave a familiar TV-type outlook for our own homedrome plus the other fighter bases in the area. Next came a dozen or more statistical masterpieces in chart form from the maintenance guy. These were designed to dazzle you with detail and prove that we never did anything wrong. The detail included all facets of the operation, past, present and forecast for the next day, and wound up with a statistical and numerical rundown on the nature and quantity of all of our on-hand aircraft spare parts and munitions. Then came the photo officer who spelled out how many feet of film went through how many of which type cameras, plus a breakout of which cameras worked, which did not work, and again a monthly percentage of success. Next to last on the program was the safety officer who harangued on ground, air and missile safety to include the detail of which Thai driver dented which contractor's fender on which truck. The temptation to editorialize during this phase must have been great, and coming as it did at the tail end of a long hard day, this pitch often went wide of the mark.

The finale came when the boss got up on the platform and discussed anything he wanted to discuss. He ranged from

McDonnell F-4C "Phantom"

what had happened to future plans. Mostly we talked about visitors for the next day and how we would operate in spite of them. It was a good gimmick, and it sort of kept you up to speed on what was going on; however, I found that after listening to it every day for months it lost some of its effect, upon me at least. One thing that we did have on occasion that spiced up the stand-up was the presentation of awards to our aircrews and to our support folks.

We would usually have these at the start of our stand-up briefings and would try to get all of our people who had received awards through this exercise at one time or another. In order to present the awards properly, the citation was read from the platform and the senior officer present then pinned the specific award or decoration on the recipient's chest. At these ceremonies, we presented such things as Air Medals, sometimes Distinguished Flying Crosses, Commendation Medals, certificates for outstanding performance and the like. DFCs and up were usually saved for one of our many visiting general officers and we asked them to hang them on the chests of the guys who had earned them. We had a particular award called the 13th Air Force Well-Done Award. It was awarded to pilots who had been recommended by their commanders and whose recommendations had been approved by the 13th Air Force. They were for handling an aircraft emergency in an outstanding manner, usually highlighting the fact that they got the machine back where it belonged rather than parking it in the jungle, or parking themselves in the jungle. It was the closest the 13th Air Force ever got to combat aircraft or jungles. We presented these at the stand-up and a little plaque went along with the award. On one such evening, we presented this award to a very sharp and shiny young man whom I'll call Bob.

His citation said that Bob was number four in a four-ship strike flight that encountered very heavy flak and numerous Migs while attacking its target, and that during his run, he lost his utility hydraulic pressure that runs all sorts of equipment on the aircraft including the afterburner and the cannon. These are both quite essential elements in Mig country, and the loss of these systems makes you a poor match for a Mig. He was dramatically alerted to the lack of burner when he tried to engage it coming off the target in order to close up the flight spacing from his number four position. No burner light simply meant that he could not keep up with his faster-moving companions and that he was number one Mig bait. The Migs have an uncanny sense of knowing when you have a flight member in trouble and, as they so often did, they rose from their sanctuary and struck at this separated flight. While they somehow failed to position themselves properly for an easy attack on Bob's partially operative bird, they did wind up in good position for an attack on the rest of the flight and a workable, if less than optimum, pass on Bob.

Knowing that his buddies would sacrifice their own speed to attempt to get him back in the envelope of mutual cover-age, and that this action would make them pigeons for the Migs that he could now see clearly and that the other flight members could not see too well, Bob determined that the course of action to save the flight lay directly in his lap. He coaxed the maximum speed out of his machine as he got rid of the tanks and all other external garbage that further slowed him down and, with a sick bird, he turned into and pressed an attack on the entire Mig flight. Since his cannon was nothing but excess ballast, he had no hope of shooting them down and he knew that his only hope was to scare them off. Scare them off he did, as he flew directly into the middle of them, scattering them all over the sky. All airplane drivers abhor the thought of a midair collision and the Mig pilots saw

Bob as another one of those crazy Thud drivers trying to ram
them. The ruse worked perfectly and the scattered Migs
regrouped and went off to seek less aggressive prey. The
flight was able to recover their limping protector and they
herded him back to the nearest airstrip where he accomplished a faultless recovery and landing with the systems he
had left. Quite a combination of guts and skill.

Bob was certainly an impressive young fellow. He was a big
guy and he flew with the same squadron I flew with. Here
was a youngster in his early twenties, extremely clean-cut
and healthy, a big strapping example of American manhood.
He looked like the All-American Boy, and he flew extremely
well. He was eager and most anxious to please, and on the
several missions I had flown with him, I was most impressed
by his professional manner and his approach to his job of
flying combat. He acted far more mature than his years and
had all the prospects of being a great combat leader.

He was particularly impressive on the evening when he
received his Well-Done award, as he was the kind of guy who
matched the citation. All present were taken by his appearance and we knew we had ourselves a good boy. The next
morning, Bob was flying number two in Crab flight and, with
the rest of the troops, he loaded up with two 3,000-pounders
and a center-line fuel tank and proceeded with his assigned
task for the day, going to downtown Hanoi.

In the month that we had started moving closer toward
downtown Hanoi, the defenses had become more intense,
almost frantic. The flak was spread out all over the area, but
there was plenty of it, and the Russians were providing the
North Vietnamese with all the Sams they could launch. By
now, with the Migs, Sams and guns well coordinated, the
defense was probably as intense as the Northern forces could
muster and the Migs were particularly active. They would
orbit in a specific area and you would have to fight first
through them and then through the Sams. The Migs would
stay pretty well dispersed so as not to soak up the Sams, but
there have been occasions when the Migs have not done their
homework too well and have wound up right in the middle of
their own ground fire.

Generally, however, you could see steady improvement in

their defense coordination and as you moved down the Ridge you would go through a definite Mig area where the Sams, although they might be actively operating their radar, would not be firing. Once you broke through that quadrant, the Sams would start filling the air. The ground fire was always present during this phase and in the area of the target itself. As soon as you came back up off the target, you would usually find the Migs shunted in against you, and you would have to fight your way back out. The Migs found out that once we dropped our bombs, with the speed we had and the power that we had available, we were not too attractive as targets. The Migs were not too pleased when they found that by then we were really carrying a head of steam and that their aircraft could not compete with us down low. They found, to their sorrow I'm sure, that the unloaded Thud was more than a match for them at low altitude as long as we didn't try to turn with them, and our buddies in the F-4C Phantoms gave them fits at higher altitudes. They got a few, but although we got a lot more of them than they ever got of us, it is important to remember that there is a significant difference in Mig drivers and in Mig models. I can recall one go, coming up off a target along the Red River when I had the lead flak-suppression flight, that turned out quite well. We dropped our bombs and came racing back up to altitude, remembering the Migs we had experienced in the area all the way down the Ridge. The Avis wing was working over on the other side of the Ridge at the same time, and the Migs were pretty well mixed up with them also. The Migs had been orbiting out to the west of us as we bombed and, as I came zooming up off the target heading back to the north, my first view was a head-on pass from a Mig who did not appear to be too well coordinated or satisfied with his attack. He had failed to take my speed into consideration, and by the time he actually tried to line up on me, he had already lost the battle and was all for getting out of the pass. I didn't get an opportunity to shoot at him and the resultant head-on pass turned into nothing more than a near-collision that scared me and, if he had any sense, should have scared him. We went zipping past each other canopy to canopy with a closing speed well up in the 1200-knot range.

About this time, Paul, my number two guy, on my west side and a little high, came into my field of view quite clearly. He really caught my attention, as the first time I saw him after we came up off the target there was a Sam bursting directly behind his tail pipe. Fortunately, it was fired at a right angle to him as he passed, a most difficult shot, or he never would have made it. The thing burst just perfectly on his tail pipe and covered about half of his aircraft with that horrible ugly orange ball, and to my surprise, he came flying out of the side of the orange ball. Some of his equipment was not working properly, and knowing that the Sams had his range and elevation, he had no choice but to roll over and hit for the weeds. He had to get down behind the Ridge before they tapped him. This, of course, left me without a wingman, which is not the greatest feeling in the world. My element was coming up off the target and were to my east, but my left side was quite bare. Bending to the right, I noted that I was lined up to the west of the Ridge and pointed right at Phuc Yen; in fact, I was very nicely lined up with the hometown runway of these guys I was fighting with. The ground gunners were sure lighting up all around the airfield and I was able to do battle with them with my trusty Vulcan cannon. That's not the kind of duel you engage in for any lengthy time period and live to talk about it, but it is satisfying to be able to at least give them a shot in their own backyard. It would be much better to knock their whole ball park out completely, but I guess that would keep them from shooting at us and that wouldn't be fair—or something.

I spotted two Mig-17's in a very sloppy echelon that put them almost one behind the other. They were under me in a lazy turn to the west and south away from Phuc Yen. I still had a bag of speed and I had my cannon and a heat-seeking Sidewinder missile, which requires multiple switch actions to set up—it's not difficult, it's just time-consuming and at the instant I did not have the time. The four separate switch

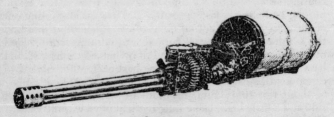

Vulcan cannon

actions that you have to take to go from the bombing mode to the missile mode did not lend themselves to this situation. With one more hand, I could have utilized the missile but I just could not fumble fast enough on this particular pass to get it set up. I closed on the two Migs like mad and they stayed in their gentle turn and did not appear to see me. I thought, I'll go through my switching action and set up my missile—but if I do, I'll have to wiggle around a bit and delay, and they may see me in the interim and initiate a break. If they do, I can't touch them as they can turn so much tighter than I can. Or if I get the missile set up, the chances of it guiding are less than a hundred percent, and if it goes streaking across the sky, that will alert them and they will be off and running and I'll never get a crack at both of them. I thought I might get one of them with that missile, but I was greedy, I wanted them both. So I jammed the throttle forward and got inside their turn and was closing beautifully. It was an ideal gunnery pass, just as pretty as it could be.

I started to fire as I pressed to within a thousand feet of the second Mig and I was doing pretty well on him and he started rolling over and to the right like a sick fish. I figured, OK, I've got this guy, now I'll just keep pressing in and get the one up in front of him. About that time, the importance of the fact that I had no wingman to look around and protect me became painfully apparent. My element was now in pretty good position and John, my seeing-eye major flying number three, called me to break right immediately. It seems that another Mig had entered the scene from above and was moving into position above and inside of my turn and was about to have at me. I stayed as long as I figured I could, and then rolled down and under to the right and as I pulled through the maneuver, threw the third Mig off me and over the top of me.

While this was going on, all my other flights were active and Carl and Phil both managed to get a confirmed Mig out of their head-on hassles coming off target. My wingman pulled up off the deck after shaking his Sams and got himself a probable to go with my probable. Things then turned into a three-ring aerial circus as the Phantoms, who were in the area with us, wanted into the act and had come down to our altitude. They had managed to get two Migs who had been on our tails on the way into the target and they wanted more.

About this time I spotted another Mig spinning down to earth that one of our guys had hammered. Rob got one with a missile and it was a beautiful hit. The entire rear end of the Mig was burning, and you could see the skeleton of the aircraft as it burned and went straight line all the way across the valley in a descent, never wiggling, and hitting at the base of the Ridge. (I never have seen any chutes from any of the Migs we have hit.) Here we had Phantoms going round and round, Migs going round and round, and Thuds going round and round. Our total bag for the effort, which took only a few minutes, was six Migs destroyed and two Migs damaged and probably destroyed.

The Phantom troops got a little concerned when our guys started hosing off those Sidewinders because from some angles the Mig and the Phantom look quite similar, and in a fast-moving fray, it is easy to get a silhouette where they look very much alike. Once you fire that missile, it has no sense and just tries to do what it is supposed to do, look for a hot tail pipe. Once our Sidewinders started flailing through the air and Migs started falling out of the sky and guns rattled all over the area, one of the Phantom drivers said, "Hey Chief, they're shooting Sidewinders. Let's get the hell out of here," whereupon they lit the burners and went back up to altitude and allowed us to finish up our work. We got a call from the Phantom wing boss that evening congratulating us on the fine work but protesting that Mig-killing was supposed to be their business.

After Rob got his Mig, he was quite low on fuel as he had been in burner for a long time. He was also right down among them at the edge of Phuc Yen, and had maneuvered to a spot behind us where he had managed to corner two Migs at his six o'clock position, a clever maneuver calculated to get you shot down. He called his plight and indicated that he was in trouble. I turned the force back toward him as he pushed his bird right down on the grass and got going as fast as he could. With the speed that the bird has at that altitude, he was able to shake his pursuers and we again turned the force out of the area. That was quite a wild melee and I think, perhaps more than any other day, taught those Mig drivers some respect for the combined forces that were lined up against them.

*   *   *

Sidewinder missiles

This was the environment that Crab flight, with Bob as Crab two, had to penetrate that day—all the way down to the bottom of the Ridge, bomb, turn, and all the way back. As they turned the corner at the north end of the Ridge, their 650-gallon external tanks were dry and they elected to drop them, since by then the Mig opposition was obviously up and ready to tangle. They pickled the tanks, pushed the power up and started down the Ridge at about 580 knots. Knife flight was just ahead of Crab and was the first flight actually to get wrapped up with the Migs. When they called a flight of four at ten o'clock high, the Migs were pickling their tanks, which they also do to lighten their load prior to engaging, and Knife started a slow turn into them. Knife didn't want to start a radical turn as that would take him away from his desired run-in and defeat the purpose of the mission itself. This was one of the Migs' goals, and if they could draw us off course or get us wrapped up in something that would force us to drop our bombs, their mission had been accomplished. But Knife did start a gradual turn into the Migs to keep them in sight and also to keep them from getting into position on any of our flights prior to or during the bomb run itself. Crab lead spotted the Migs also, but seeing that Knife flight had them under surveillance, he announced to his flight that these particular Migs were not a threat to Crab flight.

Crab lead called for afterburner and was forced to descend down toward a cloud deck that was about 4,000 feet above the ground. He dropped down to be in a better maneuvering envelope should he encounter more Migs, to be better able to combat the Sam launches he fully expected and also to align himself better for the bomb run he would have to make despite the marginal cloud conditions. The target itself was a particularly tough one to find, a dinky little thing that blended with the surrounding terrain and construction. The radio chatter was really picking up about this time—in fact, it was so dense with all the Mig and Sam warnings and everyone shouting directions and commands that it was almost impossible to interpret what was going on. This is a real problem and once it starts, it just keeps getting worse and worse and is almost impossible to stop. About the time all four Crab flight members had secured a good burner light, Crab three spotted a Sam heading for the flight from the three o'clock position and hollered on the radio, "Take it down, take it down." This is a most difficult situation, in that you see something that you know you have to tell other people about in a desperate hurry to protect them and to protect yourself, and the temptation is to blurt it out as quickly as possible without using the proper call sign. The result is that everyone in the air immediately gets a shot of confusion and wonders who is talking about whom.

The desperate question, "Who is that call for?" almost always triggers a return call and further increases the critical chatter level.

Crab three felt that he had alerted the flight and for self-preservation he broke sharply down and below number four. At this stage four was concerned with keeping three, his element lead, in sight, and he was also nervous about the Sam heading his way. He pushed over violently on the stick. After a control movement such as this, especially at speeds of about 600 knots, the aircraft reacts violently. All his maps, charts and checklists, in fact even the fuel selector knob which is part of the control panel, flew up into the air and filled the canopy and windscreen. Everything that was not tied down came up. Four's immediate reaction was to pull back on the stick and he entered a porpoise. A porpoise is a vertical oscillation where you are just a step behind the aircraft and can't physically keep up with the machine; each control movement only serves to exaggerate the problem. In other words, when you are heading down, your reaction is to pull back on the stick and you usually pull too much. You may already have pulled back enough but by the time it takes effect you have probably gone too far and need to come back the other way, so the cycle repeats and you go up and down in increasingly violent gyrations and find that you can't see where you're going or what you are doing. It is better known as a J.C. maneuver. The best way to get out of it is to let go of everything and say, "OK, J.C., you've got it. I'll take over when you get it straightened out." The control situation, plus the visibility limitations caused by things flying around the cockpit, the close proximity to the ground, a Mig trying to set up on the flight and a Sam coming their way was further complicated as all the guns at Phuc Yen opened up, and there are many, many guns at Phuc Yen. This flight was in severe trouble early in the run.

Number four finally let go of the stick which was about the only thing he could have done to get out of this porpoise condition; he could never have caught it, especially with his bombload, and after riding through a few more violent ups and downs, the aircraft dampened itself out to the point that he could regain control. As things began to come back into focus for number four, he observed the lead element, that is, number one and number two, high and out to the right and screamed out to them that they had Sams coming at them from their nine o'clock toward their one o'clock. The Sams streaked across the lead element but far enough away so that they did not detonate. Crab lead, while trying to dodge the Sams, which he did successfully, called out three Migs at the flight's three o'clock position. Perhaps you can feel the tempo of this thing increasing, and you must remember that it is all crammed into the space of a few minutes. The three Migs in the three o'clock position were initiating an attack at the same time another call went out, again without a call sign or an identifier. The call was meant for Crab lead to tell him that he also had Migs initiating an air attack from his six o'clock position. To add one more twist to this rapidly compounding situation, Crab lead had lost the stability augmentation system on his aircraft. This is the device that dampens out control pressures and oscillations and allows you to fly rather smoothly even at high speeds. Without it, it is almost impossible to maintain even straight and level flight, and turning or climbing or diving the aircraft is impossible to do smoothly. When he heard this call of Migs at his six o'clock position, Crab lead had no choice but to believe the call and was forced to push his nose down. In no time, without control augmentation, he too was in a violent high-speed porpoise that threw him all over the sky. At that speed and with that bombload on, Crab lead found himself only seconds from the target and, for all practical purposes, out of control. This put Bob, in Crab two, in the difficult position of trying to stay on the wing of his leader, not daring to separate yet faced with an impossible aircraft-positioning job. He had to avoid being run into as well as face all the other problems at hand. In the attempt to maintain position, he too entered a porpoise condition. As he was bouncing out of rhythm with the lead he popped up about 500 feet above the lead and suddenly his aircraft pitched violently down and to the left. In other words, this translated him from the right wing position with the element sitting over on the left-hand side, through a pitching motion, and down and to the left into a new position underneath three and four. By this time, the entire situation was completely out of control. There were tremendous speeds and weights involved and these massive weights were flung through extreme maneuvers that exceed the control capabilities of the machinery and of the men. With the defense's guns shooting heavily from the Phuc Yen area, Sams firing from all quadrants, especially from the city itself, and Migs in the area but backed off momentarily in order that the close-in defenses might have their chance, the situation had become nothing but grim.

Number two bottomed abruptly and stopped the downward pitch or porpoise almost as if he had gained control of the machine. Actually, he was probably hit at some time during the porpoise, perhaps when he was forced up high above the leader. He apparently took a vital hit at that time that knocked his aircraft down and to the left and the abrupt bottoming probably occurred when he caught the aircraft and at least momentarily regained control over the machine. As he bottomed, his bombs and tanks separated from the aircraft, which would indicate that he knew he had been severely hit and that he did not have adequate control of the aircraft and needed to get as much of the weight off the aircraft as he could by hitting the panic button, a switch that electrically jettisoned all external loads. His hope was that a lighter load and a change in airspeed might give him a chance to control his wild machine. The big problem was that he did not have any place to move at a time like that, especially with an aircraft as sick as his obviously was. If he went up all by himself, he would in all probability have been gobbled up by the Migs who were just waiting for a stray to fall out of the formation, or, for the instant, he would more probably have been hit by the Sams which were thick in this area close to downtown Hanoi. If he went down, he would have been faced with the intense small-arms and automatic-weapons fire that even extended down to handguns; and don't ever think that a handgun can't knock down a big bird if it hits the right spot. When the bugle blows and thousands of people lie on their backs and fire small-caliber personal weapons straight up in the air, woe be unto him who is unfortunate enough to stray through that fire.

Without freedom of movement, he was trapped. In this case, it didn't make too much difference because Bob came on the radio and said, "Crab two is hit." This, of course, alerted everybody to the fact that one of our guys was in big trouble and that there was an out-of-control aircraft traveling close to 600 knots in the immediate vicinity. A vital hit in a sensitive area of the Thud will very rapidly deplete the hydraulic systems that operate the flight control systems. The degree of depletion depends on the location and nature of the hit, but once that pressure is gone, the controls go with it and there is no way to control the aircraft even momentarily. This was the plight of Crab two; he was riding in a hurtling, out-of-control, heavyweight monster in the middle of a hostile environment determined to kill him if at all possible. Thus, only seconds after he had been hit, Bob apparently lost all control and knew that he was about to hit the ground. He evaluated his position in who knows how many microseconds, and had no choice but to take the high-speed ejection right in the middle of a hail of lead from all sides, rather than simply crash and be destroyed along with his dead aircraft. He called and said, "I'm bailing out," and out he went, right into the inferno of Hanoi under attack. His aircraft hit the ground at a speed in excess of 500 knots.

The two-ship element, led by Crab three, had become understandably confused during the wild gyrations that had occurred and initially thought that Crab one had struck the ground out of his wild porpoise. In an area like that there is absolutely nothing you can do for a pilot who has jumped out, you can't really even stop and look. If you observe the impact of the aircraft, it is strictly by chance. Anyone who stood still or retreated long enough to even try to find out what was going on would also be shot down. So that's part of the code, the name of the game. Anyone who is hit and has to jump in that area does it strictly solo.

It took Crab flight a while to sort things out and get organized coming back out of the target area, and there is little doubt that this particular strike will go down in the annals as one of the wildest and toughest rides that any flight has ever had to go through. They did manage to get reorganized and return to base safely.

It was a real heartbreaker. Bob was such a nice guy, and in this business you naturally gravitate toward eager young people who seem to have all the spunk and drive and desire that you are looking for. Bob was one of those guys we all felt very strongly for, and his loss got to the squadron and the wing, but especially to the guys in his flight. Bob's brother was over there at the same time and had been at our base visiting Bob shortly before this particular flight. He is also a fine young gentleman and is in the tanker business, refueling us as we go in and come out of the North. As soon as the flight got back on the ground and went through their formalities, they got in touch with Bob's brother and he came right back to see what he could learn. Unfortunately, you have a tough time explaining these things in exact detail and it often takes an amazing amount of mental research to reconstruct things that happen so fast and so violently. However, when Bob's brother came to the base we did everything we could to explain the situation and spell out our ideas of what had occurred.

I saw his brother that evening and that was a tough one. What do you tell a guy? You don't want to discourage him completely because you don't know what happened to the individual. You don't want to pump him up too much because you know that the chances of survival from bailout at that speed are mighty slim. You know that the flak-filled air that he went down through during his short descent was extremely dangerous. You know that his chances of injury on landing were extremely high. But here's a guy whose brother is at best missing, going back home to tell his brother's wife— what? I don't know. I appreciated his attitude and he was a wonderful man to talk to, but it was an awfully lousy conversation.

That same night, Hanoi Hanna came on the radio and announced that the same day an American aircraft had been shot down while raiding the Hanoi area. They have the usual line of chatter that all propaganda broadcasts use and a lot of it you can't believe at all. But this particular night, Hanoi Hanna said that one of the American pilots, a fine, young healthy boy had been shot down and severely injured, and that despite the best efforts of the North Vietnamese doctors, had died in the hospital shortly afterward. You can't always believe what they say and only time will tell if the announcement in itself was the truth, but I think it most interesting to note the terminology used in the broadcast. Most of the references to the Americans coming out of Radio Hanoi are highly uncomplimentary, and we are referred to as bandits, air pirates, Yankee dogs, rotten imperialists, and so on. Yet in this particular case, the individual is referred to as a fine, healthy, good-looking American boy. I wonder if this is an extremely clever bit of writing and narration designed to pluck at your heartstrings, or if perhaps young Bob impressed even the North Vietnamese as much as he impressed all of us.

7.

BEHIND THE FLIGHTLINE

Throughout my tour at Takhli, the basic rule held firm that it takes a lot of people to run a wing and to run a base. We had quite a community, and when I left, it was up to about five thousand men without a round-eyed white female in sight. The command section of a unit such as this is in many ways like the office of mayor in a small city. We had all the problems that you would expect in any municipality, and these problems were compounded by the fact that it was a constant battle to scratch what you needed out of the jungle. Funding is controlled at higher command echelons and you seldom find those holding the purse strings sharing your operational enthusiasm for the things you feel you need. In short, making a first-class operation out of a bare strip in the jungle is plain hard work plus an awful lot of frustration.

The bases in Southeast Asia vary enormously from one to another, and some of them were pretty jumbled up and sorry. The differences were due in part to mission requirements, physical location or the varying degrees of higher command interest, but the big difference was the drive and the desire of the individuals running a particular unit. Southeast Asia is usually a one-year tour for those in command and staff positions, and there is always the temptation to let the tough things slide for the next replacement to worry about. This is especially true of the flying commanders, as things move very rapidly from the operational end and there is a lot of ground to cover. Thus, you often do not get the opportunity to put the emphasis you want on the physical facilities.

The word "jungle" conveys different images to different people—quite naturally, because the jungle itself has many faces. The image of vine-entangled trees, with Tarzan about to swing across the steaming pool of quicksand, seems quite apt in some corners of Asia. I took a small group out in the wilds north of Takhli in search of the engine from one of our Thuds that had crashed shortly after takeoff, and after three days out there I felt like the great white hunter when I returned. A couple of our pilots arranged a few days off duty and hooked up with a native Thai hunting party over toward the border of Burma, and their impressions were similar to mine, when they returned without a tiger. Other areas of the "jungle" are simply rolling green fields with trees that vary from sparse to nonexistent. I always enjoyed dropping down to a few hundred feet above the green carpet when it was practical to do so on the last hundred miles of the return leg of a combat mission. The color, the stillness and the variety are fascinating, and, to me, relaxing to view. It is not uncommon to see 200-foot-high trees with 75-foot trees nestled under them and still another 25-foot bramble of green undergrowth covering the jungle floor. Within a few hundred feet you may well see a native, who knows and cares little about your presence, scar farming a patch of burned-out open land that he will abandon when the urge to move on seizes him.

I personally thought the climate in the Takhli area was great. It got a bit soggy at times, and it was the home of the king cobra, but we had driven the cobra back with the noise of our jets and the bustle of approaching civilization. Temperatures topped 110 degrees during the extremes, but at that time of year the humidity was at its low ebb. Generally, the temperatures were moderate, the breezes were cool, the sunshine was bright and there was lots of good fresh air. When it rained, it rained like nothing I have ever seen and it was common to see 6-inch puddles of water accumulate within a few minutes.

We were fortunate at Takhli in having exceptionally good

people, hard drivers who wanted to get the job done properly and rapidly; and the base showed it. We had the finest physical facility in Southeast Asia this side of Clark Air Base in the Philippines. Of course, Clark had about a fifty-year head start on us and I doubt that anyone will catch up in the next few days, but we were head and shoulders above anyone else in Vietnam and Thailand.

It was not always so. The first time I saw Takhli a few years ago, things were pretty grim. As far as air bases were concerned, Takhli was at the bottom of most anyone's ladder, anyplace in the world. We had a runway, a taxiway and a bunch of wooden hootches. (A hootch is a long, single-story, stilted wooden building of typical Thai rural design. The stilts discourage the cobra and his companions from sharing the building with you, and the sides are open and screened.) Through the cooperation of the local Thai military, we hired Thai labor, used Thai materials, and supervised the construction and placement of our first attempts at housing and working projects. Our original hootches were definitely of the low-rent-district type and we had to cram thirty men into each one to give people a place to sleep.

We had nothing resembling roads except the mud trails serving the runway area. The jungle was all around and very much in evidence; in fact, the first time I got there you couldn't even see the runway lights because of the vegetation around the runway. Snakes were prevalent at this time and nobody with any sense wandered far from the tramped-down area. Other bases in the country had received more emphasis and were in far more promising condition than was Takhli. Korat, the home of the other F-105 wing, was a far better looking base, and Udorn, in my opinion, was the most promising of the whole group. General John Murphy was the big gear at Udorn at that time and he had some fine plans for developing the base. It did not turn out that way. Takhli, on the other hand, was in the soggy jungle and did not look like it would ever amount to anything but a hellhole.

Takhli became first class with a wonderful set of base shops, good housing conditions, good recreational facilities on the way although not fully operational when I left, paved roads, and even street lights and extremely functional and attractive buildings. From an operational standpoint Takhli is far superior to a great many bases in the States.

North American F-86 "Sabre"

So how did we get from number ten on the ladder to number one on the ladder? I could extol the efforts of any number of great people who immersed themselves in the growth of the Thailand operation, but I have chosen to tell a bit of the story of two individuals to illustrate the people we had doing the job. I will try and take you behind the scenes with a distinguished combat veteran, Lt. Col. Gordon Atkinson; and I want to show you something of a most distinguished nonflying lieutenant colonel named Max E. Crandall. From their stories you should be able to get a feeling for the support that goes into building and running a tactical fighter wing at war.

* * *

I was known around Takhli as Mister Vice. Mister Vice, being the number two colonel on the base, winds up with all the cats and dogs and all the things that the boss doesn't want, but that must be done. It is more than one guy can do effectively by himself, yet the command section is authorized only a very meager staff. For example, they are not authorized a wing sergeant major, or first shirt as he is known from the stripes of authority on his sleeve, in my opinion an absolute necessity. Who ever heard of running the show without a first soldier? I would have thought that the necessity of this position was an established fact, but not so in the banana and coconut air force. In our case, we took it out of our hide, the same way we solved so many other manpower problems. The Air Force has an empire known as Manpower and Organization, which supposedly splits up the goodies peoplewise and insures that all necessary positions are justified and properly documented. I am sure that this is a big job but so far as the operating units are concerned, these manpower folks have yet to realize why the flying force is in being. Each of the three separate headquarters that we responded to from Takhli looked like a zebra farm from all the stripes, but the tactical units of 5,000 men are not authorized a first shirt. Our assumption was that all of the senior noncoms were working in manpower at the headquarters, but we didn't fight the problem. We just picked the best qualified man we could find on base and used him where necessary, and the big books stayed balanced. It is the commander's job to juggle his people and get the job done. The problem of too much headquarters, too much staff and too little at the operating level has never been properly addressed or solved.

Shortly after my arrival, I began agitating for an unauthorized executive officer. In other words, I was looking for a Vice for Mister Vice, an assistant upon whom I could unload some of the many responsibilities that I had. I wanted somebody whom I could trust to utilize the mature judgment of a seasoned combat commander yet someone who was enthusiastic enough and yet detail-minded enough to be sure that administrative niceties, visitors and physical arrangements were properly attended to. It was not too easy to sell the boss on this concept at first, as he did not feel the weight of detail as much as I did and he was not anxious to spread the badge of authority of the command section over any larger area than necessary. I finally convinced him that we could accomplish my aims in this project and still select somebody who would represent us proudly. It worked like a charm.

I found my boy in a balding, round-faced major named Gordon Atkinson who was operations officer in one of our fighter squadrons. I had not met Gordo prior to this tour but was immediately impressed when I did. At the time I got there he had some eighty missions in the theater and was highly respected by his people. I asked Gordo about going to work for me and at first I don't think he was pleased with the thought of being Vice to Mister Vice. However, after a bit of serious conversation and some explanation of what he might be able to learn from the position, but mainly by expressing my need for someone of his caliber, I managed to get Gordo to consider extending his tour and coming to work for me, with the consideration that he first be allowed to complete his hundred missions.

About that time I got an unintended assist from the personnel people. We worked on a reassignment system that involved throwing a card into the machine back in the States to determine a pilot's next assignment after he had been on board for a few months. This piece of paper, full of holes, represents the man; the holes spell out the specialties he has accumulated and are matched with more holes representing demands that have been fed into the same machine. When they matched up, the man was off to his next task. Gordo was an old fighter pilot who had been shanghaied into bombers when there was a large-scale program to that effect throughout the Air Force. He had served with distinction and generated a spot promotion to lieutenant colonel but had never ceased fighting to get out of the big loads and back to fighters. He finally made the grade with an assist from Ho Chi Minh, surrendered his spot promotion—he returned to the grade of major—and fought the battle of retraining and more schools to get his specialty changed back to fighters and to get assigned to our wing.

He was overjoyed at having the magic specialty numbers changed on his records and when the time came for him to forecast for his next assignment after Takhli, he volunteered for any fighter assignment anywhere in the world, spelled out a few places he would prefer and stated that he was very opposed to any assignment that would return him to any facet of the big-bomber business. His card made the rounds and in due course returned to announce that not only was he going back to bombers, he was going back to the same location and to the same bomber outfit that he had just beaten his way out of. What a reward for fighting a good war. He was distraught, and we immediately started screaming for and with him. At first it was just "tough luck," and then we made the big discovery that the reason for the malassignment was that he was still carried on his little number card as a bomber jock, although all concerned acknowledged that this was not proper. It seems that the personnel weenies had improperly processed his card and had sent him into the machine for grabs based on the wrong number. We screamed some more and felt that surely the system must be responsive enough to acknowledge the error of a group of administrative people, compounded by an unthinking machine, and that he would be assigned where he was eager and qualified to go. *C H I Dooey*—sorry about that—the machine had spoken and the system had spoken and that was that. I found this most difficult to accept but although Gordo had been hurt, he had not been hurt as badly as some people by our goofs, and we still had a few angles left. We have done some grim things in handling our people.

One of the worst goofs we made was due to the insensitive nature of this huge system we live under. In anything as big and impersonal as the Air Force has become, we are all made out of tickey-tackey and we all come in little boxes, and we are just numbers once you get past the immediate command level. We were badly tied up in little rules and regulations about borders, prohibited zones, forbidden zones and the like. If you were standing still and examining the rules under classroom conditions, they were not easy to comprehend and the pilot was hard pressed to catalog all the do's and don'ts and correlate them with the job we laid on him. When you got this same problem moving at 600 per, under lousy weather and navigation conditions, and admitted that a lot of people were trying desperately to kill you, you had a problem that was difficult for the best to solve.

Two of our shiny ones failed to solve the problem to the satisfaction of our bosses. These two were trying so hard to

deliver the maximum effectiveness on the task assigned to
them that they pressed too hard in the farthest reaches of
North Vietnam. They committed the unpardonable sin of
flying across the self-imposed line that we have stretched 30
miles below the wandering and crooked line known as the
Chicom border. They flew across this line while seeking their
target. No matter what the conditions that forced them to this
position, they crossed the line, and we picked them up on
our own radar and turned them in to ourselves. They were in
deep trouble with the powers that be, and they knew it. As is
so often the case, the censure they knew was coming forced
them closer together than before, and they even flew together all the time, daily risking their behinds while they waited
for the administrative ax to fall and stunt the careers they had
dedicated to their country. They were bad guys in the eyes of
the big men and they knew it, but they never quit. While
they were flying far to the north on a particularly gloomy day,
the paper work that constituted their official, career-terminating
reprimand was making its way up the unfeeling channels to
the very top of the Air Force. A sin had been committed and
someone must pay lest we arch our backs and stand up for
our people. The paper travels through and past the all-wise,
who are nonrated, or who have a comfortable view of the
fighting, and have no desire to exchange places with those
they send to give their all in a hopelessly restricted and
prohibitive climate and whom they censure for things beyond
the control of the normal man. The vitriolic contempt and
rage unleashed by the nonfighting 99 percent of our force
appalls me.

These two got their reprimand, and their lack of professionalism and their failure to abide by established constraints
was lamented all the way to the top. It was formalized and it
was signed, and it was sent back to these two swine in the
field. But on this day one of the swine was struck down by
the enemy ground fire as he attempted to deliver his bombs.
His three flight companions were dangerously low on fuel, so
his buddy in trouble, his unprofessional companion and fellow border violator, volunteered to stay on the scene to cover
his buddy while the other element raced for a tanker and
attempted to establish a doubtful rescue attempt. When the
element returned, he too was gone. He had met the same
fate while attempting to cover and protect his downed com-

panion. They both went down and we suffered—but not the system—it couldn't care less, except for the cold and formal statistical notices that must be sent. And we sent the notices; we regretted to inform you that your son and husband, and all that rot. But, in this case, the next of kin got two letters. One expressed sympathy and the other blasphemed the two noble lads for their lack of dedication. The system couldn't respond, and these stricken folks had the two young pilots' reprimands routed directly to them, since the lads were no longer at their former address. Their relatives received official reprimands on two of our finest, along with a missing in action notice. How clumsy can you get! I hope the next of kin saved those black papers so that if we are ever fortunate enough to recover these two fine young men, they will be able to see how much we thought of them.

But Gordo's case was not so grim and we saved the day. It was apparent that further frontal approaches to the personnel forces would not be effective and we had to play their game. We slowed Gordo down on his missions for a few days so that statistically he was behind the curve that would finish him on his projected tour completion date. We coupled this with a blast on operational necessity as regards the shortage of qualified aircrews and supervisors, and since the personnel types were the ones who were supposed to keep us up to speed on numbers of crews (actually, they never did), we were one up on the system. They didn't dare make any more fuss as we had them dead to rights on the deficits in combat crews, and with Gordo's concurrence, we extended him for another tour and turned him loose on his missions with the understanding that he would come to work for me as soon as he got the magic one hundredth. Meanwhile, I had our personnel people sit on their thumbs for a few weeks while I got a few letters off to friends in the States and then had them request a new assignment for Gordo using the proper numbers on his card. The letters and the reforecast and the correct numbers combined to do the job and Gordo got a good assignment next time around. Now, isn't that a silly way to have to do business?

Gordo on the ground is so decent, friendly and calm that you wonder how this guy can be a tiger in the air. Yet he is just that and while I was anxiously awaiting his arrival in my office and piling up all sorts of goodies that I would put off until Gordo came to work for me, he distinguished himself twice more and almost didn't make it to the point where he could come to work for me.

The first time that Gordo was awarded the Silver Star was one of the hairier missions that we had over there. He was given the assignment of developing a scheme to deliver weapons in North Vietnam under adverse weather conditions, not associated with the normal radar delivery techniques of which we are capable in all of our various sizes of machines. This was a little different slant on the problem and the question was how you can get into a North Vietnamese target with low ceilings and poor visibility, and get your bombs on the target when you are not preplanned for such tactics, nor for higher altitudes and radar modes of delivery. It was a particularly demanding task in that everyone knew that it would involve low-level, high-speed navigation, coupled with weather flying under dangerous and most demanding conditions, and we also knew that it would place those who gave it the try in an extremely hostile environment. It would force them into the area of enemy ground fire where even the kids fire slingshots at you. The complex weapons systems that we are operating these days—airplane is too simple a word to indicate their complexity—can be knocked down and the pilot can be killed dead with a pistol just as well as with a 100-millimeter or a Sam, providing the hits are in the right spot. We were asking in effect that Gordo get in, on the deck, in lousy weather and prove to us that we could or could not survive in such a situation and still get our bombs on the target.

Obviously we were not talking about a conventional dive-bomb approach to the target where considerably more ceiling and visibility would be required. We were talking about armed reconnaissance under substandard conditions that would perhaps uncover lucrative targets and allow us to destroy them and still get our forces safely back out of the area. A challenging assignment to be sure, one fraught with danger and that could only be proven by actual flight. Gordo prepared himself and his people most thoroughly for this mission. The thoroughness and attention to detail demonstrated in this assignment were to appear to me many times in the

future as he devoted the same energy to the more mundane
tasks that I laid on him. He picked his day quite well. He
picked a day when the visibility was rotten, a day when the
clouds were practically on the ground, and he picked a tough
target. This was to be the true test and he pulled no punches
nor did he make anything easy for himself. He laid it on as
realistically as physically possible.

Inbound to his target he was forced down in heavily
defended areas by the clouds and the rain to altitudes sometimes as low as 100 feet above the ground. When he arrived
in his selected area, he conducted a successful armed reconnaissance under about the worst possible conditions. His
preflight planning and his talent paid off as his flight was able
to destroy several automatic-weapons sites that fired on them
while they were in the process of spotting and destroying a
fuel convoy. The fuel truck drivers and convoy masters obviously never expected the stupid Americans to come hurtling
at them out of the clouds and rain through which they were
driving their trucks with a sense of security and safety. Gordo
and his boys dispatched them as well as the flak sites along
the way which had been bent on protecting the convoy.
Although he had already completed a highly successful mission, his day's work had really just started for him. Having
expended most of his ordnance, he took his flight back up
through the weather and back out of the hot area to the
poststrike refueling area. As he hooked up on the tanker for
the fuel that he would need to get him back to home base, he
was informed that another pilot, Finch two, had been shot
down north of the Red River in the heart of the heavily
defended zone he had just left.

He took on a full load of fuel and promptly made himself
available to the Rescap people to fly cover over the downed
pilot during the rescue attempt. He turned and headed back
into the country where he knew the weather was poor and
where he could now expect fully aroused defenses, even
more alert than they had been in the previous portion of his
mission. The best weather that he had going back in was 800-
to 1,000-foot ceilings with rain. With this backdrop he was a
perfect target for the many guns in the area as the gunners
knew the exact height of the cloud deck for fuzing purposes
and were also able to spot him quite easily as they looked up
toward the cloud deck. He had the further disadvantage of

having to move slowly enough to be able to search carefully for the downed pilot, which is a difficult assignment even under ideal conditions.

He searched in the hottest corner of North Vietnam under poor conditions for thirty minutes and as he approached the area he had worked before, the weather, getting worse all the time, again forced him down to 100 to 200 feet above the ground. He was unsuccessful in his search and when he could not find the downed pilot he was forced to return to the tanker for more fuel. At those altitudes and at the power settings that he was using, the fuel consumption was fantastic and time on target was short. Gordo was not the only one searching for the downed Finch two, as Finch one, the lead aircraft in Finch flight, had gone back and attempted the same type of search that Gordo had undertaken. Unfortunately, Finch one was not as successful in his search efforts as Gordo, and by the time Gordo returned to the tanker for his second poststrike refueling, he was informed that Finch one had also been shot down. He again picked up fuel and headed back into the same mess, now realizing that he had two people to look for, that the chances of success were not great and that the probability of a safe exit was diminishing with each exposure. He never faltered as he accepted the challenge and reentered to do everything he could, even if it meant losing himself, to try to save two of his nameless buddies who had been downed.

Back on the job again, he received an additional surprise. Although the Sams are supposed to have a low-altitude limitation, we have seen several occasions where they have been launched and have performed at altitudes at which they are not supposed to be able to perform. As Gordo plodded through the rain and murk under the low ceiling, he found, much to his amazement, that a Sam was headed directly for him. The Sam was not arching up above the weather, the Sam was coming at him underneath the weather. It was difficult to see and it was difficult to orient upon, but there it was, pressing in on him at the terrific speed that the Sam can generate as it accelerates. This left him with a difficult decision. If he went up into the weather he would lose his ability to keep visual track of the Sam's progress toward him. He would also lose contact with the ground and this would disrupt his search pattern while he spent priceless time and

effort seeking an area where he could safely bring his charges
back out underneath the low clouds. If he went up he would
also be moving back into an area that was more compatible
with the Sam's tracking capability. On the other hand, it was
no secret that he was in the area and every gun that could be
brought to bear on him was after him. To descend now,
especially under the hazardous weather conditions, was a
pretty risky business, but he chose that as the best of the two
available courses, and down he went and up came even more
of the ground fire that had claimed two Thuds in the past
hour. The ground fire was fierce, but he outmaneuvered the
Sam so that it crashed into the ground, and somehow or other
he came back up through that hail of fire being thrown at
him.

As he continued his search he found something he wasn't
looking for. It seems that the day before one of the reconnaissance pilots from another wing had crashed and had been
given up as lost, captured, killed or who knows what. While
searching for Finch one and Finch two, Gordo suddenly
heard a beeper, maneuvered his aircraft to locate the beeper
and found, to everyone's surprise and amazement, the pilot
who had gone down the day before. He had been sitting
coolly in the jungle, waiting for possible rescue but certainly
not expecting it under the horrible weather conditions pre-
vailing that day. Spotting the downed pilot from the day
before, Gordo alerted the search and rescue forces and called
for more Rescap plus Spad and chopper support to come in
and get the pilot out. While he was orbiting, pinpointing the
position and calling on the radio to advise the rescue controllers of the situation, Sam again sought him out, and he was
faced with the same situation all over again. He again went
down to the deck through the withering hail of fire,
outmaneuvered the Sam, came back up out of the ground fire
and found himself still flying, with still more to do.

Now his fuel was exhausted again, so he climbed back
through the weather and returned again to the refueling area
and took on another load of fuel. He resumed his coverage
where he had spotted the downed pilot, only to find the
weather still worse than it had been before. He searched
eagerly for the two pilots who had been clobbered that day
while he directed rescue operations for the pilot he had found
from the day before, and he was constantly plagued with

CH-3E Rescue helicopter

weather and defensive conditions that would shake the
staunchest of pilots. He stayed until his fuel was almost gone,
and having successfully directed the slower-moving rescue
forces into the area, he once again withdrew to the tanker.
The rescuers were able to pick up the reconnaissance pilot
safely and bring him back. As Gordo squirmed and wiggled in
the cockpit, he took on yet another load of fuel and returned
to home base seven hours after he took off, ten hours after he
briefed, elven hours after he got up. You might say that he
had put in a demanding day, and had demonstrated a tena-
cious attitude for a soft-spoken, efficient and truly brave
young gentleman.

As Gordo approached the one hundred mission mark, he
again demonstrated the bravado and plain guts that he pos-
sessed. He received a second Silver Star shortly after his
first, again for heroism demonstrated in the Hanoi area. His
promotion to lieutenant colonel came through about this time
and his continued success as he directed his squadron's
operation was most pleasant to behold. On the occasion of his
second Silver Star, he was flying in the number three position
of his flight, acting as element leader while he checked a
newer pilot out on the complicated task of leading a strike
flight into the Hanoi area. We made haste slowly with our
new folks, taking the ones we felt would make good flight
leaders up the steps gradually. The finishing school for flight

leaders was always a downtown strike with a highly experienced leader flying in the number three position. If he was able to satisfy the old-timer, with his prejudices and his personal likes and dislikes, the new leader was ready to be turned loose on his own to lead in the North.

The particular flight that Gordo assigned himself to that day had the mission of flak suppression along the route the strike flights followed into the Hanoi area. Flak suppression is a most demanding mission in many ways, yet it gives you more latitude and freedom of movement than other assignments within the strike force. You are not looking for a precise pinpoint target as much as you are looking for an area of intense ground fire, and there is absolutely no problem in finding that in the ring around the delta capital. They light up for you like the Fourth of July and the problem is not one of finding a place to bomb, but of determining which site is most likely to harass the strike aircraft coming after you, and then doing your utmost to eliminate it. There are obvious drawbacks to this particular facet of the operation in that before you can bomb you have to be sure that you have singled out the most fearsome of the many sites you place under surveillance. We have found through bitter experience that the only way to do this is to expose yourself to the full might of the guns and then duel with them in an attempt to destroy them. To accomplish this properly the flak suppression flight must climb to altitude directly over the target and manage their power, airspeed and position in a manner that allows them to look, evaluate, strike and still get out of the area in one piece. This sometimes involves hanging in an inverted position for several seconds while all the guns get the chance to light up. It may be only seconds but when you are in that particular position the seconds seem like hours. The flak suppressors get a great deal of satisfaction when they defeat the guns and allow the remainder of the force to accomplish their mission. They also get a great deal of defensive activity and are highly vulnerable for an extended time period.

Gordo did an outstanding job, as usual, and positioned his aircraft perfectly to draw maximum ground fire. As he prepared to roll in and drop his bombs he was abruptly presented with three Sam launch warnings, but he continued his attack and lined up on his selected site. At this time he was frantically advised by other members of the force that the three Sams had progressed through the warning stage and had launched, and were headed directly for him. The advice from his fellows was strictly academic as he had already spotted the three Sams and knew they were looking for him and for him alone. They were tracking and they had accelerated. Here again we have the fighter pilot making the split-second decision as to what to do. Does he toggle his bombs and concentrate on evading the Sams and saving his neck or does he press the attack to neutralize the flak and thus protect the approach of the strike force now pressing into the target area and insure a better chance of success for the strike? With a man like Gordo, no real decision-making process was required. He pressed on. He hurled his aircraft toward the barking guns and directly through the formation of three Sams that climbed rapidly and approached him from a head-on attack position in their chase to destroy his aircraft. Down he went, right through a flight of three supersonic missiles with his name written all over them. He beat the missiles and he dropped his bombs directly on a large flak site that immediately closed shop and lost all interest in the approaching fighters.

His flight leader had not been quite so fortunate and had taken a severe hit as he hung over the largest flak site in his zone of responsibility. The balance between getting the gunners to expose their full position and overexposing yourself is a very fine one. The leader called out the old familiar alert that he had been hit on his run and was in trouble and Gordo immediately diverted all of his attention to protecting a fellow flight member in distress. As his leader struggled to maintain control of his aircraft and grasped for precious altitude, his problems were further compounded as the rapacious Mig-21s, waiting, looking and hoping to pick off a straggler, spotted the sick bird. The lead Mig-21 pressed his attack on the obviously crippled Thud. It took Gordo only seconds to spot his limping leader and to assess the completely vulnerable position he was in.

The leader could not maneuver, he could barely remain airborne and he had to scratch for altitude and distance in the hope of getting himself and his machine into a more favorable area should he have to bail out. As he climbed he entered ever deeper into the area of sky where the Mig's performance

envelope increasingly surpassed his own. But, as in so many
cases up North, there was no choice. He was forced to fly
slower than he wanted to, he climbed higher than he desired
and he limited his maneuvering almost completely as he
attempted to nurse his impotent machine toward relative
safety. Gordo spotted the Mig formation, stroked the burner
and fearlessly waded into the middle of the fray. Those
following were alerted to the situation and would have helped,
but distance and speed made them merely observers. They
hastily advised Gordo that the next two Mig-21s, hanging on
the perch and waiting, had spotted him, had correctly assessed
the fact that he was bent on saving his leader, and had
initiated pursuit in an attempt to knock him off their comrade's tail.

The Migs had it all going for them as regards numbers,
altitude and maneuverability. The possibility of Gordo's surviving the scissors he now found himself between was not
great. There could have been no censure of a decision on
Gordo's part to disengage; in fact, the course of action he was
pursuing would seem to almost certainly invite heat-seeking
missiles up his own tail pipe. But Gordo calmly acknowledged the warnings and pressed to the aid of his stricken
comrade. The lead Mig was forced to maneuver and slow
down to position himself for the final kill on the stricken
leader. With full burner, Gordo was able to close from the
Mig's rear, and as soon as he reached firing range he unleashed
a heavy burst of fire from his Vulcan cannon. His two
pursuers were rapidly closing to lethal missile range on him
and the event would be decided within the next few seconds.
The lead 21 driver was not as dedicated to his task as was the
Thud driver, and as the 20-millimeter slugs ripped through
the air around him, he chose to disengage and immediately
split from the scene. This made Gordo's odds a bit better and
left him with only two superior performing aircraft on his tail
and in firing position. He racked his beast into an immediate
and violent series of evasive maneuvers that even he cannot
describe to this day. Who knows where he went or what
strain the Thud survived, but it was enough to throw his
pursuers off course and to cause them to overshoot both
himself and the handicapped leader. The Migs promptly
decided that they had more than they had bargained for, and
they disengaged and exited before this crazy American Thud

driver could further compromise their position or their sanctuary. With the leeches off his tail, Gordo rolled his aircraft upside down, spotted his crippled lead behind and underneath him, executed a split S and rolled his aircraft up and onto the leader's wing to escort him safely out of the area and back home.

So this was my new administrative assistant, my exec—this dedicated combat tiger was about to slip behind a big desk and help me shuffle the papers, and help he did as he was in on everything. He used to irritate me a bit because he worked so long and so hard and carried the complete dedication he had demonstrated in the air into his administrative tasks. I used to order him to close shop and get out of the building at eight or nine o'clock at night and he always beat me to work in the morning. He did more to streamline the administrative effort, the intricacies of serving three separate headquarters, and the cumbersome command structure, than any individual I have ever known.

He did everything from monitoring the recurring headache of housing 5,000 men on the base to wet-nursing the cocktail parties and the hundreds—literally—of visitors who floated through the Thailand circuit. The instant experts who were constantly with us were one of the larger problems in balancing time and effort. If it had not been for Gordo's abilities, I personally would not have had an opportunity to balance my time between flying or leading and maintaining my supervisory position as Mister Vice. He was constantly worrying over me about smoking too much and not getting the proper rest, constantly advising me on which problems needed my attention and which were so *nit noy* (Thai for little thing) they could be overlooked.

When Gordo left, he got the job he wanted. He is now working at Nellis Air Force Base for my most esteemed friend, Col. Chester L. Van Etten, who has painted the name "John Black," his old fighter radio call sign, on so many of his fighter aircraft that he himself is known to many as John Black. I am sure they make a number one team and continue to do a number one job. However, Gordo was not happy when he left. Shortly before, a new policy was established by our Air Force personnel folks offering regular commissions to some people who were currently on active duty in a reserve-officer status. Once again they managed to miss Gordo's bracket and he is highly representative of a fine group we have in the business who are not regular officers.

You see, Gordo is a reserve. As a reserve he will be kicked out of the Air Force in less than two years. When he reaches twenty years of commissioned service, this superior gentle-man, who should have demonstrated to the satisfaction of all concerned his merit as a leader and a hero, will be unceremoniously booted out to make room for a nonflying ROTC second lieutenant who will in all probability accept a commission in the regular force, play with it for a couple of years and then resign.

We have only so many spaces, so the book says. I will never argue with the fact that young talent is necessary. I will argue the point that we need Gordo Atkinson in this business just as long as he wants to stay, and we need the other capable reserve folks just like him. To dismiss them arbitrari-ly on a time and space basis makes little sense.

While we grew in combat effectiveness as a well-organized and cohesive unit, we also grew as a physical plant, and if this base was so superior to the others in the country, a logical question would be who was responsible. One man was re-sponsible and that was Lt. Col. Max E. Crandall. The first time I saw Max was a few years ago when he was first checking in at Takhli. He had just arrived and was in a temporary sack in one of the colonel-type trailers and as I had just ferried a bird into Takhli for the wing's use, I was also bumming a sack for the night. I was most happy to see large numbers of my friends whom I had not seen for some time and did not really spend too much time in the trailer except to note that I shared it with what appeared to be a grumpy old lieutenant colonel. We introduced ourselves briefly and Max advised me that he was just checking in as civil engineer for the wing. Since the place was still a complete quagmire, full of mosquitoes, snakes and jungle, I wished him lots of luck and wrote him off as a crotchety older civil engineer type who would probably leave after a year of nonproductive sitting.

How wrong I was. Max had previously served in the

European area and had built the base at Sidi Slamain. He was a bachelor and a glutton for work who apparently took one look at this mess and decided that with his talent and with the things that were available to him, and with the things that he had learned in Africa, both good and bad, this poor excuse for an air base was his personal challenge. His challenge was to make this piece of jungle into the finest base in Southeast Asia. He set forth with this as his goal and he succeeded.

Max was a scrounger, a good scrounger who could come up with materials and get jobs done when nobody else could make the grade. He knew his business inside and out, and he knew which corners needed to be cut at which time. He reminded me of a good motorcycle racer—he always operated right on the verge of losing control. He would be so close to sticking his own neck out past the point of retrieval, yet he was always a winner. That is the way to race motorcycles and that is the way to build bases under wartime conditions. We were investigated and we had people point the finger at Max for doing things in an unorthodox manner when he should have surveyed the situation and sat on his thumb for a few months. But these were all Monday morning quarterbacks who did not have the gumption to do the job that needed doing. Max did the job and he never got himself or his commanders in trouble. You could ask Max for the moon and tell him that it was operationally necessary for the troops who were flying and fighting the war and Max would spare no effort to get the job done—first class. He could come up with the impossible in the middle of the Thai jungle, and he did just that quite frequently.

Max was no spring chicken and he worked so hard that he finally collapsed with pneumonia. We were all most concerned and made certain that the flight surgeon had him properly doped up and put to bed in his trailer. However, a day later Max, the walking-pneumonia case, was right back on the job, refusing to be put down, refusing to quit.

Usually there is a running battle between the fighter pilots and the civil engineers—no matter how good things are the pilots don't feel the engineers are supporting them well enough. This was not the case at Takhli, and I have never seen a bunch of fighter drivers so sold on a support manager as they were on Max. Everybody on the base sweated like mad when the old man had to go over to Clark Air Base in the Philippines for an operation, with the possibility of malignancy hanging in the background. You would have thought that each of our pilots had bagged his twenty-fifth Mig when word came back that all was well. He infected his own troops with such enthusiasm that long after he left the base they were still carrying on as they knew he wanted them to.

The original hot and overcrowded hootches that Max had inherited were now obsolete. He had replaced them with a vastly expanded complex of clean, airy attractive quarters that blended the native Thai talent and teakwood with American know-how on rain protection, drainage and sanitation. Each of our aircrews flying combat had a spot in an air-conditioned building, and the pilot who flight-planned, briefed and flew to Hanoi from two in the morning until two in the afternoon could now collapse under a cooler and sleep in the afternoon heat before rising to start the cycle again. He built a command center where we could think and move with some semblance of order, and we had an air base that looked like an air base should. He provided the facilities we needed to do the combat job better.

He also gave us a most adequate building known as the officers' club. This was the only place for the officers to eat and as we were on a 24-hour-a-day schedule, the kitchen was always open. We also had a bar and game room and this was the off-duty rendezvous for both the Americans and our Thai military friends in the area. Colonel Rachain, the local Thai military commander, actually owned all the real estate we occupied and practically owned all the Thai labor we employed. He was most cooperative and pleasant, a fine gentleman without whose help we could never have progressed as we did. He got us the best help available to run this all-day operation and they turned out to be quite a snappy crew. The challenge of taking a fifteen-year-old girl out of the rice paddies and putting a white shirt, black skirt and shoes on her is one thing, but making her an English-speaking waitress is another. The Thais are the happiest and most industrious group I have observed in the Asian area and progress was rapid.

We kept the menu on the number system. One was sliced pineapple, bananas and papaya, which was delicious; number thirty-nine was the closest thing to steak available for the day; number forty-one was some form of chicken; number sixty-two was orange ice cream—which is a delicious concoction I have never seen the like of any place else in the world. It only took a short time to learn the menu by heart and ordering was a numerical recitation. We tried to break it up with Thai food prepared in our kitchen on a few occasions, and invited Colonel Rachain over to sample our first attempt. He was most polite, but allowed that Thai food American style—or American food Thai style—was a bit short on the hot peppers for his taste. We had him back for the second attempt and he attended, but gracefully indicated that he preferred to stick with old number thirty-nine.

The Thais identified themselves very personally with all of our efforts. From force of habit we each tended to eat in one section of the dining area most of the time, and the little girls could usually outguess us on our meal order. They brought us flowers from home, they brought us Thai gifts when they went off on trips or visits to their relatives, they cried when their officers went back to the States and they cried when their pilots did not come back from Hanoi.

The housegirls, houseboys, barbers and the like were much the same. Most of them lived in the Thai military complex on the other side of the runway from our area, and they were almost exclusively Thai military dependents in one form or another. Colonel Rachain called them "my family," and he controlled their employment and welfare in the firm Asian manner. He was the boss, everyone knew it, and there was no monkey business. The girl who cleaned my place up and did my laundry was named Boonaling, although we never got far enough through the language barrier to figure out how that should be spelled in English. Her husband was a Thai Air Force sergeant, and in Asian fashion her mother stayed home and cared for her five children while she and her husband worked. Like all the rest of the Thais, she could hardly wait for the annual spring water festival. This three-day affair signals the end of the dry season and the start of the rainy season. The name of the game is to douse everyone you see with a water pistol, a bucket or a push into the swamp, as a token of luck. My boss lived next door to me and Boonaling caught him in a grumpy mood, coming out of his front door with a clean uniform on, and let him have it right in the face. He was furious for days, and there was little doubt in anyone's mind about that. It failed to dampen Boonaling's

spirits and she broke through the language barrier far enough
to refer to him as Colonel God Damn from then on.

It is not supposed to rain on the first day of the festival,
and that was the time for Colonel Rachain to entertain all of
"his family" and his friends. He invited us to all of his
functions and they were most enjoyable. Thai food, Thai
style, is exotic and the results can be wild. The morning after
his first exposure to one of Colonel Rachain's spreads, my
buddy Sam decided that the experience must resemble that
of having a baby. The monsoon got twelve hours ahead of
schedule for this particular party and we arrived in the midst
of a monstrous thunderstorm. Nobody even slowed down and
it is a wonder that we were not electrocuted from the
makeshift extension cord network that threaded its way through
the wet grass and puddles to the light bulbs hanging from the
trees around Colonel Rachain's house. The rain went on, the
ceremonial dances with their fabulous costumes went on, and
then as guests of honor some of us got to dance with some of
the Thai ladies. This is something else, and since the man
leads by progressing in snake-dance style around the dance
floor to the rhythm of an oriental beat, and the woman follows
behind, I never did know how close I came to doing it
properly, but we all had a great time, Thai style. When we
got ready to leave we found out that someone had stolen
Colonel God Damn's raincoat.

Max and I had one project that we never did complete—a
go-cart track. You might think that the middle of the jungle is
a pretty crazy place for a go-cart track, but we had a real
problem devising things for our folks to do when they got a
rare bit of off-duty time. Max and I figured that we could get
together and scrounge enough equipment, materials and
money to make this thing a going concern. We struck out on
this one because it did not meet the approval of some of the
folks up the line.

At the end of his normal one-year tour things were not
complete and Max had not polished his base to his satisfaction. It was still head and shoulders above everything else
but it wasn't good enough for Max, so he extended his tour.
At the end of his first extension he was still not quite
satisfied. It was better than ever, but not quite what he
wanted, and he wanted to stay until everything he had
started was complete and in number one order. Max put in

another extension and would have stayed to manicure and polish the fine installation he had established, except for our command structure. I was forced to justify his extension, which is a reasonable requirement, so I submitted the justification to one of our three headquarters. Max proceeded, as we all did, under the assumption that the request would be approved and that we would have the opportunity to utilize his talents for many more months. As the date for his departure approached, we fired an inquiry to yet another one of our headquarters where we thought the paper work would be by that time, even with slow action, and found that they knew nothing about it. We traced back down the line to our next headquarters and lo and behold, the formal request of this terrific gentleman had been sitting in an uninterested commander's personal in-basket, without action, for three months.

This was a heartbreaker to Max. The thought that the system had so little regard for what he had done and for his desire to follow his base through to completion was hard for him to accept.

But talent like that is hard to hide and Max got a call from the number one civil engineer in Washington and was offered a good spot that the big boss had picked out for him. Max came to me seeking advice; should he fight to stay or should he go on. I advised him to go, and I'm sure he did a bang-up job in the new spot. Before he left he said, "You know, Colonel, I think it is about time you and I got out of here." I think he was right. I didn't hang around too much longer either.

8.

FIFTEEN SAMS FOR GEENO

As we took the belated and hesitant step of pressing the attack against North Vietnam's symbolic experiment in industrialization, the Thai Nguyen steel complex, my buddy Geeno was notified that his next assignment in the States would take him back into research, back to the big puzzle palace. Although Geeno was one of our more aggressive leaders and gave it all he had every time, he had already gone the advanced education route to the big degree that led him to a strictly support position. Only the real-life facts of the Vietnamese operation—the Defense Department does not like to call it a pilot shortage in so many words—had allowed him to escape to the fighter pilot's primary job of driving a machine in combat. Now, as the war heated up, he was not too pleased with the prospect of heading back into the administrative jungle. How much that thought pressed him to overextend himself while he had the chance I shall never know, but he sure pulled it all out.

The personnel mill seemed to be constantly out of rig, not sending enough qualified pilots down the pipeline, or once in a great while sending too many; and there is a never-ending flow of people like Geeno who are unhappy with the friendly personnel officer and their new assignments. Some of the reasons why it works like this make sense of a sort. Others don't.

You can't have the same younger people fighting the battle interminably or they run out of longevity. Even if they don't, you can only put a guy in the way of getting killed so many times before he loses his enthusiasm for the role. And besides, you get just plain tired. So you replace them with older men pulled in from some remote installation who once flew fighters or maybe never did but wear the set of feathers on the chest anyway. Now, even the most single-minded fighter pilot will admit that someone has to fill these vacated spots, but that is a lot less easy to accept when it applies to you as an individual. The real catch, however, is that it takes a different breed of cat to drive a fighter properly. For years we have shuffled our pilots into jobs that have little or nothing to do with combat, but they aren't standardized components and they don't convert back from a desk or a transport simply because a computer spits out a set of orders. Conversion or retraining takes time; often, it doesn't work. Aging, too, is a factor that should not be ignored where it means that the pilot has been forced to lose the razor-edge of frequent and demanding single-seat flight. If some of our best people are lots older than they were back in Korea and still going strong, it's usually because they have been close enough to the machines to keep their hand in, growing and aging with the machinery, learning to use to perfection every assist the system affords.

All of this is by way of trying to give you some idea of how Geeno, and too many others like him, felt as he neared the end of his tour. When I got to the base, he was the operations officer of one of the squadrons and, in conjunction with his strong and feisty squadron commander, ran about as tight a ship as can be run. Trying to get that pair to bend gracefully to a decision that offered assistance to anyone other than themselves was like ramming your head into the wall. To say they were strong-willed would be to water down the facts. They were just plain stubborn, but fortunately, they were quite often correct. One of the challenges that a combat commander faces is that of recognizing strong people and blending their smarts and their drive into a successful operation. I was able to do this in the case of Geeno and his boss quite easily, perhaps because I too have been accused by some of the learned ones of being of a somewhat hardheaded nature. Naturally I deny this, you know; we all know someone who is this way but naturally it is not us. Besides that, I made out their efficiency reports.

It is a big kick to me to see how people evaluate others on the efficiency report (ER) system that we use as a report card on our folks. If you read between the lines you can often get a fair overview of the person. If you read only the written words, you are bound to get a phony picture as the ER has become the most abused weapon in the history of military warfare. It is the manna of the promotion system, and bastardized descriptions of the performance of officers, as the promotion pendulum swings from extreme to extreme, are something to behold. If we had people who were as good and as bad as they are described in the hallowed ER files of the Pentagon, we would have no trouble winning the war with Ho Chi Minh. We could well afford to take all those who show up so badly and arm them with sticks to become a sacrifice force to walk through Laos to the North Vietnamese border. While these worthless souls paid the supreme price for failure to please their rater with their social grace, or their overdedication to some facet of their mission, the other group could walk up the waters of the Gulf of Tonkin and sway the land of Ho and perhaps that of Mao with their documented abilities to "get along well with peer, subordinate and supervisor alike under even the most demanding situations" or their "clearly superior ability to see the big picture that allows him without fail to solve any problem in the most cost effective and timely manner." If you think that I consider this system to be a farce you are correct. The only nice thing I can say about it is that I do not have a better system up my sleeve. The problems associated with ranking such a huge group as the Air Force into a neatly cataloged mass of tickey-tackey defies true solution. The ability to hire, fire, pay, train and reward those who work directly for any given supervisor has been so completely withdrawn into the bowels of the system that if you accept the career you must accept the rating system. You don't have to like it but you must

Grumman A-6 "Intruder"

accept it—it is all-powerful, something like James Michener's
Oro, the red god of Bora Bora.

The ER is good for a laugh once in a while. Since your fate
in this business hangs on it, there can be considerable
consternation if you have one coming up and you know deep
down inside that you have riled the powers that be. Geeno's
boss had no problems with me, but there were those in our
channels who looked upon his determination with less enthusiasm than I did. By the same token, he knew that I was the
drone who prepared the actual papers that were later
emblazoned with the big signature, and he knew that I would
somehow or other manage to allow a peek at the finished
product. Another facet of this monster that I confess I do not
understand is the current vogue for not showing the report
card to the man being rated. We used to, and I personally
thought this gave people a fair understanding of how they
stood with the guy they worked for. I hate leaving work at the
end of the day with that gnawing in your stomach that
indicates you don't know how well you are pleasing the one

who has so much go or no-go power over your future in the Air Force. Perhaps it is difficult for some to talk frankly with those who toil for them, and to be constructive in their criticism. In that I do not personally have this problem, I am intolerant of those who do, and I would suggest another block on the form to be filled in by those with such a problem. It could just say, "I am too chicken to discuss this man's performance to his face, yes or no." In fact, the man being rated is not precluded from seeing the report: he can do so simply by traveling a few thousand miles to the major air command headquarters and making an appointment to review his records file. Now I ask you, is this cost effective?

When it came time to prepare the ER on Geeno's boss, I decided it was time to have a bit of fun out of the grim business that took all of our conscious and many of our less than conscious moments. I sat down at the typewriter on a Sunday afternoon when I was not flying and dashed off the report that follows. I then went up to my trailer and called him on the phone saying I had something I wanted to discuss in private. He responded, and when he entered the trailer I managed to have the report on my desk, not quite concealed, where he was bound to see it. The curiosity factor was tremendous and he about flipped trying not to look at this all-powerful piece of paper that had his name and some wildly out-of-place markings on it. After a few minutes of idle chatter, I broke down and showed him the farce with a straight face. Concern changed to disbelief and then to laughter as he read through the paper. It went like this:

This Lieutenant Colonel is a most impressive officer with an intense interest in flying. *Fly, fly, fly, that's all the son of a bitch does. Every time you need him to get something done he's airborne. Try and pin him down for a decision—"the Colonel is flying."* During this reporting period his squadron has set several records for combat flying time and for the biggest number of fighter combat sorties from a single squadron. *Sure—what's so tough about that? He's got those poor pilots so scared of coming in second in anything that they pad more time than they fly. Who ever heard of a seven-hour mission to the bottom of route pack one? And those bandits in his maintenance section—those bastards would steal a rose off their grand-mother's grave. The rest of the poor slobs on the flight line work their tails off and his guys run around all night stealing parts and switching aft sections.* He has welded his entire squadron into a tightly knit and cohesive unit. *You bet your ass he has—they all lie and cover up for each other like a bunch of cell mates. Call him on the phone and what do the airmen say? "Sorry sir, he's in an important conference and asked not to be disturbed." He's in the sack and they know it.* His dynamic personality has made a lasting impression on the local nationals and brought about a new era in Thai-US relations. *Who'll ever forget the night the Thai commander had us over to his place? He even ran our host out of Thai whiskey—and that funny little dance he did in his bare feet between the broken bottles.* He has been decorated, and decorated, and deco-rated. *That's all those poor Lieutenants and Sergeants do down there is make up decorations for him. They even tried to get him another Silver Star for making last week's staff meeting on time—for once.* I recommend that he be assigned at the highest possible staff level, preferably to the Pentagon. *That place is so jumbled up and big, that with his ability to get lost in the shuffle it is hard to see how he can do any harm up there.*

As we progressed through the lines, we decided the levity was too good to hold to ourselves so I called the other two squadron commanders over and we all had a big guffaw. One of the other squadron commanders was now Geeno. When we had lost Don, we wanted to replace him immediately with a strong commander from within our own resources. Geeno was the logical choice, and though he took Don's job with the heavy heart that we all shared, he waded right into the problems he faced, and within a few days you would have thought that he had been a combat squadron commander for years. Unfortunately, we were not to have the benefit of Geeno's tough but gentle personality for very long. He believed in his mission too much, and he immersed himself so far in the details of his charges that a few weeks later we lost him.

* * *

It was a Saturday morning and Geeno had drawn the early briefing and takeoff as the mission commander for both the Korat wing and ourselves against that lousy Thai Nguyen railroad yard, which served the steel mill (at that time we had not yet been turned loose on the mill itself). This was one of the many wild setups over there and the North Vietnamese naturally wanted to extract the maximum price for letting us clobber that complex. They had enough stuff in there to protect both the rail yard and the steel plant, but as they were always pretty sure of our restrictions and what we could and could not hit, they could quite well afford to orient all their guns toward the protection of the rail yards and trust to luck and intelligence for the protection of the steel plant. We made their tasks lots easier in many respects.

Their Sam and Mig defenses were not hampered by being divided between the two targets lying one on top of the other, and they had excellent area defense. They had positioned their Sams in such a manner that they could cover our ingress to the target area of Thai Nguyen from any angle and protect both the yards and the mill. They had the benefit of lots of practice in tracking us as we came down Thud Ridge; and because they knew we would avoid both the Mig sanctuaries at Phuc Yen and Kep and the magic inner circles at Hanoi and Haiphong, they were able to look at us all the way in and have a fair shot whenever the missile gear indicated conditions to be favorable.

The Migs were also in a favorable posture since they were based on both sides of the Ridge—at Phuc Yen to the west and Kep to the east. I have often marveled at the Migs' amazing lack of success, I know airplanes very well and my three years of leading the USAF demonstration team, The Thunderbirds, did nothing to dim my perception of relative maximum performance capability among different aircraft. I have fought with the Migs in two wars now—be they declared, recognized, popular or not—and I have yet to see any general indication that the Mig drivers we have faced thus far are using the maximum skill or technical capability available to them. I don't think you will find a truly professional fighter pilot who would not sell his front seat in hell to be a Mig squadron commander in the face of an American fighter-bomber attack, should such a transformation be possible in our world of reality. Please remember I am only speaking professionally and am not expressing any desire to go the rice and fish route. I am simply saying that they could murder us if they did the job properly.

They don't go first class and our guys are both good and dedicated. I guess that is the difference. I have had a batch of them on my tail when they have had a better aircraft that could go faster, turn better, and outaccelerate me. I have been on the low end of odds as high as 16 to 2—and that's pretty lousy. (In this particular case of the poor odds, they hung me up for twenty-three minutes, an almost unheard-of time period for aerial combat even in the early Korea days when this occurred. They didn't scratch me, only because their cannon couldn't hit the round side of a broad.) I have had them come up from under my tail spewing red tracers that looked like a runaway Roman candle burst at the seams. Had those guns been properly harmonized, they would have nailed me without a doubt.

They have still not learned their lessons well and I suspect they do not do their homework properly. With the advantages they have going for them, I am sure glad that the majority of those we have tangled with to date are not as clever in this game as our guys are. Anyone who reads the air-to-air results and feels that American technology has scored another victory over the competition of the world is sadly misled. We have been able to take advantage of their mistakes and they have not seen, or have ignored, or have been inept enough not to take advantage of, our mistakes. I scream caution at the top of my lungs that we have not yet met the first team of Mig drivers but I have failed to observe a flow of listeners to my door. As a matter of fact, it becomes less popular and less rewarding each day to scream about basic convictions in the conduct of any struggle between men and machines. I feel very strongly that our inability to talk of practicality or to accept the word of those who physically do the job is hurting us all the way from the drawing board to the battlefield. Is our level of incompetence so high that the doer can never be heard? Is it inconceivable that a captain could know something from practical experience that a general doesn't know? I often wonder if Hannibal had any elephant drivers who tried to get the big message to him at the base of the Alps, but were swallowed up in a system that wanted to hear only good about itself.

But Geeno's problems were faster moving than Hannibal's and the Sams, the Migs and the flak were all zeroed in and waiting for him that bleak morning when he headed north for the last time—and he knew they were waiting. Like the rest of the Thud drivers, he never lacked a knowledge or appreciation of the forces aligned against him, but only a few flinched from the blanket of steel that waited, always active, always eager, never compromising. We had only four who couldn't hack it, only four whose fear overcame them and dealt them the gravest defeat man can suffer—to surrender to the cowardice that made them quit in the face of the enemy while those they had lived with went forth to take their chances on dying or rotting away in prison in order to defend their supposed right to default on their brothers-in-arms and still go forth unblemished. This is wrong and our system is wrong to tolerate it. You try and change it if you will. I have already tried and been rebuffed. No matter what demands the leadership imposes, the combat soldier who falters and fails in the face of the enemy's fire is an unspeakable wretch whose own insides must someday devour him.

There is no telling what type may display the unpardonable sin of reneging under fire. Our four covered the spectrum. We had one who had been a professional fighter pilot for about ten years. He loved the travel, adventure and challenge of the peacetime forces. He liked his aircraft and thought well of her demonstrated prowess on the gunnery range with the practice bombs and shells. When the press of events called him to the day when the gunnery range fired back and airplanes exploded and people died, he crawled on his belly and surrendered his image of a man because he was afraid. Another was a bomber guy who got caught up in the personnel conversion to this different machine. He was out of his element, almost as far out of his element as those poor slobs who have been rotting in Hanoi for over two years, so he fell on his face and cried, "I can't take it." He had been professionally raised under a banner that unfortunately says "Peace Is Our Profession" and he wasn't capable of transforming himself to the knowledge that war is our profession, as most of the rest of the bomber guys did. Our third failure was a lieutenant who almost cracked up earlier while pulling alert pad duty with nobody even shooting at him. Perhaps I should have spotted him then, but it took only a few lousy

37-millimeter shells, bursting woefully out of range, to surface this clever dodger in uniform. He decided that he would
like to be a ground officer during the period of hostilities, and
the last I heard he was getting away with it.

Our fourth was our worst. He wears the U. S. Navy ring of
an Annapolis graduate. I always knew the Navy was smart,
but how they figured this clown out ten years ago and got him
transferred to the Air Force is beyond me. He was the worst
in that he knew better and had demonstrated the capability,
under fire, to do the job. He quit around the halfway mark
when he was approaching the stage where he would have
been of real value to us. Among other things, he developed a
fear of heights after ten years as a jet pilot. He learned all the
rules and all the angles and he played them to the hilt. When
all else failed him, he managed a hardship discharge. Hardship indeed, that this leech defaced the profession as long as
he did.

So do you suppose that Geeno was scared as he blasted off
in the murk of a predawn departure from our own private
piece of jungle? I suppose he was. Anyone who isn't scared is
an idiot. It is completely plausible and quite a scintillating
experience to be able to translate this being scared into the
most dynamic courage and a determination to get the job
done properly. Geeno knew what his job was. He had to lead
two wings of F-105's to one of the nastiest targets in the
North, and he and his three flight companions were to still
the flak so the first wave of strike aircraft could penetrate and
get the job done.

Republic F-105 "Thunderchief"

When you are in the spot of leading both wings and are also the flak suppression flight for your own wing, the first one in on the target, you can't help feeling a tremendous sense of responsibility. In this situation, more than any other, you know that the responsibility for the whole tribe is in your lap. More than that, you know that the success or failure of the strike itself is your baby doll. No matter how well it is planned and no matter how many instant experts are sitting on the ground ready to advise on something they have never done, you have the ball. Your word is sought after in the confusion of the departure. You call the shots as men and machines struggle to the end of the runway and fight to leave the arming area in proper order. Your burner light is the infallible signal to all concerned, "Yes, this is it, we're really going," and the degree of confidence, calm and expertise that you exude does more than you know to determine the results, and even the survival of your troops.

This was brought home to me most clearly during a discussion with one of the docs who was working on a potential fear-of-flying case. Actually the guy had the fear, and it seemed like every time he moved he got exposed to something else to increase his fear, but he was a good man and he utilized every bit of smart and stamina he had, and while I am sure that he never beat the fear, he controlled it and stuck with the task. While trying to help this pilot, the doc was discussing the emotions people faced daily with the violent loss of those they sweat next to and he said something to the effect that all rational men had a sense of fear. He said, "Don't you think the colonels who lead you in this wing feel fear?"

The pilot responded in amazement, "You mean they actually get scared too?" It's what you do with the emotion that counts.

Geeno picked up his specific responsibility for this Saturday morning mission the evening before. When the frag arrived there was always much interest in what we were doing the next day and a shuffle to see who would fill which spot. In a wing like ours where the leaders led, you always had to give the boss first crack at the next day's work. Depending on who had to meet the visitors the next day— and there were almost always visitors—who had what meeting or what additional duty plans, the boss would decide on

his availability and choice of mission time. Other things being
equal, that 0200 wakeup was not too popular with those of us
in the command bracket. It is great to be skimming along
when the sun comes up, and you get the feeling that you are
in the saddle on this new day and that you are running things
and all will be good. You also get a feeling of accomplishment
when you land early and know that before most people have
stirred you have done a good job. And you get so tired you
hurt. The primary duty jocks who have been flight planning
most of the night could sneak away to the sack for a few
hours, but the leader always had something to make that
move inappropriate, and the next thing you knew you had
worked yourself out of daylight and into night. We all gave
the continuing early schedule a try at one time or another,
and we all managed to get falling-down sick doing it. So on
this particular Friday afternoon, both the boss and I declined
and the early one rotated to Geeno, the next squadron
commander in line.

Immediately after the stand-up briefing he gathered his
flight leaders and his planners in the big briefing room and
they started through the mass of detail necessary to select
and chart the route for the next morning. Every detail of
ingress and egress was probed and once the mission commander was satisfied with his plan of action, the selected
individuals from each participating flight set to work to
prepare the maps, charts and cruise data for their flight
members. This particular planning session did not have to get
too involved as most everyone knew the area and the target
quite well. There was not too much freedom of choice on
routes, and there was nothing new to say on defenses in that
area. They were all still there and everyone would get to see
all of them in the morning. Having put his charges to work
there was little else for him to do other than to make sure he
knew each and every particular of the route he had selected
as well as the details of the drill he would employ in
marshaling and leading the next day.

Very little went right in the morning. The first problem
was getting enough aircraft in commission. After much has-
sling and reconfiguration the last-minute efforts of the flight
line people and the harried schedulers paid off and aircraft
numbers, pilots, flight call signs and bombloads started to fall
into place. It is most important that all the scheduled blocks

be filled so that each flight performs as a flight of four. The
maintenance troops are always hard pressed to get enough of
the occasionally recalcitrant monsters all the way in commission, with all systems working. Should they fail to do so,
which they seldom do even under the worst of time compres-
sions, it results in more than a departure short one or two
aircraft, worse than an effort launched with less than planned
bomb coverage on target. It becomes an effort wherein one or
more flights are no longer self-sustaining portions of the
strike, since they cannot render mutual support between the
elements of two. The offensive as well as the defensive plan is
short one pair of eyes and one man and machine combination
that fits perfectly into the jigsaw of mutual support. The flight
short one man automatically becomes a pair plus a straggler,
and Thai Nguyen was no place for stragglers.

This particular predawn scramble paid off and the full force
was launched as planned. Geeno ran into weather on his
refueling effort but managed to get the job done in style, and
all his charges dropped off the tanker, and headed for Thud
Ridge. As they approached the target area the weather they
had experienced during refueling was still with them and by
now had become a threat to the success of the mission. From
the river on in, the area was covered with a middle layer of
broken to overcast clouds. While a cloud layer of this kind is
not in itself too difficult to penetrate, it makes a great
difference in your tactics against the defenses and your actual
run on the target. Whether you stayed above the clouds,
went below them, or tried to hide inside them, you were in
for trouble.

If you stay on top on the way to the target you can look for
Migs, but you cannot see the ground for that extra double
check on your approach, nor can you see the Sams as they
kick up a boiling caldron of dust when they leap from their
launch sites. If you can't see them on the way up when they
are relatively slow and struggling both to accelerate and to
guide, you are in trouble, for by the time they come bursting
up through the undercast, accelerated and guiding on course
for you, your chances of evading them are slim. If you duck
just under the clouds you have a better visual shot at the
Sams and better visual navigation, but you give both the Sam
people and the ground gunners a perfect silhouette of your
force against the cloud backdrop, at the same time telegraphing

your exact altitude for both sighting and fuzing purposes. If you go far below the clouds, up goes the fuel consumption and up goes the exposure to smaller guns on the ground. About the only other piece of airspace available is inside the clouds themselves, and herding a large formation of heavily loaded machines through uncontrolled airspace that is full of turbulence and rocks, thundering blindly into and over an area where the defenders have no qualms about firing guns or Sams into the clouds if they or their radar even think you are there, is not a generally approved tactic. It was a tough decision that constantly faced fighter commanders going north.

Geeno was in the process of initiating a gradual descent to a position under the clouds that appeared to be the best compromise available under the conditions when Sam helped him to expedite both his decision and his descent. Three Sams launched and headed directly for the lead flight like lumbering white telephone poles. It quite obviously does not take them too long to get out of that lumbering stage and the closer they get and the faster they go the more rapidly you must react. Geeno still had visual contact with the ground and was able to spot this flight of three en route toward his charges. He bellowed out the warning on the radio and took his flight down to the deck, under the approaching missiles. You can practice all you want and brief all you want, but when those things are pointed your way, the old adrenaline flows, the palms get sweaty and the voice gets squeaky. If you are worried about your circulation, a few rides in that area will convince you that the old pump is really putting out.

The rest of the force had been well alerted by Geeno's call and were able to watch the air show as he and his flight parried the Sams and continued on toward the target. There was little doubt that the defenses were ready that morning and when you started getting tapped that far out you could bet the rest of the ride would be wild. In one way it sort of helps to have some successful action of that kind before you get right on the target, as it seems to act almost like a warm-up session before a deadly ball game. As long as you win that first one you have some feeling of accomplishment along with the definite knowledge that the ball game is on. It does not do a thing for the radio chatter, however, and a lot of

people immediately have a great number of important things
that they just have to say right now. This was the worst
possible time for a garbaged-up radio channel. You want the
air clear for calls alerting the rest of the flights to the posture
and actions of the defenses. There is no telling how many
people and aircraft we have lost simply because some blab-
bermouth was making a worthless transmission that blocked
out a warning call. It was a problem requiring constant
attention and it was not uncommon to have to chew some guy
out on the radio and tell him to shut up.

Fortunately, the chatter died rapidly or Geeno would probably never have made it to the target. He was now definitely
committed to an approach under the clouds and the countdown proceeded as the tick marks fell behind on the run-in
line on his map and the exaggerated pencil mark alongside
his course line said silently that two minutes from now all hell
would break loose above the rail yards. This was where you
liked everything smooth, so you could navigate perfectly and
get the approach and roll-in that you wanted without slinging
some poor wingman off by himself as the speed built toward
maximum. But there were no smooth skies available at the
two-minute marker that day. A second volley of three Sams
hurled clouds of dust and dirt on their masters and leaped
eagerly toward the lead flight. Navigation be damned, you
had to beat those Sams or the navigation would be of no
value, so Geeno sounded the alarm again and hauled all of his
flights down to the treetops at breakneck speed. The maneuver was too much for the Sams' stubby little wings trying to
accept their radar's guidance, and two of them stumbled
hopelessly, only to stall themselves out and tumble earthward, while their lone companion screeched ballistically skyward, ever accelerating, to explode in isolation at the end of
its snow-white contrail. But the Sams had accomplished one
thing: they forced Geeno into a major decision at a time when
he would just as soon have had nothing to think about but the
mechanics of the attack. He had to decide whether he would
blast that Sam site or continue as planned.

By this time in our war, a Sam site that revealed itself was
fair game, one of the targets we liked to destroy. This guy was
wide open and had showed his colors to an entire strike force
loaded for bear. The three dust pillars from the launch pad
stretched upward like three large surveyor's poles saying,

here, right in the middle of these three, here is Sam, and nothing Sam's masters could do would make those indicators disappear for several minutes. It was a great target, the kind a fighter pilot loves. There would be guns protecting the site, more missiles on the launch rails and maybe more in concealed storage, and that silly little control van in the very center. A few loads of bombs could do a lot of good in the middle of that site. It would have been a legal decision nobody could criticize, but the thought wouldn't go away that he was the leader, the guy who had to get this wing and another wing in and out of that gruesome rail yard. He was also the guy they were depending on to draw that flak at the yards and then paste it good so that all following could have a better chance of completing their runs. He knew it was going to be hard as hell to straighten this gaggle out after the Sam-evading maneuvers and get a decent run at the target, but the yards were the target, the one they had briefed on for so long, the one they wanted to knock out so badly so they wouldn't have to come back here for it again. The decision was instantaneous and automatic and Geeno squared his forces away and pushed for the yards already coming into view at 600 per.

(I faced a similar one about that time when I was suppressing the flak around a cozy little spot closer to town. The flak was fierce and my course took me right over the hallowed sanctuary of Phuc Yen airfield, which was still off limits. As I pulled up there were four Mig-21's in run-up position on the end of the runway, getting ready to take off and jump the guys behind me in the force. They, of course, were taboo as their wheels had not yet bounced off the concrete, but I had weapons on board that would leave no big postholes for identification and it would sure be great to knock those four out all at once. But the guys behind me could probably outdo the Migs, one way or the other, and I knew that the flak in front of me would get nothing but more accurate unless I hammered it for the guys behind me. I pressed on to suppress the flak. As advertised, they rolled down the runway, sucked up their gear, made a 180-degree turn, and were all over the second flight behind me. It's probably a good thing that I didn't cream those four Mig-21s as somebody would have squawked about it, and with my luck they would have court-martialed me. I'm so dumb about things like that, I probably would have told the truth anyway.)

Geeno's problems were compounding rapidly and as he reached up for bombing altitude he found the cloud deck lowering right over the target and another decision was upon him. The weather wasn't as good as it had looked and the flights were coming up from behind like six hundred. Was it good enough? Could these pros get in under here, knock the target out and get back out with their skins? The microsecond evaluation by the trained eye said yes—yes they could change the mechanics of their prebriefed attack, they could convert dive angles and airspeeds and sight pictures to change the amount of lead angle required to get the bombs in there. They could get whatever altitude the clouds and the gunners would give them and as they rolled in, they could tell how high they were and what the angle was to the desired impact point and they could tell when it looked just right and bomb and get the hell out of there. Yes, it was a go, and Geeno so announced on the radio.

The dizzy guns didn't light up the way they should have. The fire was only light and yet he knew that a goodly portion of the defenses in the North were concentrated down there. To bomb on the minuscule elements that revealed themselves would have helped, but only a little. What was the matter with those clods, were they asleep? Surely he hadn't surprised them, not after they had been hosing Sams at him for five minutes. He went as high as the clouds would allow and he had to make a move right away. This was Geeno's big decision, the instantaneous awful decision of a lifetime and he did the unheard of. He stayed up on top, and he calmly circled over the wildest array of weapons ever assembled in the history of ground-to-air warfare. He circled because they would not fire at him and if they did not show themselves he could not blast a channel for his strike aircraft and some of his boys would get hurt.

As he swung past the end of the yards, Sam broke the relative lull and the seventh, eighth and ninth launches of the day reached for him. As he swung violently out of their guidance capability he tried to set his lead element up to bomb the newly revealed and threatening site, but his evasive gyration had not only thrown the Sams off, it had swung him out of position to strike the site as its defending guns let fly all the lead they owned, since their charges had revealed their position during launch. His third and fourth aircraft, in the second element, were in good position, and satisfied that they could knock out this threat, he directed them to hit the site, calmly turned his back on them and proceeded to weave his way between the clouds and the rising crescendo of heavy gunfire that now committed itself fully from the other end of the yards. Those were the ones he wanted, the big ones that had remained hidden and were now making up for lost time.

He somehow made it back toward them and knew he had found the target he wanted. Two bombloads were on the Sam site and he still had his own and his wingman's bombs for these guns. Up and over he went for his bomb run and the timing was great as the first strike flight was approaching their own roll-in. He had to hurry—but not too fast. Sam had other ideas and, in the day's duel between Geeno and Sam, Sam was not to be denied. A site commander who had remained concealed must have realized the gravity of the threat with the suppressors on the run and the strike birds right on their tail, and he salvoed all six of his Sams directly at Geeno in a desperate attempt to get this wild one who had flaunted the strongest of defenses by loitering above them. There was no warning and there was no evasive action. All six Sams guided perfectly, all six proximity fuzes functioned, and Geeno was obscured in a six-sided puff ball of ugly red, brown and gray.

His Thud flew out the other side of the blossoming cloud, faltered for a moment, then rolled over for its final dive. His wingman had been wide of the burst and his bombs did the job. I hope Geeno knew.

Things were still moving at breakneck speed and the strike force was at work. There was no faltering, no hesitation, just deadly split-second precision work. You don't look for anybody else and you don't think about anybody else during these seconds when your ass belongs to Uncle Sam. Most of the time you can't assimilate anything else, and you definitely can't analyze it until later anyway; nor, even if you could, could you do anything about it. Each one of us understands that, but we don't particularly care to dwell on it. The strike was a beauty and everyone put them right in there and everyone got out. Everyone that is, except Geeno—the fighter pilot commander who bet his life that he could knock out the toughest guns in the world and save his buddies.

9.

THE LONGEST MISSION

Pilots get to be a superstitious lot as they approach that magic 100-mission mark. You can't get a 95-mission man to change his flying suit or wear a different pair of gloves—they won't do or wear anything differently. One friend of mine got a St. Christopher medal from his wife when he had only about five missions to go. He quickly put it in his footlocker reasoning, "Whatever I've got going for me now, I don't want to change." Another clown got hit on his ninetieth but made it back and swore he wasn't ever going to change his drawers or his socks until he got that hundredth mission.

My mother tells me that when I was a little kid I used to say, "Sunday is the best day," but in our wing we hated Sundays. It was one of those stupid superstitions, like accidents coming in threes, Friday the thirteenth, and all that. We didn't really believe it and consciously we ignored it, but when we really got clobbered, it always seemed to be on Sunday. One particular Sunday must certainly have been the longest day in the world for Leo and all the rest of us. It was so long, it finally ran into Thursday.

Leo was in charge of our Wild Weasel crews that flew the F-105 Fs and his business was clobbering Sam sites. We put these specialists in converted two-seat Thuds that we robbed from the training program back in the States. They flew as a two-man team, and we tried to keep the same two together all the time, because their job of monitoring, finding, and attacking the sites was a tightly knit two-man effort of interpretation and flying. A weasel flight was usually made up of a two seater as lead with a single seater as his wingman and another two seater as element leader, also with a single seater wingman. Leo was good and I used him extensively as my liaison with this specialized bunch of experts and what Leo said, they did. We had them scattered throughout the squadrons, which I always thought was a mistake. I wanted to put them all in one squadron like they did in the Avis wing, but I never could sell my point. I considered their job different enough to group them together under one boss and let them fly all the weasel missions from one squadron. This would provide the advantage of always having a flight of four all playing the same game—as opposed to the arrangement we used, where you would have a flight made up of part weasels and part pickup team from the particular squadron providing the weasel coverage for the day. If I had been able to sell my point, I feel that Leo, Harry, Bob and Joe would all be with us today, or at least we would not have lost them all on the same Sunday.

Perhaps Leo's best single mission was when he took on most of North Vietnam all by himself. He spotted a Sam site and knocked it out in a hurry, moved to the next site down the pike and dumped that one also, and the route of the strike force was well defined with Sams and their supporting components exploding on the ground. The plaintive wail of a pair of beepers told him that his wingman had been hit and that two weasels were in their chutes. He spotted a Mig intent on shooting the helpless pilots hanging in their chutes—they play dirty up there—closed to almost collision range and blew the vulture out of the sky. With the Mig's wingman on his tail, Leo, desperate for fuel, outraced his pursuer as he streaked southward for an aerial refueling. As darkness approached he returned, alone, found a flight of four Migs over the downed crew, flew directly into the middle of them and scattered them, shooting down yet another Mig. When the rescue proved hopeless he found there were no airborne tankers to refuel him and only through his own skill was he able to limp through the black night, penetrate the thunderstorms and land at an emergency base with little other than fumes in his fuel tanks. Leo was no stranger to stress, but a Sunday was to do him in.

As boss weasel, Leo scheduled the other weasels and when he was short of crews (but we don't talk about shortage of crews, do we?) he would take the double load himself. He took the early morning run to Hanoi in the lead position for his ninety-sixth trip and turned himself around to fly as element leader for his ninety-seventh and last trip that Sunday afternoon. Did he goof by scheduling himself twice? I suppose he did, but somebody had to go twice and Leo was the boss, so he went.

I was leading the force that day and the mission was rotten from the start. The weather was OK and the briefing and preparations went OK, but we were in trouble from the time we started to taxi to the runway for takeoff. As we rolled down the taxi strip to the arming area, the gruesome sound of a beeper split the air. Somebody's beeper was stuck in the on position and it saturated the radio. The control tower picked it up right away and tried to get a steer on the offending airman but could not pinpoint it. Everything was laid on, tankers, support aircraft and the like, and you simply can't stop and start all over. We had to try everything we could to locate that beeper and get the guy with it to abort the mission and fill his spot with a spare aircraft. We started taking steers on each other as soon as we got airborne and managed to pin it down to Leo's flight but we couldn't tell which aircraft the beeper was coming from. Once you get strapped into that monster with all that gear on, there is no way you can check your own beeper. You can't move anything but your hands and feet and there is no way to reach behind you and examine the contents of your chute. We split Leo's flight into elements and moved individual flight members fore and aft of the tankers as we headed north and we got the tankers to try and spot the beeper with their direction-finding gear but we couldn't get a valid steer. The continuous transmission was strong enough to clutter the air but not strong enough to give a good steer at that altitude. The silly little things will transmit for a couple of days on a good battery, so there was little hope that it would go off by itself and we were in for a noisy afternoon. Just how noisy we did not know.

Another thing that we did not know—and it was coincidence rather than plan—was that three of us within the strike force were carrying miniature Japanese tape recorders. We flew so many divergent paths that afternoon, and the noise and confusion level was so high, that ordinarily it would have been close to impossible to reconstruct the activity. With a good deal of homework we were able to recreate all the sounds of that Sunday, as there was at least one recorder in the midst of the action at all times, and we had an added benefit of one recorder in the two-place lead weasel aircraft to give us some additional insight into that two-man crew. These tapes usually helped us to study and learn, but that Sunday they combined to weave a complicated tale.

I was Waco lead and my weasels were Carbine flight. I had Oakland, Tomahawk and Neptune flights as the other bombers and Dallas and Chicago were flights of Phantoms assigned as my Mig cover, though, as it turned out, those two flights might better have stayed home that day. As we dropped off the big KC-135 tanker and headed for the river, Carbine switched his flight over to prestrike radio frequency and swung away to the north to troll for the Sam sites we knew would be active. Ben and Norm were in the number one Carbine aircraft and even before we had switched radio frequencies in the rest of the force, Norm had already alerted Harry, his number two, Leo in his number three machine and Bob in number four that one of his indicators was sputtering like a rattlesnake with an ugly prelaunch warning. "Four miles to go now, strong signal. OK, Sam's up and he's off to our right. He's at one o'clock, stronger signal, now he's fading. No threat—and here's another one. He's at twelve. One at twelve, one at one."

About that time, as Waco lead, I called all the strike flights over to the prestrike channel and we checked in on the radio. It is a reassuring sound to me as the flight lead barks his call sign and the flight members crisply respond with their number in the flight.

"Waco."

"Two."

"Three."

"Four."

"Oakland."

"Two."

KC-135

"Three."

"Four."

"Tomahawk."

"Two."

"Three."

"Four."

"Neptune."

"Two."

"Three."

"Four."

Everybody was there and ready to go to work. You get so you can recognize most of the voices, and as they check in you can almost see and feel those strong alert men straining against their shoulder straps and sitting tall in their cockpits.

"Waco—Carbine. You gonna stay this frequency or go to strike channel?" Now that's a nice polite reminder from the weasels I had briefed that we would switch channels as we crossed the river. I guess Carbine lead was ready to go to the noisy channel. Everybody else would be on that one and we would get to listen to our Phantom escorts go through their preflight briefing that they should have accomplished back on the ground—but it was a necessary evil.

"Waco flights to ten, button one zero." And again, the staccato check-in followed by my final preparatory command, "Clean 'em up, green 'em up and start your music." All was now go.

"Dallas flight, let's get rid of the tanks," served to announce that our escorts were in the area, and more important, everyone must watch out as they were in the process of dropping those damn tanks through our ranks again. We never did figure out why they had to drop them right on top of us, and I can assure you that a 20-foot-long fuel tank in the face can ruin your entire day.

"Weak guns at twelve o'clock low," came from Carbine lead and then he said "Negative Sams." This was a very significant call. The lead weasel was scanning the scene and he had no indications of any Sam prelaunch activity. While it only takes them a few seconds to launch a Sam, they must go through some prelaunch activity and they were not yet engaged in it.

Next came the most significant call of the day—or what could have been the most significant. Had it been accomplished properly, it could have saved us three Thuds and four people. The flight indicator call sign was garbled and all you could tell was that it was one of the Phantom escort flights. "Drumfphe—Aaah—got two Sams at nine o'clock level." But the weasels had no indication of Sam activity and they don't miss that. Had Mig-21s sneaked behind and below the weasels and launched a pair of air-to-air rockets at the trailing element of Carbine flight? I think so. Was this the first time that one of the escort drivers had seen a missile in flight? Was he so steeped in Sam briefings that a Sam was all he correlated with something white streaking through the sky with fire on the end? Did the adrenaline garble his transmission? By his nine o'clock positioning on his call, did he indicate that he was between the Migs and Carbine flight, and that the missiles were already on the way and eating up the precious few seconds between a break call and missile impact? I think so.

"What was that?" indicated that another escort member had not understood his flight mate.

"He called two at nine level, Sams."

"No joy." The flight lead didn't see them. He was out of the ball game—and the game was lost.

"Negative contacts. Guns low at twelve o'clock. Very strong guns." Again the expert weasels in Carbine flight saw no Sams. They had to be air-to-air missiles.

"There's a flight behind us, Carbine." The last chance. Who said it? Who was it? This was all in seconds, as fast as forty people could talk at the same time.

"Say again." The radio noise was intense.

"There's a flight behind us. Rog, that's Finch." Who in hell was Finch? Were those the Migs?

"Signals up now, moderate indicator, you're thirteen miles from launch. Still have very strong guns at nine and a signal—a very strong signal—may be a presentation."

Two of them see it now. "OK, Carbine, he's looking at us, twelve o'clock." But that indicated a direction exactly opposite that from which two white objects with fire on the end were now accelerating through the sky.

And again the unidentified and unintelligible voice came from the escort. "OK, we got a Sam at—ughh—Thrush flight." Who the hell was Thrush flight? Who was talking? Was Carbine four already down in flames and did someone see air-to-air missiles on the way toward Carbine three? I think so.

And then my chief weasel, one of the nicest and most intense men I have ever known, made his last intelligible airborne transmission, and he made it in his usual precise and definite manner. "This is Carbine three. I've flamed out. Carbine three flamed out. Mayday, Mayday, Mayday."

The radio exploded. "Rog. You've got flame coming out—"

"This is Waco lead. They're at nine level. Take it around to the right—all Waco flights to the right." I had Leo's aircraft in sight and ordered all my flights to turn to cover him.

"Number three, you're out of control. Get out—GET OUT!"

"I'll get a fix."

"I got two chutes—two chutes, I got a fix."

"Look at the chutes."

"Pull up so we miss them."

"OK, who in Waco has them in sight?" I did not see the chutes at first.

"I got them up there about eight thirty."

"Carbine lead has the two chutes at about sixty-five hundred feet." The ground gunners were shooting at the chutes on the way down but they didn't hit them. No sporting blood up there.

"OK, this is Waco lead. We've got two guys out and in chutes and we've got a pretty fair chance of getting them. We're still far enough back to do some good so we're calling the whole thing off and going Rescap." I ordered my sixteen attacking fighter-bombers, my remaining weasels and escort

flights to a new task, and all but one flight of four responded
at once.

"Waco, you want us to go on?" came from Oakland, who
somehow had missed the intent of the whole operation and
was still on course for the original target. Although it made
no sense, and although it made no difference in the situation
we were faced with at the instant, I was so furious at him for
being out ahead by himself, I think I would have punched
him in the nose if I'd had him in front of me. Your emotions
get quite high in a situation like that. Little things jar you
when they don't go right.

Now, having diverted the force from the briefed strike, my
job was to organize and control this rescue operation as best I
could. You have to alert the rescue guys and give them all the
details, and you have to arrange the flights you have on the
scene so that you can give maximum cover to the people on
the ground and also cover the rescue machines when they
arrive. At the altitudes you have to work on a rescue, the fuel
goes pretty fast because you have to keep your speed up or
you are liable to join those on the ground. You also have to
stay close enough to the downed crew to strafe if necessary to
keep the enemy away from them while waiting for the rescue
machines. This is difficult to do in a high-performance jet
with a little bitty wing like the Thud and it becomes difficult
to cover those on the ground without falling out of the sky as
you rack the bird around in a tight turn it was not designed
for. I gave Carbine the job of getting the rescue forces on the
way and I took the low cover. I stacked Tomahawk, Oakland
and Neptune flights up at higher altitudes so they could
conserve fuel and also watch out for more Migs. That way I
could stay until my fuel got low, bring the next flight down in
the exact location of the downed crew and then I could
depart for the tanker to pick up more fuel and return to the
scene. We could shuttle the other flights through the same
routine while we got all the tankers we could obtain as far
north as they could come. As I circled, I remember seeing
two plumes of smoke that looked like aircraft impacts against
the hills. I noted them as I watched the two doll-like figures
floating down with occasional red tracers from the ground
guns arcing over them, but my thought was that their aircraft
must have broken apart and impacted in two sections. The

energy available for creative thought is limited at a time like this and it was especially so at the eastern end of my orbit when I found some 37-millimeter guns intent on curtailing my Rescap activities. They weren't close enough to the guys in the chutes to hurt them so I just called their position out to the other flights and left them alone. No sense in shooting them up at the moment. Just in case we didn't get out guys out, a bunch of shot-up gunner's families would probably not do them any good. I was quite confident that we had things set up as well as we could, and I looked forward to barbing Leo that night back at the base as to how come he had been shot down.

By now we were again aware of a problem that we had pretty well forgotten in the press of events. That beeper was still on and it was screeching at full power, blocking transmissions and generally making things more difficult. Until you have experienced the screech of that thing, you can't imagine how bothersome it can be, like the scraping of someone's fingernails up and down a blackboard. We still didn't know who had it on and there was no chance of going through another process of elimination now. We were stuck with it, but we didn't yet know just how significant it would be in the sequence of the afternoon's events.

As the chutes floated down, the drama continued. "The coordinates now are—Mayday, Mayday, Mayday."

"Two, you still with me? Still have them?"

"Carbine, let's go rescue frequency."

The rescue people have coordinators who are tasked with controlling the entire show when you get into a spot like this. They have radios and radars at their disposal, some airborne in large transport aircraft and some on the ground. They had a call sign for radio transmissions like everyone else, and Royal one might represent an airborne rescue controller while Royal five could represent a ground station to the south. Through these resources they coordinate and control any rescue operation, directing the fighters, the choppers who accomplish any pickup of downed crewmen, and the prop-driven A1Es who pinpoint the downed crew's location, attempt to keep the enemy away from him, and fly a protective escort for the choppers while they are making a pickup. While the A1Es are known in general as Spads, they too have

a radio call sign, and Nomad one might be the leader of a pair
of Spads working a specific rescue while his wingman might
be identified as Nomad two.

Douglas A1E "Spad"

The distances involved are critical. You often have a tough
time getting the rescue people on the radio, and until you do,
nothing gets started. Charged with the responsibility of
contacting them and getting the show on the road, Carbine
lead started acting.

"Hello Royal, hello Royal—Carbine one." The only answer
was the interminable beeper screeching in defiance.

Two more calls mocked by the beeper and Royal replied
weakly, "Carbine—Royal."

"Roger, Royal. Carbine three was hit and has ejected. Both
chutes were sighted. They have not touched down yet. Right
now they are at two thousand feet. Are you ready for coordinates? They are going down slowly and it looks like they
might be able to hit on the west side of a ridge and we are in
the area now."

Then came a most welcome voice booming through on the
radio. "This is Carbine three on the ground, can you hear
me?" Leo was down and talking to the troops he knew were
bent on getting him out of there. The answer to his urgent
call was the screech of the lost beeper. Since he had turned

his own beeper off as he hit the ground, his first thought was that his backseat partner had failed to turn his beeper off. "Bear, your beeper's still on. Your beeper's still on."

There has always been a strange relationship between single-engine fighter pilots and those who ride with them in the back of two-place aircraft on specialized missions. Very seldom do the frontseat men admit that the guy in back is doing quite a job and that the mission would never be successful without him. They carry all sorts of impolite names and are the brunt of many jokes.

The Phantom guys started calling their backseaters "Gibs," standing for guy in the backseat. Everyone has to be different so our backseaters became known and referred to as trained bears. Leo's call to his bear reverberated with the strongest sense of comradeship and the reply came back, "My beeper's off and the Bear is OK."

I was over the spot now and watched as they gathered in their multicolored chutes and pulled them back into the trees. They had hit the ground quite close together, near a narrow dirt road that ran the length of a valley between two ridges. There were rice paddies on one side and the trees covering a small ridge crept right down to the road on the other side. The road made a U-turn to go around a small peak in the ridge line and they had landed on opposite legs of the U, with the hill in between them, and thus could not see each other. I called, "Roger, Roger, we got you in sight, Leo. Roger, Carbine three, we do hear you intermittently and we do see both chutes."

"Carbine, they are on the ground and in contact and we see the chutes."

"Hello Royal, hello Royal—Carbine here—" and the beeper squealed on to tell us that it did not belong to Leo or the Bear.

"OK, Royal, they hit on a hill just northeast of the position I gave you. Second ridge over."

I had swung past their position out into the area I had just told myself and all others not to enter. "Flak. Don't get out here, baby."

Leo knew who was who and guessed rightly that I would be close by with the lead flight. "Waco—this is Carbine," came up from the paddies of the enemy on the scratchy, hard-to-understand emergency radio, with that lousy beeper

on top of it all. "Waco—this is Carbine three. We are OK and
are going to move up the ridge so—"

"Roger, Roger, I understand you are OK and are moving up
the ridge—"

"Hello, Royal—this is Nomad." This was the first indication
that the Rescap was in progress as the first of the Spads
checked in.

"Hello, Royal—Carbine here. Where in hell is everybody?
OK, Waco, this is Carbine one."

"Go ahead Carbine—Waco."

"Rog, I think I better leave the area. I think that stuck
beeper is goofing up the works and I think it is in my flight."

"Rog, I just talked to Leo and they are OK and are edging
up the ridge."

As Carbine flight acknowledged and started moving for the
tankers, the next revolting chapter began to unfold. "Carbine
flight check in. Carbine four, you on? Carbine four, this is
one."

"Carbine—Tomahawk here. How's the flak?"

"There was some shooting on the next ridge over, just east
of where they got hit."

"Carbine four, come up channel one one."

"Carbine—this is Waco. You make good contact with Royal?"

"I'll call them again and relay to you outbound. Hello,
Royal—Carbine. Carbine two, give them a call." Sometimes
one radio in a flight will do the job, for no apparent reason,
while another will not. Two was able to get Royal up on
frequency and they brought the rescue commander up to
speed and gave him some updated coordinates.

"Roger, Carbine, and how long can you stay in the area?"

"We are departing the area now as I think one of my flight
has a beeper stuck and we are clearing out so we don't
interfere with the rescue."

"Roger. Is there anyone else in the area who could maintain a tallyho on them?" This indicated trouble to come. It
was apparent that the rescue coordinator did not appreciate
the fact that there were many machines already on the scene
in a well-controlled effort to provide the necessary cover for
the rescue aircraft and the downed crews. Carbine explained
it again but the message apparently never was well understood. Those controlling the effort are understandably reluctant to commit rescue craft to a hostile area until adequate

forces are available to protect them, but here we had more than enough planes in position, had already wasted valuable time, and were to waste more before the afternoon was over.

"Rog, the whole force is in there and Waco is the commander and he has taken charge of the whole thing. If you can give me any estimates, I can pass them on to him."

"OK, it will be about forty minutes before we can get anything in there, and if you can get Waco to come up on this frequency I would appreciate it."

"OK, Waco may have to put somebody higher to relay. Stand by, I'll be right back."

"Waco—Carbine."

"Yeah, go ahead."

"I just talked to Royal and they said it would be forty minutes before they could get anyone into the area, and I told him that you would be in the area and would be in charge."

"OK, get those tankers as far north as you can get them so we can hit them in a hurry."

"Rog, I passed two good chutes and contact with the front seat, and he would like to have someone high over your position for radio relay."

"OK, Tomahawk, you're the top guy. You go high, OK?"

"Rog. Tomahawk, let's go rescue freq."

In the background a feeble transmission from far to the south forced itself through the beeper scream and gave us another indication that the wheels were turning and that we had hope of getting our boys out. "OK, Chopper lead—Royal. I've got you on my radarscope, and the fighters are in the area. They have tally on the two who are down and Waco is in charge. Both people landed safely and they have voice contact with one now, over."

"Royal—Carbine."

"Carbine—Royal two. Go." This told us that another cog had slipped into place. The emergency standby rescue controller, Royal two, had scrambled from far to the south and had progressed far enough into the area to assume his role of on-scene controller. We could hear him all the way up to the area where we orbited, looked and waited.

"Roger, Waco is low and Tomahawk is coming up this frequency to relay."

"Roger, Roger, understand, thank you."

"Royal—Tomahawk on."

"Roger, Tomahawk, how long will you be able to stay in the area?"

"We'll be able to stay about forty-five minutes."

"Roger, understand forty-five minutes, and are you groomed for Migs?"

"Affirmative."

"Rog, and I'm not reading anyone else up there. Are there any others up there we can use for Cap?" Once again it was apparent that there was confusion within the control element as to what they had to work with.

"Roger, Waco, a flight of four, Carbine with three, Oakland with four and Neptune with four plus the Phantoms in the area."

"Carbine two, you still getting the beeper?"

"Not at this time." The beeper has a limited range, even at altitude, and Carbine must now have realized that they had left the beeper behind in the area of the Rescap.

"Carbine one—two here. Let's go button three for one." Such a switch, going to a less commonly used radio channel for one minute, is the only way you can talk to your flight members when the chatter gets real bad, and Carbine two wanted to talk with his leader in private, high in the unfriendly skies of the North.

Completing the channel change he checked in, "Carbine two."

"One. Go ahead."

"Rog, I think our number four got hit just prior to Leo getting hit."

"You do?" The tone of startled disbelief was pitiful, such a familiar voice that you could almost see the leader's face. He didn't want to believe that he had lost another good young kid but he already knew it was true. Why else no contact with Bob? Nobody had seen him or talked with him in the last few crazy minutes. Bob was brand-new when he walked into our wing. He had been through the normal training routines, but the cocky little lieutenant was on his first real job in the fighter business and he progressed well. He had earned his spurs on some of the toughest ones we had, and was now one of our sharp-eyed wingmen enjoying the respect of his comrades, but his progress had come to a flaming halt against a hilltop in North Vietnam. Did he get out of the

THE LONGEST MISSION   175

aircraft? Who knows—I don't even know what happened to the machine, but now I know what that second pillar of smoke meant. This was all quite difficult to explain to his parents later, especially by mail. His Dad wrote that Bob's mother had been ill since being notified—could I tell him more? I didn't know any more. Bob's Dad said he had taught Bob to be a good woodsman and that he could go for days in the hills—did I think he had a chance of being in the hills? I didn't know.

This meant that there was only one of the lieutenants left in the squadron. We had received a group of them all at once and they were all great kids. Now there was only one left. The guys in the squadron took care of that the same evening, partly to boost the spirits of all concerned and partly to break the hex. Although the remaining lieutenant had a couple of years to go before anyone would be seriously considering him for promotion to captain, the squadron jester announced that the air in the local area was obviously unhealthy for lieutenants, and that from now on until the end of his combat tour all squadron members would address the surviving lieutenant as brevet captain. They made believe they didn't have any lieutenants and the lad in question successfully completed his tour with one real and one imaginary bar on his shoulder.

The question of what happened to Bob was unanswered, but the question of the beeper that was stuck was now pretty well answered. Carbine one and two, the two surviving weasels, were out of the immediate rescue area en route to the tanker and they could no longer hear the screeching monster. Leo and his Bear were on the ground and Leo had checked beepers off on the radio. Four was down in the area and one of his beepers was the culprit. If we could have isolated it earlier, who would have filled in for him? Would the shootdown have gone the same? For sure the Rescap would have gone better without the noise. I wonder if he was fiddling around in the cockpit trying to reach his beeper when he got bagged? I don't know. In this business it is not too profitable or comforting to think too much about the ifs.

"Royal—Carbine."

"Carbine—Royal. Go ahead."

"Roger, I cannot locate my number four man. He was on the wing of number three. I cannot get him to respond. There's a possibility he's down in the same area, over."

"Roger, so that would be Carbine three and four, positively three and probably four."

"Roger, I only personally saw one aircraft in flames. It went into a spin just as they ejected. I saw two good chutes from number three, that's a two-seater. Number four was a single-seater with one man in it. I never saw it but I can't raise him now."

"Roger, can you cycle off the tanker and go back in now?" Royal wanted Carbine and his wingman to refuel and return to the rescue area.

"Roger, if I can be sure that neither one of our beepers is active. Are you getting that now, four—or two—are you still getting that?"

"Not at the present time."

"Roger, Carbine one and two can go back in."

"Roger, you can contact control for a tanker and let us know on this frequency when you come back in."

Carbine lead switched the surviving half of his flight to the radio frequency monitored by the waiting tankers and began the lonely trip back to refuel. Here for a few minutes he was in a different atmosphere. The challenge is to find the tanker, get the fuel and get back into the fray quickly. Nobody is shooting at you out here, but the intermission is not particularly relaxing. You always feel like hell when you lose a guy, and when you lose more than one it is downright grim. In his two-place machine Carbine lead and his Bear groused at each other as they searched for the tank and tried to reconstruct the scene. In the two-place job you chatter at the other guy over a mike that is hot all the time. In a single-seater, you talk to yourself.

"Wonder what hit him?"

"Hmmm?"

"Wonder what hit him?"

"Crap, I don't know."

"I heard somebody call Sam but they never did give their call sign."

The tanker rendezvous was going at about the normal pace it always assumes when the air is charged with emergency. You can't get the right people to talk to you. Carbine lead was bouncing from channel to channel on the radio but none of the tanker control radars would respond and offer the desired steer to contact with the tanker.

"Balls." But calling the wrath of all the unnamed gods down on the controllers is to no avail and the only thing you can do is press toward the area where you think the tanker will be and try to get in contact with him yourself for a free-lance hookup.

A cross volley of curses from front and back seat was interrupted by my call ringing through on emergency channel. I was still back in the area running the low cover and waiting hopefully for the rescue craft I assumed to be on the way.

"Hello, Carbine three—this is Waco. Turn off the beeper if you read me, please."

Carbine realized that they were probably the only ones who had the answer to the beeper question. "Could be Carbine four's beeper. You better tell Waco lead."

"Carbine four is on the ground."

"That's what I said, Waco lead and the rest of the people don't know Carbine four is down."

The radar control trying to get the tankers and fighters together was coming into focus on the gravity of the problem, but they burst onto normal and emergency channels only momentarily as they and the tankers sought to establish contact. As they talked, I was receiving a call from Leo on the ground and was reassuring him, "Roger, Leo, you're loud and clear. In about twenty-five minutes we should have some choppers up for you. The whole force is covering you, over."

"Leo, you need to climb the hill, over." I thought I had him in ideal position and I knew I had the force necessary to cover the operation. All I needed was to run the fuel shuttle smoothly and wait for those pickup machines.

"Tomahawk—Waco. Relay to Royal again to move the whole tanker fleet up north. Be sure they know we have the whole force in here covering those guys."

Carbine lead plodded on, and as it was becoming increasingly apparent that refueling was going to be a problem, the frontseater and the backseater thought out loud to each other.

"Crap."

"Two stinking airplanes."

"I'm telling you, I just can't believe it."

"Did you plot that on the map?"

"I don't have a map."

"How many miles were we out from that place we were going to?"

"I've got the coordinates here."

Back at the scene I had spotted the first of the ground activity and was passing details to the downed crew. "OK, Leo, one of you is on one side of the hill and the other on the other side—just around the bend. You're OK around the bend, but there're some houses further down. WATCH OUT, there's someone walking out on the road!"

I was now very concerned about the somebody on the road but Royal, fulfilling his duties as overall airborne controller of the rescue, broke through the wall of noise on the radio in a desperate search for information. I acknowledged and was shocked at their answer, "Waco, there's a possibility that the number four man might have gone down too. Would you see if you could get me any information on that?"

"Can we work on another frequency Royal? All I can hear is beepers. You want to go to twenty?"

Many miles to the south, Carbine had wound up working mutual steers with the tanker he had finally contacted on the radio with no help from the ground controller. They had found each other and were setting up the busy pattern of refueling that was to be used again and again that afternoon and evening.

"Rog, Tanker, all I need is gas for one and two. Three and four are down and we need a full load so we can get back in there."

"Rog, Carbine, we'll give you all we got. Incidentally, nobody has any contact with control."

"That's about average. If you can get them, tell them that Waco, the force commander, is going to base all his minimum fuel departures from the rescue area on the fact that all the tankers will be north of the normal post-strike refueling area."

"Rog, if we can ever get them on the other radio we'll relay that."

As they moved into position behind the big bird that was to pass them the critical fuel, I was too far away to hear Carbine flight on the radio, but later review of all of the tapes tied the whole thing together. I was having fits back in the area trying to listen to Leo, pass information to him and keep others off the radio. "Whoever is yakking on emergency frequency get off. Leo, you're just too hard to understand. Move that mike away from your mouth a bit and try it again. In the meantime, stay put and stay out of sight. We've got somebody coming for you."

The guys in the two-place aircraft have a different job, not necessarily one that I would care for as a full-time occupation for myself, but they love it and they do a fabulous piece of work. They are strapped in that two-place monster together and where one goes the other goes, unless fate spares only one when things go sour. They realize that they are in it together, even more than any two strike pilots. They work together like a piece of precision machinery whether they like each other or not, and in addition to having to listen to everyone else in the sky, they have to listen to each other from engine crank to shutdown. Their hot mike system is installed so that when you want to talk to the other man you do not have to activate any switches or mike buttons. This is great when you need it, but you can get awfully tired of listening to both yourself and your fellow weasel breathing for four hours. The two-place hot mike seems to make two-man aircrews feel they have to talk to each other. While I personally prefer a bit more silence when I have work to do, I will admit it helps to say something or to hear somebody else who may be as confused as you are yourself. The weasels wind up barbing each other constantly just as two close and mutually dedicated friends would do over a casual drink at the bar. Carbine one and his Bear were shook about the time they were refueling, and they talked.

"Four zero—this is Carbine. I'm so damn heavy I can't keep this beast in the sky back here. How about a little toboggan?"

When you refuel, tobogganing is sometimes necessary as the fighter has to slow down to speeds that are compatible for both fighter and tanker, and any trade of that nature is bound to compromise somebody's performance. Once a heavy fighter gets into that position, especially if he has any sort of a load on board the machine, he is hanging on the engine. You get into that awkward attitude where you have some of your flaps extended, you have backed way off on the power in order to get into position, and you have killed your flying speed almost completely. You are so close to stalled out that you need full power from the engine so you can hang up there by brute force. Sometimes this is still not enough and you simply fall off the end of the boom and sink.

One remedy is for the tanker to drop his nose to form a more compatible profile so that you are both falling down hill together, or tobogganing. This is fine if weather, altitude separation and all that will allow it, and providing the tanker changes attitude smoothly. Quite often the tanker crew has been allowing George, the automatic pilot, to fly the aircraft because George can actually do a smoother job, and when they cut George out and manually take control, they tend to be too positive. When the ham-handed human pushes the control forward and the nose dumps with that huge mass of metal and fuel rotating up and over its own nose, it gets wild. The fighter pilot is already extended to his maximum control and engine power limits or else he would not have had to call for the toboggan, and when the great beast's tail rises in his face, the fighter usually manages to porpoise from positive to negative G forces while junk flies around the cockpit and that stinking fuel turns to fiery fingers of fumes that reach into the cockpit and stab at your eyes, nose and mouth. Even with a tight mask and 100 percent oxygen, you can't get away from those fuel fumes and they just plain hurt. You can feel and taste every raw corner of every sinus in your head and at times you involuntarily cry so hard you can't even see the tanker in front of you. Anything more than a momentary shot turns your stomach inside out and the sickening dizziness hangs on for some time until your body has purged the fumes.

"Auugh—" over the top they went. "Nice toboggan, chief—gad." But even the gyrations failed to block the sharp reminder spitting over emergency channel, "Orphan Annie—Mickey Mouse," and the area designator that followed spelled Leo's position.

"Sams," from the frontseater.

"Yeah, and Migs," from the backseater.

"Crap—that's all we need up there now is more of those bastards."

"Carbine," came from control. "Do you have the coordinates for Carbine four?"

"No, I didn't even know he was down, but the best we can give you is within ten miles of three. Control, don't forget Waco is running his fighters based on you getting us lots more tankers up here. And I'm sure Royal is running his show based on that also."

Carbine got no reply and internal conversation took over. "Oh, crud. That stinking fuel, I think I'll puke," came from the rear seat as the tanks filled and the boomer initiated the disconnect. The fuel in the two systems banged against hydraulically closed doors and vented directly into the pilot's breathing and living environment. Beautiful piece of engineering.

"This pig. I'm really falling out of the sky."

"You know I saw some flak underneath us on the way in."

"How about holding the stick in this bank for a minute. Don't let the airspeed get any lower or we'll sink clean out of sight."

"I'll try. Damn—airspeed I ain't got. How come you always have to blow your nose when the going gets rough. Good thing you got me back here."

"Crap."

"You know right over Leo himself we are out of range of all Sams according to the book."

"Not by much."

"Better than nothing."

A repeat of the Mig and Sam warnings coincided with the other survivor's full load of fuel and his nasal purge, and Carbine announced, "OK, tanker, we're both full and we are departing."

The tanker answered with "Rog. Good luck. We won't be here when you get back. Wish we could be."

"I'll bet he does."

"Yeah, but I still wouldn't want their job. What would your wife say when someone asks her what her husband does? My husband makes his living passing gas—"

"Gimme back the stick—" The frontseater resumed control of his aircraft and realigned his radio frequencies with "Carbine, let's go back to rescue frequency."

"Tomahawk—this is Carbine on the way back in. Give me a short count so I can home on you." When you need to find another aircraft you can have him activate his radio transmitter while he counts or talks, and an indicator in your own aircraft will point to his general position.

"Rog, this is Tomahawk holding down. I'm at seven thousand feet."

"Royal—this is Carbine. I'm back in the area with the two I've got left and I'm full of fuel."

"Rog, Carbine, hold about twenty miles out of the area and I'll call you when I want you to go in."

The series of transmissions that followed brought the next in a series of shocks for the day. "Royal five, Royal five—Royal two on rescue frequency."

"Go ahead."

"Roger, we've got everybody in position up there and we're waiting for some clearance to go. Is there anything you can do to let us know if we're going to get clearance or not?"

An irritated fighter pilot blurted out "Clearance for what?" —the obvious question as all of us who had heard the transmission blinked in disbelief. The rescue force was not just minutes away from picking our boys out of the paddies. They were orbiting to the south, across the border, while the communicators attempted to explain a situation they could not comprehend to a battle staff and a commander seven hundred miles to the south, and we sat there with all the tools and the know-how to save our guys.

"Roger, Royal two, we're trying to work on that for you now."

"Roger, we have quite a gaggle of fighters up there now and we're having quite a time trying to shuttle them back and forth and the Nomads are all ready to go."

Frustration was universal. "What the hell—who has to get a clearance?" We all realized for the first time that afternoon that all was not well with the rescue effort.

"Let's get the crap with it." We had all the cards we could possibly hold under the circumstances, but things were not going well. We were tied up in our own red tape and each of us could feel that tender something called a comrade getting tougher and tougher to hold onto. Nobody was about to give up and we all talked to ourselves, except the weasels who jollied it up together.

"How in hell did anybody get shot down over a mountain anyway?"

"I don't even know what they were in range of."

"Well, fifty-seven millimeter—"

"I know that—"

"Thirty-seven millimeter—"

"He was really on fire."

"Hmmm?"

"He was really on fire."

"I got a gun at twelve thirty," and it was back to business as usual. The backseater interrupted the weasel's own idle chatter with "Moderate intensity."

The noise was building up to an intense level again, and as the boss in Waco lead, I was having trouble getting my messages across. I had reached a critical fuel state by this time and before I could break my element off and send them scurrying for a tanker I had to yell at the whole tribe again and attempt to keep the unnecessary chatter off the air. I decided to send my element on ahead of me to the tankers and when I dispatched them, they lucked out and got contact with tanker control right off the bat. The last I heard of them for a while, they were getting a steer to one of the tankers pressing northward to accept the thirsty birds. Once they were established outbound and I knew that Carbine was back in the area, I felt free to turn the low cover over to the flight above me and start for fuel myself. As I left the area, I knew that the entire show was not on the road, but I could tell that our portion was in good shape, and I couldn't understand why the other forces were not in there by now.

"Carbine—this is Royal. Will you attempt contact with Nomad one on this channel and then I want you to escort him and Nomad two into the area."

The slow prop jobs had at least been cleared into the area. They would now pick up escort from the Thuds and press in on the deck to try and get a visual sighting on the downed crew and sample the ground resistance. If they found the situation workable, they would call the choppers in, try to get them to the spot and attempt the pickup. But it was all too slow, too cumbersome. There should be a better way and there could be a better way, but we never planned or prepared for it.

Why didn't we have a fast-moving vehicle that could fly reasonably close to us as we entered the area and then respond immediately when needed? Why didn't we have a fast bird with its own armament that could have been on the scene before those guys hit the ground? Why didn't we have a rig that could have been there and could have found them as easily as I found them? Why not a machine that could land and take off vertically from the rice paddy or the road with those two precious creatures on board; or even better, why not a machine to snatch their chutes as they floated down for five minutes with the enemy shooting at them? We can snatch the chute and recover an inanimate capsule that has accomplished its directed mission of research in space, but for two humans who have dedicated their lives since adolescence to the service of their country, two highly talented and educated husbands and fathers, for them all we can do is wait and slowly exercise a primitive system, whose chances of success are marginal from the start.

Why? Because we built this inferior system we now use out of what we had. For rescue aircraft, we took some old junkers that had been rotting in the boneyards in the Arizona sun and pressed them back into service. We tied things together with inadequate communications gear that was years behind the state of the art currently displayed for open purchase in store windows in downtown Tokyo. We wrapped it all up in a cumbersome command system of cross-checks that spelled terror to those who would act with decision on the spot, and we made sure that we had to communicate way up the line to ascertain that it was all right to attempt to save a few lives. Then we charged it all to the guys doing the job. We said we'll make it work by the guts and dedication of the drivers.

A modern system would be expensive, and in truth, it would have had to have been in the mill several years ago to have helped that afternoon. It wouldn't be used too often—so therefore it wouldn't be too cost effective, would it? Cost effective to whom? I know several hundred guys who would give you all the back pay they may get to buy that type of rig, if they ever get out of the Hanoi Hilton in one piece. Every taxpayer we own is paying a pretty penny to try and replace the skilled veterans we have left to suffer alone. We could have built an adequate system in time for that Sunday, or we could have it right now, but we don't. If we start it now, it will be a few years before we have it perfected, and by then we may not need it. But perhaps we will need it. Perhaps you will need it, or I will need it, or your son or husband will need it. Of course, it's a tough one to sell, but it should have been sold yesterday and it should be sold today, and it is not. You are automatically critical of our antiquated approach as you sit in unfriendly skies and watch talent and young hope dashed forever before your eyes. If you have any feel for the worth of man, it makes you want to vomit. And I almost did vomit, but from the bitter fuel fumes I was sucking in as my bird took on fuel from the tanker, and as I left the tanker to return to the rescue area I strained my ears and my mind to keep up with the drama taking place on the valley floor of Route Pack 6.

"Nomad, Nomad—this is Carbine." The call established the first real contact between the rescue elements and the strike force now converted to rescue force.

"Nomad here. Go."

"Rog, Nomad. Royal wants me to escort you into the area. What's your position?"

While the prop job started the chore of establishing visual contact with the fighters, the Sam warnings interrupted their transmissions to remind us that we must be on our toes. Better Sam warnings than Mig warnings at this stage of the game. Even though we had plenty of cover for the slower machines, we did not want them interrupted or disturbed as they sought out the downed men. We knew pretty well where the nearest Sam was located and we were not overly concerned with him at that moment.

"Nomad—this is Royal. You have border clearance." Great. The wheels had at least ground out one favorable decision. The prop guys could come up into the area but the choppers hadn't moved yet. They should have been there long ago, but at least the Spads were finally on the way. They were not the only ones entering the area, as the control people had started diverting other strike and cover flights from their normal homeward route, and they were loading up on fuel and coming into the area both to help us with their numbers and to allow us a bit more freedom in shuttling in and out for our fuel. There was no shortage of machinery from the fighter end, but we were powerless to do anything to speed the pickup we all wanted so much. The rescue people were now in full control of the effort.

"Carbine—this is Royal. What's your bingo time?" The control types had committed Carbine to escort on the way in, but knowing the appetite for fuel that a Thud displays at low altitude, they were planning ahead for escort relief.

"Stand by, got to figure one. Ahhh, let's see, appears to be

about forty-five minutes, Royal." That should be plenty of
time to get together and move the Spads up to the area, but
it is amazing how hard it can get to spot another aircraft at
times. When you throw in a speed difference and a bit of
haze and a bit of low altitude, it can get downright difficult,
and Carbine and the Nomads were having their problems.

"Carbine—Royal. Did you copy Nomad?"

"Rog, I understand he is about thirty-five miles out, is that
Roger?"

As the control and the two flight leaders worked together
to effect a join-up, the radio spit out a grim indicator of things
to come. "Royal—Oakland, we've got some sweptwings here.
Do you have any Phantoms other than Wedge in the area?" It
is not difficult to confuse the Migs and the Phantoms and that
is a mistake nobody wants to make. "You say Wedge has gone
out to refuel?" and everybody perked up a bit more, rechecked
the gunsight and the missiles and peered into the haze that
was increasing as the sun sank lower and lower. Time, light
and visibility were going to be more of a factor than we had at
first thought.

"Sam, medium intensity at two o'clock." More company.

"Tomahawk—Royal. Did you copy?" Royal knew that Tomahawk, which had the primary responsibility for the low cover
of the downed pilots, was the flight with the lowest full
reserve and was thus the flight most vulnerable to any Mig
attack.

"Tomahawk, say again."

"Rog, Tomahawk. We have Migs approaching the area."

"Sams up to medium intensity," came from the weasels.

"Royal—this is Carbine. I'm still trailing Nomad. Do you
want me to press on?"

"Rog."

"Carbine—this is Nomad. I'm at base plus three."

This call should have told the altitude of the prop machines
and it was passed in the accepted manner using a base
altitude that changed from day to day, and was supposed to
be passed to all pilots at briefing. By using it you could talk in
the open about altitudes and still not tip your hand all the
way to those listening on the other end of the line. "Whatever that is," came from the frontseat of Carbine lead.

"Do you have a base altitude?" Perhaps the Bear could
earn his pay yet.

"They didn't give us one today." Good deal, one more problem, but not a significant one.

"Royal—Oakland. Royal—this is Oakland."

"Go ahead, Oakland."

"Rog, Royal, you can disregard those Mig warnings. Those are Phantoms in the area." Maybe so, or maybe different people were looking at different aircraft, but the call did not portray the seriousness of the situation.

"Nomad, can you give me a short count?" came from Carbine as he attempted to use his direction-finding gear to get a good visual contact on the Spads. The Spads replied by holding down the mike button and counting forward to 5 and then backward to 1, and while they were doing that they augmented the beeper that was still cluttering up the air and making the radio almost useless. But the steer worked and Carbine came back with "OK, Nomad, we're about your eight o'clock."

During the radio transmission for the steer, Carbine's Bear had been trying to get a word in edgewise to advise his comrades that Sam was up and looking at them, and though he was quite distant, he apparently was going to fling one into the area anyway. "YOU LISTENING??? We got a valid launch—take it down."

"Launch light—look alive."

"Nomad, you across the river yet?"

"Rog."

"OK, if Sam comes he'll come from eleven o'clock—now twelve—strong indication."

Carbine lead took a look, but was forced to sort out his priorities. You can handle only so many things at once and the Sam launch was second in line as far as he was concerned at the moment. "Umm—yeah—mmmm—I don't see Sam anyplace and I've got to look out here for those Nomads." Thus the wild Sam failed to deter the effort.

As Carbine reentered the area with the Spads, it became important for him to establish the relative positions of the other flights. All too often pilots have become involved in one facet of a task, only to ignore the other fast-moving pieces of equipment in the same piece of sky, and disaster has been the result.

"Tomahawk—Carbine."

"Carbine—Tomahawk three."

"Rog, what's your altitude?"

"We're at fifteen."

"Carbine's about twenty west and we're trying to pick up the Spads."

"Crown—this is Detroit. We're at bingo fuel." The Phantoms had been covering from a pretty reasonable altitude, but now they were running short on fuel and there was little else to do except release the top cover and try and get another flight to shuttle into their spot.

"OK, you're released to the tankers." We had exposed a chink in our armor but we didn't know it yet. There was no way we could know it from our position. You just have to rely on the guys controlling the situation to keep you covered while you charge around on the treetops.

"Nomad—Tomahawk. What's your altitude?" Another smart flight leader was drawing himself a mental picture of the congestion and wanted to be sure he kept his charges where they belonged.

"Nomad, what's your estimate to the target?"

I was having trouble reading Leo now. The combination of necessary radio chatter, the howling beeper and the fact that Leo was talking rather loudly with his mouth a bit too close to the emergency radio made him tough to understand, unless you were right over the top of him. I was not over him yet, but I was back from refueling to resume command of my force as Waco lead.

"Carbine, Carbine three, if you read, say again please." I wanted to keep in touch with him for any necessary exchange of info and I was sure that a bit of chatter would be good for his spirits at the moment, but we were just not getting through as well as we should.

"This is Carbine lead. I'm almost in the target area and I have the Spads at my two o'clock position. Spads check at your eight o'clock."

"—high Sam indication." Sam still wanted to play, but we had no time for him now.

"Tomahawk, Royal wants to know how you stand on fuel."

Nomad did not understand that it was not Leo's beeper saturating the air, and once again Leo garbled as he tried to answer the call, "Carbine three, Carbine three, turn off your beeper."

"Tomahawk three, four is approaching five thousand pounds." Time for another flight to start thinking about the fuel problem. It is a great temptation to ignore it, but you just can't. Anything we didn't need was someone else down, out of fuel short of the tanker. For Tomahawk four it wouldn't have made any difference.

"Nomad one, do you have Carbine?"

"Rog, Carbine, have you."

"OK, I'm turning to the right now, down to about eighty or ninety degrees." They were in visual contact and Carbine was intent on bringing the Spads right over the spot where Leo and his Bear were waiting.

"Tomahawk, you got Carbine?"

"Carbine—Tomahawk. Go."

"Rog. I'm in the area and the Nomads are right behind me. We're about fifteen miles out."

"Tomahawk—Royal."

"Go."

"How are you doing on fuel?"

"I'm good for about another ten minutes."

"OK, if you will point them out to Carbine and the Nomads, we will get you out of there."

As all elements of the effort closed on the target area, the wayward beeper became more than ever a disruptive factor. It was difficult to relay proper instructions and you couldn't tell if you were getting your message across. The ear-splitting screech shortened already short mental fuses and blocked out vital calls to different portions of the fleet at different times. It encouraged improper transmissions, and pilots recognizing a comrade's voice tried to push their message across the radio by abandoning call signs, using first names and confusing others in the air. The next vital call was improperly given: the caller didn't identify himself adequately, and what happened in the next few minutes made it clear that the message didn't get across to all of us.

"OK, we got bogies at three o'clock high."

"Carbine three—this is Carbine one. We're about ten miles out." He was trying so hard to say, "OK, boss, hang on, we are almost there." You could almost feel the transmission.

"Nomad—this is Carbine one. How about a short hold-down on the mike?" He was pretty sure he knew where everyone was, but you can't take a chance when you are so close to getting the job done. He wanted to recheck positions with the directional gear.

"Nomad, Tomahawk is right over the area and I'll show it to you."

The lead Spad replied with a statement that seemed old hat to us at the instant but that later took a prominent place in our reconstruction of the puzzle. "I've got a continuous parachute beeper and personal beeper." This we had known for hours. "I've got a directional swing on a beacon just to the north of where we're orbiting, Tomahawk." Tomahawk knew he was directly over the spot where he had seen and talked to the downed crew. Like most of us, he didn't even know Carbine four was down. He had no choice but to assume that the Spad had received a false swing on his indicator, and his job was to steer him to the proper place. That swing must have been on young Bob's equipment, but where was he and how was he?

"Rog, he's south of us about three miles—four miles."

"This is Nomad. I'm over the plot but don't have anybody in sight yet."

"OK, Nomad—this is Tomahawk one transmitting for a steer. Tomahawk out." The Spad was over the place he had plotted on the map from the coordinates he had been given, but it is difficult at best to give a really exact set of coordinates when you are bouncing around the sky taking care of the little goodies we had to take care of. In addition, the maps are tough to read exactly unless you have them spread out on a smooth table and have a nice set of map tools to work with. Thus, the Spad's being over the plotted spot did not necessarily mean that he was over the exact piece of geography where we knew Leo and his Bear to be. The flight leads of both Carbine and Tomahawk were trying to get Nomad to keep them in sight and fly over the recognized spot on the ground.

"OK, Nomad one, how did you read?"

"Nomad one—this is Carbine. Have you in sight. The site is back at your six o'clock and if you'll do a turn to the left—" The rest of his instructions were drowned in an especially loud beeper pulsation that seemed almost to reach up and deny the airwaves at the most crucial of moments.

"Tomahawk—this is Carbine. I've got you in sight. The

Spads are off about your two o'clock—one o'clock. OK, I told him to start a left turn. OK, check at about your one o'clock—three o'clock Tomahawk." Tomahawk's wingman then spotted the Spads and called them out to his leader at the wingman's eleven o'clock position. The instant he saw them Tomahawk started working them back over the spot.

"Tomahawk is rocking his wings, Nomad, do you see me?

"...OK, this is Tomahawk one. I'm inside of your circle, turn left—TURN LEFT!" Tomahawk was seized with the hopeless realization that Nomad did not have him and that they were so close yet so far from success, and he about rocked himself out of the sky as he hollered above the beeper, "Tomahawk rocking wings, DO YOU HAVE ME?" and his frustration spilled over as he answered his own question, "Ahhhh, he doesn't see me."

"OK, Tomahawk—Nomad here. Say again heading."

"Head east, head east."

"Nomad one, did you read?"

"Roger, Nomad one."

"OK, Nomads, this is Carbine lead and you are right behind me and you are pretty well right in the area. I don't have the chutes right now." Over the hot mike Carbine's Bear called two bogies at five o'clock going away, but at this instant this was not Carbine's business and they were going away anyway.

"Nomad one, this is Nomad two. Do you want the choppers to come in?"

Of course we wanted the choppers to come in. They weren't doing us any good on the south side of the border and we were talking to the crew and the Spads were not getting shot up. Why not bring them in? That's the name of the game and one of the orbiting Thud drivers voiced it with a hearty "YES" over the radio. But Nomad one felt differently and for some reason was reluctant to act.

"Nomad one here, let me locate the pilot first."

I guess that call is the one that did Leo and his Bear in for sure, and the same pilot who had screamed "YES" now punched his mike button and sighed the bitter sigh of disbelief. Because Nomad one was running this portion of the show and those choppers to the south would not move without his OK, we lost this chapter of the war.

Another flight checked back into the area with "Royal—
Neptune. What do you have for me?"

"Neptune—this is Royal. They said send everybody home.
You're one of those they said send home." I have never
figured that one out. Who were "they" and why were they
sending fighters out of the area? The job was far from done
and we needed all the help we could get. I could not figure
that one, and I still can't, but those of us in the Thuds had
only a support role by that time and the decisions were not
ours. Had they been, the story might have been different.

"Tomahawk—this is Nomad. Will you locate the pilots,
please."

"Tomahawk—Carbine here. Will you fly directly over the
spot so I can pick it back up, please? I'm at your twelve
o'clock heading directly toward it." And then Leo tried to get
this Spad driver who controlled his future squared away. He
started steering him in from the ground, but either he would
not talk to Leo or he didn't hear him.

"OK, Nomad, the pilot was talking to you from the ground.
Carbine was talking to you. Did you hear him?"

"Negative, negative, I am unable to read him. Am I in the
right area?"

"Rog, Rog, do you have the smoke from one aircraft? Fly
east—head east, head east."

"Roger, I have the smoke from the aircraft."

"I said head east. Do you copy? EAST!" The Nomads
finally got the message but they still could not see what so
many were seeing and were telling them to see.

"The Nomads are orbiting right over them now."

"The Nomads are inside your turn at seven o'clock, Ed, do
you have them? . . . the Nomads?"

"Rog, have them." It was now painfully apparent to the
Thud drivers on the scene that they were going to have to
make their heavy strike fighters perform like Spads by turning tightly on the deck and steering the blind rescueman, and
that if our guys were found it would have to be our doing.
The Nomads were acting like they had taken gas.

"Crap."

"OK, Nomad, do you have one one-oh-five? Should be at
your one o'clock high."

"Negative—ahh, Roger, got you."

"OK, I'm headed north and I'm going to be right over the

area. It's right under me at this moment. OK, Nomad—this is Tomahawk one rocking wings. I'm directly over the area. Do you have me, Nomad?"

"Ahh, all right, I've got you now, Tomahawk one."

"OK, Nomad, you're on it now—roll out—roll out—ROLL OUT!" There was more steering still to be done and Nomad one just couldn't seem to get with it. "OK, roll right and it's at two o'clock to you right now."

Nomad seemed to have the idea now, but he was not hearing what we were hearing. "OK, I'm going down and see if I can find him."

"OK, Nomad, did you hear him?" We were beginning to think we were working with a guy who was both deaf and blind. "Nomad, did you hear him?" But Nomad was not with us.

From the air, we could not see the enemy on the ground. The valley was still and without visible movement but we assumed the enemy must be close to Leo by now. Leo's next call was so clear and so plaintive, it was pitiful. He must have realized that the beeper was giving everyone problems, and from the helter-skelter crisscross paths we were flying he must have deduced that we were having trouble getting the Spads into position. He must have realized that things were getting tense, especially since only he could know the terror of watching his would-be captors advance toward him while he watched his comrades trying desperately to provide the missing link of a visual sighting by a Nomad driver who couldn't see, but whose visual sighting had become mandatory; without this, the choppers which alone could save him would not be launched. Leo sounded like he backed off, took a look at the entire situation, calmly picked up his emergency radio, held it the proper distance from his mouth, and in a precise voice that somehow sounded smaller with each transmission said, "Pickup aircraft—this is Carbine three here, over." He saw the Spad, but the Spad did not see him, and in answer came the screech of the stuck beeper somewhere to the north. Tomahawk had pressed his fuel to the danger point, and having put the Spad on top of the downed crew and having Carbine over the crew with a still usable load of fuel, and with me and my Waco flight right behind Carbine flight, he left to refuel.

"Nomad—this is Tomahawk one. I'm going back out of the

area, I'm going back out of the area. Do you have him in sight?"

Nomad didn't answer, but as Tomahawk left, Carbine picked up the pace. "Nomad, Carbine three is calling you on emergency frequency. If you would answer him I'm sure he would appreciate it." As Carbine fought a losing battle to finish the job that was so close to completion, but that for no reason was crumbling in front of his eyes, all strings snapped to a new degree of tautness.

"*BREAK RIGHT,* Tomahawk three! Migs behind you." Those had been bogies all right, and the vultures had played it smart. They had loitered out of contention until the bottom flight, now critical on fuel, had started to gather its forces, rejoin, and climb up through the Migs' best altitude on their way out in quest of fuel.

"Which Tomahawk has Migs?"

"Tomahawk three. I'm hit and I'm burning—son of a bitch. . . . Tomahawk four—this is three. What's your position?"

"To your left. I've got you."

Tomahawk three was still flying but in trouble. Maybe he paid too much attention to his trouble, but who can say? Maybe he ignored the fact that three vultures don't quit easily, especially when they have a flamer and a potential straggler in front of them. Who is to criticize three for getting a bit wrapped up in whether he was about to blow up or not? Not me. I've been there, and unless you have you just don't know.

"Four—still got me?"

"Tallyho, three."

"Anyone behind us?"

"Four here. I can't see them." Look hard, buddy. You're the flying safety expert who has read so much and studied so much about what happens when you panic. Keep that head moving. Remember all that jazz about emergency procedures? What's the next move? How did you get here anyway? You aren't an old tac fighter pilot. You didn't even get the courtesy of a check-out in the aircraft or a school before you left the States. They sent you over here as an administrator of safety and you had to wangle a local check-out on your own guts and dedication. So this must be aerial combat. This must be where that air combat maneuvering comes in. Too bad you didn't get a chance to try it before this in practice.

But look hard, work hard, this is the big league, buddy, and you are in the spotlight.

"Three's moving around and heading south. I've been hit. OK, Carbine—this is Tomahawk three on emergency frequency." Hard hit as he was, he wanted to be sure the guys down there in the area knew the Migs were waiting for them. "There's Migs in the area. Three's hit and heading south— BREAK LEFT!"

Too late. Joe had tried hard to do the best possible job on the wing of his crippled element leader. They had started to take evasive action by diving, accelerating and turning when they first spotted the Migs, but the Mig-21 is most maneuverable, and it is fast. They were at the altitude where the Mig had it all over them and that is why the Migs waited for them up there. Their only chance, once they had the Migs on their tail, would have been violent maneuvers coupled with the action they did take. They never got to the violent stage and once three had been hit hard, it would have been quite difficult to do anything too violent; he had lost several of the systems that contribute to maximum flight performance in the aircraft. He was lucky even to be flying with the damage he had taken, and Tomahawk three and four both knew it. The Migs played it smart by not pressing their obvious advantage and overshooting their prey. They struck once, did pretty well, and hung back to wait for the best time to make their next move. They must have positioned themselves very well. On both the passes the Migs made, neither Tomahawk three nor four saw them until it was too late. Maybe Joe, as Tomahawk four, paid too much attention to his stricken element lead and not enough to clearing the area visually, but again, who is to say? They were outnumbered three to two from the start, and once Tomahawk three got tapped, the odds went up like a skyrocket, since a wounded wingman is far worse than no wingman at all. They were caught, outgunned, and outflown by a bunch of vultures working out of a stupid sanctuary in their own backyard.

"Carbine three—this is Nomad. Do you read?" At least the Spads were still trying. We never did figure out if they had finally heard Leo's desperate transmissions or had just started calling in the blind because they didn't know where the crew was.

These calls and the trouble calls from Tomahawk flight had

fallen on inbound ears and one of the Phantom flights cycling
off the tanker was heading to the aid of Tomahawk under full
steam. "Tomahawk—this is Cleveland heading inbound. How
far out are you?" Before he could get an answer, the air was
saturated by a new sound: double beepers again. One was
our old nemesis, the other a newer and stronger one from
Joe's gear as he floated earthward with all he and his family
had ever hoped or planned for disintegrating in front of his
eyes, and the saw-toothed ridges and the huge jungle trees
reached up and waited. But the show must go on. More
problems for sure, but keep punching.

"Nomad—this is Carbine. Do you have the smoke on the
side of the ridge?"

"Cleveland—this is Tomahawk three. I'm headed out, low
on fuel and in burner. There's Twenty-ones in the area."

The noise was unbearable. You wanted to take your helmet
and mask off and throw them to the floor of the machine.

"Oh, man, not another one!" came from the frontseat of
Carbine one.

The Bear said simply, "Ohhhhh."

"Royal, Royal—this is Tomahawk one. Over."

"Rog, Royal, I've got another man down. I saw the chute."

"Ohhhh, man."

"Nomad—this is Carbine one. How are you doing?" But
Nomad was not talking or he was not hearing.

"Tomahawk one, Royal wants you."

Carbine was approaching the time when fuel would again
be a problem and the spectacular lack of success they were
having with the Spads brought the thought strongly forward
that things could rapidly get even worse than they were.
"Carbine two, as soon as your center-line tank goes dry, get
rid of it." Normally, we like to hold on to those tanks in a
rescue situation so we can get maximum fuel from the tanker.
However, in this case Carbine reasoned that they were
approaching the final stages of this drama, and that they had
better get rid of all of the drag they could and stay in the area
as long as possible. Nomad had to do the job now, or there
would be little use in making plans for a return trip. The
ever-increasing slant of the sun's rays, accentuating the haze
hanging over the weird combination of jungle and mountain,
reinforced his decision. Time was running out. We had
already spent far too much time and now, with success in our

grasp, we were blowing the entire deal—and there was nothing we could do about it.

Tomahawk one had stayed in the area past his fuel minimums, trying to steer the Nomads around, and he was already hurting, but he had no thoughts of leaving. He knew that his damaged number three was screaming south in burner and should be safe from further Mig annoyance. He was shepherding his lost number four to the ground and, fuel or no fuel, he was determined that at least Joe would touch down without further lead coming his way from other Migs. He circled until Joe touched the trees and immediately established contact.

"Tomahawk four, get out of your chute and turn that beeper off." If there was one thing we didn't need, it was more beeper noise. "This is one, turn the beeper off."

Joe was a cool customer, clean, thin, crew cut, a nice guy, and from the ground came a garbled reply as he struggled out of his chute, shut down the beeper and secured the chute and himself under the giant trees.

"Turn the beeper off, turn the beeper off, turn the beeper off."

"Cleveland—Tomahawk three, I think the Migs got four."

"Tomahawk, Tomahawk, where are you?" provided an excellent example of a useless call that only served to further garbage up the air. If only we all thought before we punched the mike button—but things do get tense.

Trying to outguess the caller, Tomahawk one responded, "Tomahawk one here on emergency—" but he was blocked out by Carbine one still trying to complete the first rescue we had started that afternoon.

"Carbine here, Nomad, see that ground smoke signal up the valley? Is that theirs or yours?" But Nomad would not talk. The jig was close to up and the Spad was right there but obviously was not hacking the program.

Leo came up on the radio. "Nomad, Nomad—this is Carbine three. You are passing directly over the top of me now." But blind Tom couldn't hack the course.

"Ooohh—they're passing right over the top of him and they don't see him." Carbine could not believe his eyes and ears. "Tomahawk—this is Carbine. Will you pass to Royal that we are only going to be able to stay here another ten minutes. And Nomad's working the area and the crew's talking to them from the ground saying that they are flying right over them, but they can't see them and they haven't even started the choppers in yet. We're running out of time."

"Roger, we got to clear some of those Migs out of here before we can get our choppers in there. Which flight's in there now?" The call from Royal showed again that they did not understand the problem.

"Rog, there's no Migs in the target area. They're between us and home. You can get the choppers in here—no sweat. Don't worry about the Migs, we'll take our chances with them at altitude on the way out. The way is clear for the choppers and you're about to blow the whole bloody issue. Get them in here."

Royal countered with "Would you contact Nomad one and tell him to tell the choppers when he wants them to come in? They're holding ten miles out or ten minutes out, I don't know which. He's got the ball."

"Nomad one—this is Carbine. Will you give the choppers a call when you want them in. They're about ten out. Nomad one—Carbine. Do you read? Nomad, if you read you are supposed to contact the choppers when you want them to come in. They are standing by, ten away."

"Royal—Tomahawk. We need a tanker. I've got two birds down to three thousand. We need one bad."

"Nomad one—Carbine. *Do you read?*"

"Royal—Carbine. I've got enough for about one more turn around the target. Have you got anyone inbound to replace me?"

"I am holding Waco at a higher altitude in an orbit around you. It will be a few minutes before he gets there." Obviously the control people were not covering their slots in depth, and this was all the harder to understand because they had everybody and his brother available, and yet they had already started diverting flights back to their home bases. They probably got the word from one of the many headquarters control battle staffs down the line and did not have the knowledge or the gumption to challenge the poor decision. As a result, we were in a deeper pickle than we had been all afternoon. The sun was diving for the horizon, the haze was increasing, and we were running short on cover aircraft. No excuse for it.

Carbine knew that he could do nothing about the big picture from his spot in the action and answered, "OK, and I never did get an acknowledgment from Nomad on emergency or any other channel." The Bear came up on the hot mike to advise that he was picking up a hand beeper, as apparently either Leo or his Bear, knowing the other beeper was saturating the air, desperately turned on the beeper in their emergency radio in a vain attempt to override the other beeper and attract the attention of the Spad flying back and forth over their heads.

The frontseat acknowledged with an "Ugh" and allowed that he had better call Nomad one more time.

"Nomad, did you understand that you are to clear the choppers in when you are ready? They are standing by." Then in complete frustration over the ineptness of the would-be rescuers and his own inability to do anything about it, he added to his Bear, "Crap, I don't even know where that son of a bitch went now."

"Royal—this is Tomahawk. Will we be able to go back in and find my guy who is down?"

Carbine had now depleted his fuel to the danger point as he waited for me and the rest of my Waco flight to drop down and relieve him. I came in as he went out, repeating the sad story I had already listened to on my radio, and as his Bear took one last glance at the panorama, he noted that smoke a bit to the north and remarked, "I don't think that smoke is them." If not, then whose was it?

As we changed the airborne guard, Leo came back at us from the ground. He made a relatively long transmission, but much of it was cut out by other transmissions and the beeper. He said something about the beeper, apparently assuring us again that it wasn't his, then, "They're coming up the hill after us—get me out of here! Get me out of here!" We listened in stunned silence and none of us bothered to tell him what we already knew and what he already knew. He came on one more time with a big loud garble, then, "THEM— get me out of here! GET ME OUT OF HERE!" We didn't.

Carbine's Bear said, "What did he say?"

Carbine replied, "He said get me out of here."

As I took over the low cover again, I could not get the Spads to talk to me. I made one wide arc checking for them, then went directly over the spot where the crew had been. There was nothing. No noise, no smoke, no activity, no answer to my calls. I swung wide for another check and finally Nomad gave me a call. "Waco, I've checked the area and there is nothing up here. All I found was a stuck beeper and it is garbaging the air something awful. There's Migs in the area and there's nobody on the ground and I'm leaving the area."

I don't believe I even acknowledged his call, but I knew I was now helpless and as he left for the south, I made another pass over the spot, low and directly over the little knob with the U-shaped road bending around it. I went right down on the deck over the small house alongside the road, over the open rice paddies and skimmed the tops of the trees on the knob, lit my burner and pulled up into a big roll as a farewell salute to my buddies. He was right. There was nothing there now—nothing I could do anything about.

10.

TILL THURSDAY

That bleak Sunday was to drag on four more days. The light was fading and Leo and company were out of business, but I still had a bellyful of fuel and there was still work to be done. Reluctantly, I left the area and struck out for where I might be able to do some good for Tomahawk four. Joe—the nice young guy who had come to us as an administrative officer, even though he was a rated pilot. Joe—the shy young man who had accepted my personal mantle of authority and roared through our almost impossibly inferior safety program within the wing like a bulldozer cleaning out rat's nests. He was not a Thud driver by trade, but he scrounged an hour here and an hour there until he could leap all the hurdles and qualify himself for combat. He had a hell of a time mastering the art of hanging behind a tanker and refueling in flight, but he did it. Joe—another one of my boys who had not managed to graduate from the toughest postgraduate school in the world, the school that demanded a hundred missions over the North in a Thud for a diploma. He was now simply Tomahawk four, down over the North.

Since our superiors had managed to control away almost all the fighters we had previously assembled, I figured I had

better get with the program in a hurry. I split my flight into
elements of two to search more effectively and headed for the
coordinates that were supposed to represent the spot where
Joe was down. I knew that, unless someone climbed out of
the tanker and tied him up with a rope, Tomahawk would be
back in with the one wingman he had left, and I hoped we
could have something good for him to cover and perhaps we
could still use the Spads and the choppers. As I entered the
new area, I knew even more than before that time would be a
big factor. It was a fantastic looking spot. The hills rolled up
into small mountains and further south leaped into the sheer
saw-toothed karst that dropped violently to the winding
riverbed far below. The sawtooths were already shading the
huge trees rolling from ridge to ridge underneath them, and
my first thought was of two big hopes. I hoped he hadn't
landed on top of one of those sharp knobs and I hoped we
had a good gutty chopper driver sitting in the wings. I hoped
half right.

I swung my element a bit north of due west and started a
gradual turn that would allow me to get a good look at the
land below and would bring me out of the orbit about over
the sharp peaks to the south. There were a few trails showing
in the jungle carpet, and the ground appeared to roll gently
toward the delta to the east. Meager terraces had been
scratched out where the land was level enough to cultivate;
there were a few groups of dwellings, but nothing big. I gave
a little test on a couple of them but I could not see that
anyone fired at me or seemed to care that I was there. There
was a fire burning in the jungle a few miles away and if I was
in the right spot, that would probably be some portion of the
aircraft that had gone its own way either before or after Joe
left it. The stuck beeper had faded to the lonely north and
the air was still and intense as four Thuds worked against the
clock, the jungle and the elements of the air war in the
North. I did not have long to wait, and halfway through my
first turn a new, strong and definite rescue beeper came up
on the inside of my turn. I grabbed a quick directional steer
on him and called my number two man who verified both the
beeper and the steer. We wrapped those Thuds around to the
left like we were driving midget racers, and although the
force of the turn nearly knocked them out of the sky, we were
able to roll straight and level before we got to the spot on the

ground where the beacon was telling us our fourth downed comrade of the afternoon was waiting for us and for the help we could bring.

As I approached the spot, I skidded my steed to the right and got as slow as I could get and still stay airborne, rocked the left wing down and looked long and hard at nothing but trees. The steering needle swung to the left and then to the tail and I knew I had him pinpointed. "Tomahawk four, Tomahawk four—this is Waco on emergency. If you read me turn your beeper off."

Like the cut of a knife the screecher shut off and the small clear voice said, "This is Tomahawk four. I read you loud and clear, Waco. I am OK and awaiting pickup." I was so pleased, I almost forgot my business, and in my anxiety to get a better look at the area, I almost pulled my beast into a stall as I told the world on the radio that I had found Joe. "Waco two, I've got his position spotted. Get up to altitude and get us some Spads and some choppers in here on the double. Tell them no sweat on Migs and tell them we have to hurry. We're far enough south so they ought to be able to get the job done without making it a big production." I swung around for the spot and yanked my sweaty map out from under my left buttock, which is still the best map holder ever devised for a fighter plane, and prepared to get some good coordinates for the rescue guys. "Joe, turn your beeper on now." I fixed right over the beacon and said, "OK, Joe, turn it off, and if I just flew right over your position, turn it back on for two seconds, then back off." The reply was just like the survival movies and I knew that I was right and that Joe was both in good shape and as sharp as he could be.

I relayed the coordinates, and since the rescue system had been alerted by Tomahawk lead on his way out for fuel, it was not too long before two different Spads, but still using the callsign Nomad, arrived on the scene and went to work like a couple of old pros. They took over and my job reverted to that of top cover. The memory of the fiasco of an hour ago was with me as much as my aching seat and my weary head and back, but this one was already farther ahead than the other one had ever been and these Nomads were doing it properly.

"OK, Tomahawk four—Nomad here. Turn your beeper on for ten seconds." He lined up and said encouragingly, "OK, good steer, I'm lined up on you. Turn your beeper on and

leave it on till I tell you to turn it off." Completing his pass,
he got a good low-level swing and was able to bend his little
bird around in a tight turn that allowed him to keep the area
in view. "OK, Tomahawk, beeper off. Are you on top of that
ridge I just flew over?"

"Nomad—Tomahawk. I am on the east side of the ridge
you just flew over, about halfway down to where it levels off
into a little plateau. I have plenty of flares. Over."

"Rog, Tomahawk, hold your flares." The flares are a good
spotting device and can be a big help to the searcher. By the
same token, they can be a big help to those searching from
the ground. We have lost people by the premature use of
flares that have allowed the bad guys to get there before the
rescue people. Sometimes it is necessary to use them, but
they are better held until the choppers are on the way or
until the Nomad feels the area is clear enough of enemy to
use one to pinpoint the downed man in the thick tree cover,
so that the Nomad can set up a quick in-and-out run for the
choppers. The multiple layers of trees go as high as 200 feet,
and a man gets pretty small under them. "Spread your chute
out as well as you can, Tomahawk. I'm on the way back in."

This Nomad showed a completely different picture of the
rescue pilots than the one we had just attempted to work
with. He was sure enough of the position and condition of his
man and knew how critical the time was, so he called the
controllers on his second radio and directed that the choppers
start inbound on the now relatively short trip that they had to
make. All the terrain there was relatively high as far as
ground elevation was concerned, which would make the
choppers' job more difficult, but all in all, things smacked of
possible success. Pulling up abruptly over the suspected spot,
Nomad announced, "Rog, Tomahawk, think I've got you. The
choppers will be here in a few minutes. Get ready for pickup
and give me a red smoke flare now so I can be sure I get
them to the right spot from the right approach direction."
Joe, like many of us, figured that those flares and the radio
were two of the most valuable pieces of cargo you could carry,
and he had several extras strapped to the outside of his anti-G
suit. He took one out, carefully selected the end that would
emit a thick red smoke that would float up through the trees
to stain the twilight sky and momentarily show both his
position and the direction of the wind before it drifted away

into nothing, held it skyward and pulled the lanyard. "Rog, Tomahawk four, I've got your smoke. Sit tight for a couple of minutes."

But the minutes dragged, the sun sank lower, and the haze thickened. I had been stooging around on the deck for quite some time and could not delay too long before departing for the night rendezvous with the tanker that I now had to have, or else I would have to park this bird of mine in the jungle. But I knew the tankers would be there. I knew it because Tomahawk lead and two were on the way back in and told me so. Joe should be picked up by the time Tomahawk got here and I could blast for the tanker while they escorted the rescue troops out. Where in hell were those choppers?

"Tomahawk four—this is Nomad. I hate to tell you this, old buddy, but one of the choppers thinks he has a rough engine and has turned back and the other one has decided he will go with him in case he has any trouble. We can't get another one up here tonight so I guess you better pull up a log and try and get some rest. We will try and get back in the morning— and by the way, there is a stream about fifty yards downhill from you if you get low on water. *C H I Dooey*, (Thai for sorry about that) old buddy." At least the Spad driver got right to the point. He knew we were screwed and so did Joe.

"Roger, this is Tomahawk four, understand. Thank you. I'll be waiting for you in the morning."

I couldn't believe it. So what if one of the choppers did have a rough engine—we'd had rough engines all afternoon. If the first one decided he was going to crap out, so what— why did the second one want to go back in case of trouble? We had trouble we hadn't used yet right here, and we had the rescue in our hip pocket. I still can't believe it. I try to think nice things about the situation and about the actions and decisions I saw that day, but I can't.

Tomahawk lead couldn't believe it either but it was dark and the deed was done. He headed for home with his still goodly fuel load and I stumbled off to find the tanker that would give us what we needed for the trip back to base. But we weren't through yet. Nomad's wingman split the evening ether with "Mayday, Mayday, Mayday—Nomad lead is hit and on fire." In his frustration he had wandered too close to someone on the ground, and once again unseen small arms had scored a hit.

Oh, boy, what next! I knew that Nomad was far slower than we were and the only place that he could be was behind us, so I forgot the fuel and wheeled 180 degrees and back we went.

"Nomad—this is Nomad four. You're on fire. Bail out, bail out, BAIL OUT!" I was ready to commit us to another attempt at cover, knowing before it started that this one would not have a chance. When an airman in trouble calls, you have no choice, and one of our people was in trouble. I got a feeling of encouragement from the next two transmissions. The wingman repeated his call, "Bail out, you're on fire."

With lots of calm, Nomad came back and said, "Negative."

Not negative because he was not on fire, but negative because he was not about to park his Spad over the dark noplace where he knew four fellows had withered in the sunlight. He was not about to leap into what would have been either death or prison, knowing there would be no rescue for him that night. He knew what the odds were, and he was going to take his chances with the machine. He had apparently wandered into the wrong area at the wrong altitude as he egressed from the messed up effort that had left the guy he had located and talked to and even flared sitting on a stump waiting for the bad guys to pick him up. He knew that there was no rescue this day and he was not about to become number five if he could help it. There is little doubt that he knew he was on fire. In a bird like the 105, you cannot see the wing, and besides the wing seldom burns. In the Spad you can see the wing, and he was burning severely from the wing root. Very close to the sort of thing that causes wing separation and rapid departure from the scene. His judgment was swift, and I am sure that his head was filled with many thoughts of things other than himself as he made his move.

He rolled his flaming Spad over onto her back and dove for the deck. His wingman got the natural impression that he had lost control of the machine and that resulted in a few more panic-stricken calls in the black unfriendly night. Down he went, pointed at the hills, the hills he could not see but those he knew were there. If he got the ancient warrior going fast enough he could blow the flame out. He could starve the fire, he could divert the airflow, and the fire would go out and

he could limp home. And if not—why not try. He did, and it
worked, and while it was working his wingman and the Thud
drivers still left in the area marveled and wondered what the
next step would be. The next step was a big batch of silence
and lots of hard breathing. After what seemed like four hours
and could not possibly have been more than a minute, the
not-so-calm-but-ever-so-pleased voice of Mr. Nomad announced
that the fire had gone out, that he was pulling the nose up,
and that he had plenty of fuel to get back to his homedrome.
The night was black, but not nearly as black as my thoughts. I
wheeled once again, and more than seven hours after I left
Takhli I touched down on that remote piece of concrete and
unstrapped from the belts that bound me to the machine. I
was beat but I was not through fighting.

You have no idea how tired you can get from a physical and
mental ordeal such as that, but tired or not, you don't quit.
You couldn't quit even if you wanted to, because you have to
talk to people, you have to analyze, you have to debrief, you
have to make the next plan, and you have to sign off on a
bunch of administrative details to the families of four brave
men and that hits you right in the gut.

I got on the hot line to the big bosses as soon as I got into
the operations building and found them ready to talk. They
were, of course, anxious to hear what had happened from my
view, and I told them. I was anxious to know what had
happened from the rescue guy's point of view, but nobody
was ever able to explain that to my satisfaction. My big points
to them, as you can't live in the past in this racket, were let's
get Joe out—we know he is there—and let's go clean house
on those lousy Migs. We had been forced to set ourselves up
like a bunch of pigeons that afternoon, but I wanted to go
back in style and clean their clocks while we got Joe out. The
weather was rolling into that area and things did not look
overly promising, but I did get a guarantee that the electronic types would keep a watch on the area all night and there
would be visual and electronic help in the morning at first
light. I got an acknowledgment of understanding of my
request for a sweep against the Migs but that was all I got for
the moment.

While I cleaned up the details and grabbed a bite to eat,
we got the word "go" on my proposal for a combination
rescue effort and Mig sweep for the next morning. It was

already close to midnight and morning meant something like
4 A.M. for this one, so the press was on again. All the aches
and pains faded rapidly in the light of the new challenge and
I set to work with my maps and my planners. We sectioned
the area we wanted to cover where we thought we had the
best chance of hammering the Migs and of protecting the
primary searchers while we did a bit of searching on our own.
We picked our flight lineups carefully, charted the routes and
pinned down the timing. We decided to leave the bombs at
home since we weren't after ground targets on this one and
we wanted to go clean. About 2 A.M. I started to get the
wearies badly, so once I had the plan going the way I wanted,
I turned it over to some of my troops who would not be flying
in the morning and went to the trailer for a quick two-hour
snooze.

Morning came quickly, but the challenge pushed aside the
need for rest. The weather in the area where Joe had parked
was as advertised—rotten. The clouds had stacked up against
the hills and the electronic guys who had been watching the
spot all night reported no signals, but cloud right down to the
deck. There was little possibility of visual search that morning, but we could still run our part of the plan and perhaps
wax some Migs and hope we would keep them away in case
the rescue effort could get in gear with an unexpected
weather break. It was an eager bunch that launched that
morning—eager to look for some of our troops and eager to
shake up the Migs. And shake them up we did. They
expected to charge into a string of lumbering, bomb-laden
Thuds and have their normal easy game of commit if it is
favorable or run back to the home-free area if things don't
look too good. They waded in and were immediately surprised. There were Mig fuel tanks jettisoned all over the area
and once they discovered the name of the game, they were
not at all eager to play, but they found it a bit difficult to turn
loose of the first of us they engaged. I can recall the enthusiasm of one wingman in the middle of the fast, swirling fray as
the action went right down to the treetops and erupted in a
blast of fire and dust when he hammered his Mig and drove
him exploding into the hillside: "I got one! I got one!" His
flight leader beat me to the mike button to say, "Shut up and
go get another one."

But when the first Mig flights discovered our intent, the

rest stayed on the ground. We made another swing over the entire area but they wanted nothing to do with us. Why should they come up and fight when they were safe in their havens to wait for another day? The weather stayed bad in the area where Joe was, and although we strained our ears and eyes, we added nothing to the rescue effort. It was a fun mission, though. When I landed, I had logged twelve hours of single-engine jet combat time in the past twenty clock hours. When you consider the incidentals that went with those flights, that leaves nothing but a few quick bites of food and those two hours of sack time I squeezed in. I wasn't very sharp that afternoon, but none of us could relax because we could not forget the halfway job up north that needed to be completed. Despite the fact that Joe was in a rather lightly populated region, there are very few areas up there that don't have enough people to give a downed airman a rough time. There was little doubt that they knew exactly where he was, and his chances of getting out were diminishing by the hour while the weather that hampered us made it that much easier for the bad guys.

When nothing good had been reported by Tuesday morning we realized that if we were to do any good on the now slim hope that Joe was still on the loose and still waiting for us, we were going to have to get the ball rolling ourselves. The afternoon mission seemed to provide a good vehicle and I loaded it with our best people. It was an interesting one as it was headed for one of the better targets right in downtown Hanoi and although everyone knows that your chances of coming back from one of those are not the greatest, there were always people crawling over each other trying to get on them. That is something about a fighter pilot that is both unique and hard to describe. Tell him you are going to send him to hell, and that things will be rougher than he's ever seen, and he will fight for the chance to go. He may be petrified half the time but he will die rather than admit it, and if he gets back, most of the time he will tell you that it might have been a bit rough but not so rough that he doesn't want to go back and try to do it just a little bit better next time.

This mission was especially attractive as we were to be

allowed to provide our own Mig cover flight for a change. On
an approach somewhat similar to the sweep of the day before,
we were to take one flight without bombs whose only job was
to fly like the normal strike aircraft but go get the Migs if
they showed. I was forced to take that flight in the face of the
wails of my three squadron commanders. My flight call sign
for this one was Wabash, and I picked myself three sharp
flight leaders from the squadron and put them on my wing.
That's how I wound up with Ken on my wing as Wabash two.
We charged around the course despite the fact that the
weather forecast was quite dismal. (The weather is seldom
what you would call really good, but there was quite a bit of
doubt that we would get in that day.) We got down into the
Migs' backyard but they did not rise to the bait. They knew
better than we did what the weather was downtown, and
figured we were just spinning our wheels and would not be
able to get in to our primary target; there was little sense in
exposing themselves. They were right. We had to divert
about three-quarters of the way down the Ridge and eat
another frustration pill.

The rest of the flights went to their alternate targets. My
flight was purposely not assigned to an alternate strike as I
had other ideas. As soon as I cancelled the primary strike I
headed for the last spot we had seen Joe. Once in the area, it
was no problem to identify the exact position, and I split my
Wabash flight again, to cover more area, and set about the job
of trying to raise some sign of Tomahawk four. After a few
circuits in the area I started to get the action I was looking
for. I had been crisscrossing the ridge and the little plateau
where I knew he had been on Sunday evening, but I was not
sticking solely to that spot as I knew he might have been
forced to move even though he could not go very far in that
country by himself. I switched to the emergency channel I
knew he would be monitoring—if he still had his radio, if the
battery was still working and if he still had the freedom to
operate the radio as he wished. All three were pretty big ifs
by this time but the events of Sunday had left such a bitter
taste in all of our mouths that we wanted to exhaust every
possibility. As I moved I alternated radio calls with "Tomahawk four, Tomahawk four—this is Wabash lead. If you read
come up on your beeper," and the next circuit I would give

him, "Joe—this is Wabash lead. If you read me, Joe, come up on emergency channel. Give me a call on emergency, Joe."

And up came the beeper. Weak to be sure and with nowhere near the piercing tone that it had belted out a couple of days ago, but it was there. It was so weak that I could not home in on it the way I wanted to and thus could not get a really accurate fix, but it was very close to the same area. "Tomahawk four—Wabash. I read your beeper. If you read me shut your beeper off now." There was always the possibility that Joe, or whoever had his beeper, had not actually read my earlier transmissions but had simply turned it on when he realized that the Thuds overhead were looking, not simply passing by. Of course, if the wrong people have the beeper and you sucker in a little too close you are liable to be met with a blast of ground fire. Even though we all knew this and even though we have lost some machines and people to this ruse, when you pick up the scent that could be one of the guys, you acknowledge this possibility and press on regardless.

The beeper operator responded perfectly and the pitifully weak beep left the air as directed. Well, we were on the trail of something and the mere thought that there was some remote possibility of pulling this thing out of the dismal sack that it was in was exhilarating. I called my element lead and told him to get back to the tankers as fast as he could, pick up a load of juice and come back to relieve me. While he was gone I continued to work the beeper but could not pin it down to a specific ridge or group of bushes. I would start in on it, get my directional indication and then it would fade, just like a weak radio when you are trying to catch the prime line or note of music on your favorite radio program. I couldn't hack it alone and I quickly decided it would take another full-scale effort, with the help of the rescue specialists, unless I got a big breakthrough soon. Try as we might, neither my wingman, Ken, nor I could get what we wanted out of the beeper, nor could we get any voice contact.

While we were working our hearts out in a vain attempt to get the specifics I knew so well I would need if I was to persuade my bosses to launch the rescue fleet again, my element was encountering delays on the tanker rendezvous, and this was the first indication that a more exciting afternoon was ahead. I did not want to leave the scene until I had at least the other part of my flight in the area where they could give one more try for something that would be a firmer hat hanger when I tried to sell the case. We played our fuel right down to the minimum and they were not back yet. The time of day indicated that we would not be able to get the show in gear and get back that night, but there was time for the element to work a bit longer. They did not show, as they were hung up on the tanker and I played the fuel to the point that everything would have to work just right on the way back, or Wabash one and two were in trouble.

I had in effect bet heavily on the fact that the ground controllers and the tankers would appreciate the seriousness of the situation, and that they would do their job of getting me where I was supposed to be, and get a tanker up to us in time to avert fuel starvation and the resultant loss of machines and maybe people—like me and my wingman.

They should already have been aware of what I was doing, and I had all sorts of gear on board my bird to let them know where I was and that I anticipated an emergency situation, and after all, a nice guy's future was at stake—but it turned out to be not such a good bet. When I could wait no longer, I called the element and brought them up to speed on my results so far. I told them to get back in as soon as they could and repeat my efforts. If they got nothing better than I did they were to hit the tankers again and head for home where we would recap the situation and make our pitch for another rescue attempt. This accomplished, Ken and I reached for all the altitude we could get and I started screaming for ground control to get me with a tanker, quickly.

As we leveled at maximum altitude, we should have been within voice range of the control people. We called and called but received no answer. I knew we were transmitting OK, as I could hear and talk to other fighters and tankers in the area, but none of us could get the control guys to answer or assist. I turned my internal radio gear to the emergency position which is supposed to knock every ground controller right out of his chair as he sits in his darkened room and surveys the air picture, but to no avail. We desperately needed help and nobody would help. As Ken and I tried not to believe the story our gauges were telling us, we both knew that it was most doubtful that we would be able to get ground control direction to a tanker in time. We didn't know why they wouldn't answer, but we knew time was eating fuel and things looked grim as Ken punched the mike button and passed that simple phrase that means more to a fighter pilot than all the fancy emergency calls: "Boss, I'm hurting."

One of our tanker friends was listening and was trying as hard as we were to rock someone off his seat and get some steers going. He advised us that he was blasting away with both of his big radios on all channels and, like us, could get nothing. We started to try a freelance rendezvous and hookup with him using his internal gear and ours, but it became immediately apparent that we were just too far apart and that there was not enough fuel left to get us together.

Then someone awoke to that lonely cry of emergency to the north and the radio spoke to us, "Aircraft on emergency, what's your problem?" I spit out my answer as tersely as I could but I obviously did not have the regular crew chief, as I got the most frustrating of answers, "Stand by."

I couldn't stand by and barked back, "Listen, I can't stand by, I have two Thuds at minimum emergency fuel and I have got to get to a tanker right now. Give me a steer to the nearest tanker, quickly, or we are both going to flame out."

As I looked over the side at the rough green carpet below I subconsciously remembered that this was the area where the little people skin captives alive. Some of the more vivid horror stories I had heard made a fast lap around my head, only to be jarred out of position by my friendly controller's reply to my desperate plea, "Emergency aircraft—this is control. I am having trouble hearing you and don't quite understand your problem. Proceed further south and give me a call later and I will set up a tanker for you."

Balls, better that clod should have been looking down at these headhunters than me. I hoped he fell out of his swivel chair and bumped his little head on his scope. The tankers screamed at him and Ken and I both screamed at him and he wouldn't come back up on the air. But someone in that center must have heard and understood, because within about thirty seconds a new voice came booming through loud and clear from the center, but unfortunately as he shoved Clodley out of the way and took over the scope, he must have alerted all other control agencies within a zillion miles that he had two birds about to flame out, because all at once we had more

help than we could use. They all wanted to help now, and
they all wanted to do it at once. Within sixty seconds we had
calls from every ground operator who could get a hand on a
mike and who could make his mouth work. They each wanted
us to cycle the emergency equipment, they each wanted an
identifying turn or a dogleg, and they each wanted a detailed
explanation of the problem. It was tough to get a word in
edgewise but Ken finally managed to get through with "Boss,
I'm down to five hundred pounds." I had seven hundred and
either quantity is about enough to take a Thud around the
block, and that's all.

The next two minutes were critical and it was clear that the
controllers were out of control. I held the mike button down
for a few seconds hoping to cut a few people out and
announced, "OK, all control agencies shut up and listen. This
is Wabash lead. I've only got a couple of minutes of fuel left
and I must have a tanker. Now, whichever one of you has
good contact with me and has me identified for sure, take
control of me. Sit back and take a deep breath and go to
work. You've got to do it right and if you don't I'm going to
park these two birds in the jungle, and so help me if I do, I'll
walk back and kill you. The rest of you get off the air."

One kind soul accepted the challenge and tried to get with
the program, but he was unsure of himself and his resources
and he was stumbling. When Ken came through with "Two
hundred pounds, boss," I figured we had about had the
stroke.

Then out of nowhere came the clear voice of White tanker.
"Wabash—this is White. I think I have a beacon on you. I've
passed all the gas I am authorized to for the day, and I just
have enough to get back to home base, but if you are hurting
as badly as I think you are I'm willing to give it a try. Have to
land at an intermediate base and get my wrist slapped.
Deviation from plans, you know."

At last. Someone who sounded like he knew what was
going on. "Rog, White—Wabash here. You call the shots but
make it quick."

"OK, Wabash, turn to zero nine zero and drop down to
twenty-four thousand. I should be about forty miles back on
the inside of your turn. OK, Wabash, roll out, roll out.
Steady on. Now look at eight o'clock. Eight a little low."

"OK, Ken, we're going past him. There he is about seven to you. A little low."

"I got him and I'm showing zero on the fuel."

"I've still got two hundred pounds. Go get him. Pull your nose up and roll back to your left. You'll fall right down on top of him."

As Ken rolled up over his left shoulder and let the big nose fall through, there that big fat beauty was, and Ken's engine started chugging as the pumps reached for the last drops of fuel.

"White—Wabash two. Got you in sight and I'm flaming out now. Toboggan. Go down. Go down. I'm flamed out. Hold two fifty and go down. Come on fellows—give me a chance—toboggan."

"White, he's flamed out, STUFF THAT NOSE DOWN. He's got to coast up to you. Don't miss, boomer."

As the big load with the lifesaving fuel pushed over into a dive, the now silent Thud coasted into position behind him and Ken almost sighed as he said, "Come get me boomer." And the sarge in the back end of the tanker lay on his belly, took hold of the controls of his flying refueling boom, aimed one time and rammed the boom into the Thud's nose. As the hydraulic locks bit into the receptacle, Ken was hooked up and being towed along for the ride. As the fuel poured into his tanks and the engine restarted, I was delicately charging into position on his wing as my fuel needle bounced on and off the empty mark. As his tanks registered a thousand pounds he disengaged and slid to the side while I moved into the slot, and before I chugged to silence the same expert gentleman stuck me and the fuel flowed. After I filled up, Ken came back on the boom and filled up and we left for home.

"Nice save, White. Where are you going to land?"

"I'll have to go into your place."

"Good, we'll see you on the ground. Beautiful crew, and that boomer is absolutely gorgeous."

"Glad we could help. See you later."

All the way home I didn't even talk to all the various control guys whose areas we passed through. They were all very efficient now that we didn't need them, and it was not because I was pouting that I didn't talk. I just didn't trust

myself to speak to them at the moment, as I am sure that I
would have hurt someone's feelings. My next task was to get
on the phone to my big bosses, which I did as soon as I got
on the ground and again thanked White Tanker for his save.

One of Ken's additional duties, for he was a wing staff
weenie, was running our Standardization and Evaluation
program. The program directed that masses of records be
kept on each pilot certifying that each was up to date on all
the recurring courses of instruction and examinations as the
various headquarters saw fit. Even in war we got inspected
by inspection teams of as many as forty-five men from each of
our headquarters, as often as four times a year. They stayed in
Bangkok and commuted to the jungle daily in our C-47
gooney bird. It was an almost unbelievable farce, but they
got combat pay for it. Among the other things we had to do to
satisfy the inspectors was to document each pilot's proficiency
at least once each six months. When our Stan-Eval guys had
to complete and file a two-page report, with lots of signatures
on it, documenting their flight checks on each of our pilots.
I figured that if we had to play this silly game, then each
time a Stan-Eval guy flew in a flight of four to Hanoi, the
other flight members who made it back safely had demonstrated
"proficiency," and they were automatically credited with a
flight check, and another absurd square was filled on another
absurd chart. A few days after we landed from this particular
flight, Ken stopped by the office and advised, "Boss, you
were due for a headquarters proficiency flight check," and
handed me my report card. It said, "Colonel Broughton was
given a proficiency evaluation while flying as Force Commander on a combat strike mission. His demonstrated ability
to command and control an entire strike force is outstanding.
He was able to cope with several critical and unforeseen
problems with cool and decisive action. Flight was debriefed."
We almost laughed ourselves sick.

It takes a lot of maneuvering of forces and some significant
changes in plans to mount a sizable rescue effort such as we
would need to try what I wanted to try. I thus had to
convince those further up the line that we could be relatively
sure of gaining something from the effort. If you launch for
this purpose, you have to give up some more routine mission
that you are scheduled for and this often causes raised
eyebrows in some quarters. I guess they knew I felt quite

strongly about this one and since we had verified the fact that there were signals coming from the area, and since we knew that Joe appeared to be in good shape, I got the OK for the next day. We provided the fighter cover and configured for that specific mission. The rescue people came up with the Spads and the HH-3C Sikorsky choppers, better known as the Jolly Green Giants, and we pre-briefed to rendezvous crossing the border. We staggered our fighters so we could have good cover through both the search and the rescue, should that come to pass. It didn't come to pass. The Spads looked and got nothing. No noise and nothing visual. We escorted them back out through the quiet countryside where nothing moved, and nobody even fired a round that we saw. That was officially the end of the attempt. We had done all we could.

The next day, leading a flight, Ken was able to swing back over the area again. He repeated our previous pattern and bigger than hell the beeper came up on command. He called for voice contact expecting the same void that we had received two days before, but this time the beeper talked to him on the emergency channel. Only problem was that it was talking in an Oriental voice. It was not until then, on that Thursday afternoon, that the mission we had started on Sunday was finally all through.

11.

THE EASY PACKS

When your daily job is to attack difficult targets in the Hanoi area, you sometimes take your alternate targets too lightly. Nobody can outguess the weather, especially in a place like North Vietnam where you may well get only a few really good days all year, so on each mission you have to plan to go any one of several ways. That's the reason for all the complicated mission planning I mentioned earlier. When you bank on going for the big one and at the last minute find yourself diverted to one of the easy Packs down in the southern part of North Vietnam, the emotions are bound to be varied. (A Pack, remember, is short for what the Air Force calls a Route Package.) Some feel mostly frustration that the prime job will not be done that day. Some feel a degree of fatality: nothing to be done about it and some of these kids will live longer because of it. The ones I worried about were those who had never learned, or who had forgotten, the bitter lesson that anyplace where they may shoot at you can be a source of dire trouble. It is a great temptation to ignore some of the rules you live by in an intense area when you are called upon to work in one that is not as intense but nevertheless hostile. There is nothing sadder than to lose a Thud and a pilot on an easy target, but it can and does happen for several reasons.

If the weather is bad enough to cancel the primary target, it is likely to be less than rosy in the rest of the country—not always, but quite often. Two particular weather bugaboos over there are far worse than they are anyplace else in the world that I have flown, and I've flown most places. The first is the thunderstorms, or even bumpy cumulus clouds that are in effect very junior thunderstorms. The big ones go up like nothing you can imagine, and when a good-sized cloud system sets into an area, you can expect it to be there for days. The clouds run from right on the deck to well above 50,000 feet, and as they grow, they roam back and forth and bump into each other, causing more thunder-bumpers and confusion. There is no going under, over or around a big batch of them, and if they are stretched across your path, you most often just have to grit your teeth, hang on as best you can and press for the other side. Any thunderstorm is a rough ride, but these are rougher. The monsters and the cumulus type are alike as far as visibility is concerned—unbelievably bad.

The second phenomenon that makes Asian skies uncomfortable is the continuing poor visibility. Upon the arrival of a major or fast-moving weather system, the visibility will clear and the weather will be beautiful. Flying over there on a day like that gives you a sense of luxury. All the rest of the time the visibility varies from poor to dreadful. I have done my share of flying in smog and city-polluted air as well as dust over the deserts and smoke over an area like Tokyo, but they do not hold a candle to the murk that hangs in the air from Hanoi to Bangkok. In most reduced visibility conditions you can see straight down or at least penetrate the restricted visibility on some axis. Not that stuff. It is like somebody painted your sunglasses white. I guess some of it comes from the fact that everyone from India to Tokyo seems to be burning something, and part of it comes again from the heavy, wet air, but regardless, it is plain awful as far as seeing where you are going when you are flying a fighter.

Another thing that costs us on the easy ones is the appearance of the countryside and the lack of a skyful of flak to meet you upon your arrival in the target complex. The easy Packs look like the other side of the moon in lots of spots. The

North Vietnamese have little need to clean up or rebuild the many crossings, fords, bridges and the like that we have destroyed in the past, as it is much easier to build a new route or find a new crossing. The hulks of the old targets scar the countryside. Moreover, nobody moves when you are flying over the area and only when you surprise something like a stray convoy of vehicles or construction equipment do you get any sensation of actuality or life below you. The guns are there, nobody doubts that, but they are not there in the concentration that you find up North. Many of the guns are on the move, while others have specific facets of the constant southward flow of men and equipment to protect. When you come upon this scene with a small maneuverable unit like a flight of two or a flight of four and gaze on the silent bomb holes and the silent roads and villages, and when you are excused from the rattle and burst of the heavier guns of Hanoi, it is easy to make the big slip. It is easy to forget that they will shoot. They are smart in the easy Packs, and most of the time they will hold their fire until you stumble into a position where they have a good chance of zapping you on the first try.

Another reason for Thud losses in the easy areas goes back to the combination of man and machine tempered by experience. Lots of us have flown many of the machines of the recent past as well as the present, and we have flown them on a variety of missions. Each one is different and each handles differently as you force or coax it through its performance spectrum. Like boats and cars, each model has its strong and its weak points, so that each one is best suited to a particular kind of mission. I would argue violently with the thought that any single machine could be designed and built to accomplish all missions satisfactorily.

You can fly them all through the same sky, but that is a great deal different from doing the best possible job on each mission. The basic differences in speed, altitude, maneuverability and weapons delivery just do not make it good sense to assume away the differences and try to build one vehicle for all tasks. Pilots have a tendency to wish all good things from all machines they have flown into the one they are presently flying, and this can mean trouble. Those who have horsed an F-102 around a corner like a midget racer on dirt don't forget it, and someplace way back in the computer is the feeling

Convair F-102 "Delta Dagger"

that all century series fighters should turn like that. Those who have violently changed direction in the F-106 while still maintaining perfect control don't forget that. Those who have strapped the neat little F-104 onto their backsides and experienced the sensation that "I can make this baby doll go anyplace, anytime" do not forget that. Yet, when any of us fly the Thud with its almost complete lack of these sporty characteristics, we love the way we can whistle along on the deck with the big, high-drag bomb, tank and missile load, as we race down the Ridge to Hanoi with little fear for the Mig. However, when we take this same Thud and try to play maximum performance close support over terrain that often rivals Denver for elevation and rarefied air, we sometimes forget that we have a skinny little wing originally designed for high-speed, straight-and-level, on-the-deck nuclear delivery. When we forget that we can't turn like a deuce, honk like a six or skitter like a four, we ask for trouble and we most often find it.

We had a good example of the weather problem the day we lost Pete—the visibility was so bad you couldn't believe it. We had been reporting this to the head shed for several days, but were unable to convince anyone that it was too poor to work in safety. The show must go on. Although Pete was relatively new to us, he had made a great impression, and he had a wealth of experience to back it up. He was supposed to have been our next new squadron commander and with this in mind, we had him out getting his fingernails dirty in all the areas we flew in. That day he was flying number two and finding out what the wingmen felt like in the nasty visibility of the near North. The big headquarters executed his flight to work with a forward air controller flying a slower prop aircraft, who would direct the fighters against targets he had identified on the ground. We figured the visibility would make the forward air control portion of the mission a loser from the start, but they had to go, and sure enough, by the time they arrived in the area, the airborne controller had aborted the mission because even in his slow prop job, he could not see his hand in front of his face, to say nothing of having adequate visibility to control high-speed fighters against pinpoint, sensitive targets. The controller had a change in plans for them and sent them out on their own to work an area that was no better as regards visibility but far less sensitive.

Once in the newly assigned area, the lead knew they had their hands full, and as he searched for his target and attempted to roll in on it, he instructed Pete not to go lower than 10,000 feet, but to attempt to keep him in sight as he attempted to split the murk. The lead hurtled down the chute, but lost all visual contact and bombing references, aborted the pass and recovered his altitude on instruments. Back on top, ready to give it a second try, the lead attempted to call his number two man on the radio, but to no avail. He stayed up on top and milled around over the target area trying in vain to locate his flightmate by visual or electronic means, until low fuel forced him to drop his bombs on a target of opportunity that he was able to see and head for home as he alerted the rescue forces that his wingman was among the missing. The rescue people searched in vain, and the only thing other fighters called in to support the rescue managed to locate was an active heavy radar-controlled gun battery. When the lead recovered at home base, we found several hits in the underside of his aircraft, but he had no knowledge of when or where or how he had taken the hits. It was supposed to be an easy one, but we had one bird shot up, and we never again heard from, or about, our prospective new squadron commander.

* * *

The weather system that made the visibility so bad moved further north, but then we lost John on a well-traveled route in the easy area that everybody knows waxes hot and cold. I was in command of the force that day and we launched on the primary target way up there in the face of a weather report that looked impossible. Someone up the line got the same impression, but not until we were on the tankers, and we were diverted to a series of alternates that we had sagely planned for in advance. After sorting out mission planning cards and target photos, and jamming now worthless maps into odd corners of the cockpit, we all got squared away, and the flights split away from what had been the strike force to go after their individual and lesser defended targets. I was the first flight across the line and as John's flight entered behind and to the north of me, his flight leader further split his flight into elements, and he took one half of his assigned route, while John with his element took the other.

John flew over the spot he eventually bombed but elected to continue to the northern end of his route while lowering his fuel load to make his Thud lighter and more maneuverable while checking the entire route for possible targets. When he swung back over the original area, he set up his element and rolled in on his run without opposition, but he didn't like the way the run looked and figured he could do better with another try, so he aborted the pass and pulled back up over the target for his third exposure over the same point. His number four man had rolled in behind him as instructed and had completed his bomb run, leaving no doubt in the minds of those on the ground as to what the Thuds were after. John readjusted his position, rolled in again, and, sure enough, got hit hard as he was dropping his bombs. The ground gunners had received all the tracking practice they needed and knew they had one in their sights, and when they opened up, they did their job well. He got the nose up and managed to get a little way past the target before she locked up on him and he had to step out.

We found out later that afternoon that there was plenty of firepower in that desolate section of the world, and later intelligence info indicated that the target he had picked was a sizable group of well-organized and well-equipped troops who were moving south with their weapons. If we had been able to control the winds, we probably could have recovered him, but the wind was blowing directly in his face as he leaped out, and no amount of pulling or tugging on the risers could keep him from drifting backward, and he landed right smack where the enemy troops were. By the time I had responded to the Mayday call, he had hit the ground directly on the road he had been bombing, and he and his chute had disappeared the instant he touched down. It was quite apparent what had happened, but we still wanted to be sure. I had the exact spot pinpointed by both coordinates and description, and when I arrived, the flight lead and number two had been forced to head for the tanker for fuel, and the number four man, on his first combat mission, was somewhere between disoriented and lost. Once again I was running a Rescap, and the first thing I did was locate the neophyte number four man and get him squared away and on his way back to the tanker. He later turned out to be one of our shiny lads, but unfortunately he was killed in a midair collision toward the tail end of his tour, as he himself was shepherding a then-new sport around.

When the first Spad arrived on the scene, I found myself and my number two man as bottom cover and we were able to get the Spad almost over the spot, yet displaced a couple of miles to the north to take advantage of the protective cover of the hills. The Spad and I decided that the only way to determine whether further rescue was feasible or necessary was for him to take a close look at the spot where we knew John had hit the ground. We figured that if we both headed west for a few miles, he could stay on the deck with his slower aircraft and turn in toward the spot while I could light the burner and pull my element up several thousand feet as I did a wingover to the left to line up with the road. The combination of the burner noise and the up and over maneuver was calculated to get their attention, and then we could roll in and race down the road with our cannon blazing while the Spad came in on the treetops. Halfway down the road, about over the spot where we had seen John, I would light the burner again and do another wingover and come back down the road shooting up the south side as he passed the spot and broke north for the cover of the hills. We executed the maneuver, and as I approached firing range, I noticed that the hills sloped rather abruptly upward on both sides of the road, making in effect a valley. Small arms, .50 caliber and who knows what all else spit from every rock and ditch along the roads and up into the foothills, and I realized that we had stumbled onto at least a battalion of North Vietnamese regulars. Those guys were dug in, and they were loaded, but it still looked like good shooting for me for the first few rounds. I fired, and then the stupid gun jammed and not another round passed through it that day. I cursed the gun, and I cursed the troops on the ground, and I flew to the spot and started around, knowing full well that my gun was done, but that the Spad was behind me doing his part. Around we went for part two and this time I felt like I had a toy airplane flying through real bullets as I pulled the trigger on the dead cannon and screamed for nobody's edification but my own, "Drop dead, you bastards."

The Spad hugged the trees to the north, and I hugged them to the south and thirty seconds later all the nasty tracers and noise had gone away and he said, "There's nobody there, no sense in losing any more birds. We better call it off. Sorry, old man—thanks for the cover." I concurred, and that was the end of that.

It's easy to say, why press? The target wasn't worth it, but John had a job to do and he wanted to do it to perfection, and God knows he tried. He hung it out over the target for them to shoot at, and I know many who will tell you how bad that is, but I have a lot more experience and a lot more combat than John had, and I hung it out twice without even a gun to shoot, and what's more, I dragged my wingman with me, and we both knew exactly what we were getting into. I guess that is what combat is made of.

The weather refused to change and my old buddy Ralph bit the dust on an easy one fighting the same old rotten visibility, but also fighting the aircraft. He was element lead on a point target on an early morning go, and when they got there, the haze was even covered up with a low cloud layer. There was no choice but to fall back to the planned alternate of road reconnaissance, so they split into elements and started to work. Ralph had been in my squadron for a long time when I had an F-106 outfit. He had flown F-102s before that and was one of my best. He and I worked up a little acrobatic routine that I thought was quite good—but don't tell anybody about that as it's not authorized. I helped arrange an F-104 assignment for him when he left the squadron, and he performed with distinction in his new assignment until Southeast Asia called and he joined us.

Lockheed F-104 "Starfighter"

Part way down the route of the road recce, Ralph called out a truck and wheeled to attack it from low level in the haze of early morning. He still had all the bombs on his aircraft, and he was low and slow, heavy and sluggish, but he had a target in sight and he was after it. I never did figure out if he was going to bomb it from a very low angle or strafe it with his bombs still on the aircraft. All I know is that neither approach is healthy in the machine he was in, and I know that the ground gunners had a more lucrative target in their sights than Ralph had in his. I wonder if for an instant he was flying a batwinged F-106 instead of a clipped-wing F-105. He was only about 3500 feet above the ground, and his speed was well below 350 knots when he took a direct hit from the previously silent guns. They ripped his belly section out and started a fire that in turn caused other large pieces of structure to separate from the aircraft.

His flight leader called him three times to bail out, but the canopy never separated from the aircraft, and there was no bailout observed. The bombs were still on the aircraft as it impacted the ground. Number four reported that the last thing Ralph said was "Oh, no." I'm sure by then he knew what was happening. All for a lousy beat-up truck, but if you are going to take a bunch of guys and feed them gunpowder and raw meat while you tie one hand behind them, this is what you have to expect—losses. It just hurts worse to lose them on the easy ones.

12.

UNHAPPY HUNTING GROUNDS

Everyone who flies a combat tour in fighters finds a favorite area to work in. You find places you detest and have no desire to fly into, and you find other places where you feel more relaxed, more competent, more aggressive. The index is not necessarily the severity of the defenses, and in fact a flier's favorite section may be very heavily defended. It is just a case of feeling that you can master all the challenges in one spot and adopting that section as your personal hunting grounds. When you make that identification, it is amazing how well you can manipulate both the schedule and the conduct of the mission to allow you to comb your hunting grounds regularly.

I despised the northeast railroad. I didn't like the long haul that we had to make to get there and I didn't like the approaches to the targets, even though it was easy enough to get there and the landmarks made navigation no problem. While there were plenty of people shooting at you on the way in and the way out, the gunfire was not an overriding factor until you got to the target itself. The targets were blah targets, and they were all heavily defended. We smashed most of the worthwhile ones fairly early on, and after we had knocked out the better targets in other complexes to the west of the railroad and toward Hanoi, the North Vietnamese loaded the railroad with guns from these other areas and then moved them up and down the rail line as needed. Our plan of hitting the same places again and again helped them in their arrangement of guns, and there were not too many places where they couldn't hammer you pretty hard from all sides. Nobody wants to bust his rear end, but I abhorred the thought of busting it for some crummy beat-up piece of railroad track or a couple of used railroad cars.

I didn't like the egress route either, because once you got past the guns that chased you to the coast, you would have to look at all those ships lined up waiting to get into the port at Haiphong with the flags of many nations we had knocked ourselves out to help flapping in the North Vietnamese breeze. It was rough to watch some kid blow up in your face and moments later watch your supposed allies unloading more equipment to be transported to the gunners so they could either work you over the next day or ship it down south to clobber some poor grunt crawling around in the mud. I didn't like the refueling on the way out because everyone was always hurting for fuel, and the rat race to find your tanker and hook up with him was always more confused out there. And I didn't like the long haul home. As far as I am concerned, all single-engine fighters still have an automatic rough running engine once you pass the shoreline and look out at all that water.

My favorite bombing and hunting area started around Viet Tri and went straight south past Hoa Binh, then west along Route 6 up to Son La. I never went into the area that I didn't find a good target for my bombs and I always managed to find excellent armed reconnaissance targets after I had dropped the bombs. When you pick a favorite area you get to know it quite well, and you know where to look for the elusive targets. It thus becomes easier to generate a good mission. I have found as many as fifty trucks in convoy in there; I have played games with the Migs in there; and I have hammered countless buildings and supply caches and a goodly portion of them have gone boom. This has not been completely one-sided, and I hasten to add that I have been hit three times while working that area and there have been several moments of doubt as to my chances of getting out.

It was a murky gray Sunday afternoon when Sam hit me

just to the east of Hoa Binh. I am very pleased to be a member of that exclusive club of aviators who have been hit by a Sam and lived to tell about it, and I have to admit that it is quite a sensation. I was leading both wings that afternoon and we were after a sprawling barracks area stretched out across the flatlands just east of the mountains. As usual, visibility was poor and we expected a cloud deck about 8,000 feet but we were unsure of the extent of cloud cover the deck would provide. If it was too extensive we would be out of business.

My electronics guys must have taken gas on Saturday night, because the birds were not in great electrical shape and there was a shortage of spare aircraft. I was not too happy with my personal machine but I had to take it with some of the gear not operating. There was no choice as there was nothing else available, and while I admit to toying with the idea of shafting one of the lieutenants or captains with my halfway machine and taking his, I couldn't quite see that. I figured I was better able to get the job done with less than the optimum available to me than was one of my wingmen, and I pressed on with my own machine. By the time I got hooked up on the tanker I found that the tank hanging crew must have taken some of that same gas, as the huge 650-gallon center-line fuel tank I was carrying under the belly to match the bombload was not functioning properly. This piece of equipment was another one of our frequent offenders and we never managed to get them to work as they should. My malfunction of the day was a bit different than usual as I could get all the fuel from the tank to the engine without any problem, but something in the plumbing was goofed up and would not allow me to accept a full load of fuel from the tanker, either in the belly tank or in the main system. I bounced on and off the refueling boom a dozen times and I pulled circuit breakers and worked switches for all I was worth, but to no avail. I had my number three man back off and pull out all the emergency instructions and read them to me to see if I had missed anything, but I had not. I wanted a full load of fuel. We did not have too much to play with under ideal conditions, and if we got wrapped up with Migs or anything else unusual, things might get tight. While I crammed as much fuel into her as she would take, I had number three back out again and get out his hand navigation computer and figure out how I would make out on fuel if I left the tanker with a partial load, used the fuel in the belly tank first, and then jettisoned the tank to reduce the overall drag on the aircraft. I did not want to abort the mission. Nobody wants to abort, but when you are leading, it is sheer torture to turn your force over to someone else. Number three came back with the answer that I could just make it—probably.

As we dropped off the tankers and headed out across the hills, I was paying particular attention to my fuel consumption and waiting for that tank to go dry so I could dump it. About halfway in, I got the empty light and punched her off. Those monsters stand up on end in the airstream and just barely clear the aircraft, most of the time, and I was relieved to be rid of it, and relieved to have transferred the partial load of fuel into my main tanks where I knew I could use it. I wasn't relieved for long as the dizzy oil pressure gauge started to weave back and forth in my face. With the engine we had in that bird, a fluctuating oil pressure indication was a real red flag and was the typical first signal for a series of rapid reactions that left you minus engine. We were only a few minutes out from the target now and I wanted desperately to continue. The weather was now definitely marginal and I wanted to make the go or no-go decision. I didn't want to turn loose of my two-wing force, but the needle refused to stop its methodical up and down, up and down. I am constantly amazed at the wide range of thoughts that whistle through your head while you are flying combat. I wanted to convince myself that the fluctuation was not going to stop me and that the engine was not about to come unglued, and I managed to do it. I remembered one of my old midget-racing friends who had worked like a dog to get his machine in shape for one of the big races up in the northwest. His efforts paid off, and his driver pushed the car out in front and was holding a comfortable lead with three-quarters of the race completed when he suddenly pulled into the pits. Pogo, the driver, started to climb out, explaining that his oil pressure was fluctuating and he was afraid he would damage the engine. Ralph, the owner, wanted that race in the worst way and he practically gave Pogo a compression fracture as he stuffed him back into the seat and back onto the track. He had lost too much ground and they lost the race. There was nothing wrong with the engine, and the first thing Ralph did was cover the oil

pressure gauge with tape. To my knowledge, he has never
had a pressure gague visible in any of his cars since. The
microsecond it took me to recall that story whizzed past and I
continued on to the target.

The mountains rise to about 5,000 feet in that section of
the North until you have passed Hoa Binh, and then they
drop rapidly to the flat sea-level floor of the delta. While we
were not too far above the crests of the hills as we thundered
off the last ridge, we still had to push the noses down a bit to
get the approach altitude I wanted, and we had a real head of
steam as we broke out over the flatland. The visibility was
good enough to work, and though I found out to my surprise
that the cloud deck at 8,000 feet was a solid overcast, I
blasted out the code word for go and the strike was on. I
knew that because of the ceiling the guys would have to alter
their preplanned dive-bomb passes, but I also knew that
these pros were good at that and that there would be no
turning back in this wing today.

The target was harder to pick up than I had anticipated.
The target photos that we had to work from were pretty sad
and often outdated, and the first time you went on a new
target that photo was usually the only clue you had on the
details of what you were looking for. The countryside up
there changes a great deal with the seasons, and rivers,
streams and reservoirs can look completely different depending on the amount of rain that has fallen. This one had
changed, and bore little resemblance to the target photo I
had studied, and I had to turn almost 90 degrees further
toward the north than I had intended. My number four man
was actually the first one to get his bubble leveled and spot
the target and as he called it out, I pulled hard to the left to
line up for the attack. As I tugged at my 49,000-pound
monster and prodded it around the corner, I was straining my
head to look to the left and line up on the target. I tugged a
little too hard along the up-and-down axis, and the tremendous bag of speed that I was carrying threw number two and
myself up as well as around to the left. Since I was concen-
trating back over my left shoulder I could not see that I was
approaching an underhanging bank of clouds to my right
front. I dragged number two and myself up into the murk in
a hard left wingover at 600 knots and found myself with a few
problems that required rapid solution. I had to convert from

visual flight to instrument flight and depend on my instruments to help me control the aircraft. In that I was really ricocheting along and was in a most unusual flight attitude this was not the easiest of transitions, but I managed to accomplish it. I needed to get back under that cloud deck so I could bomb and get out of there, and every second I stayed up in the murk took me further past my target, but I had to stay up there for a few seconds to give three and four a chance to gain a little displacement. They had been able to avoid the cloud and I didn't want to run into them as I came spitting back out the bottom. This is where the failure of my electronics guys to get my bird in shape almost did me in and I must have made a pretty picture on Sam's radarscope as I pushed over and got two and myself back out under the clouds. The Sam controllers knew the height of the ceiling, and as we emerged at the bottom, three Sams were upon us. We never saw them coming and I can only guess at their site of origin. One of them must have been set for detonation at the base of the clouds and the other two were using their normal fuzing and as the preset fuze detonated a bit short of the base of the clouds and directly under the belly of my aircraft, the other two shrieked between John, my number two man, and myself. With their tails now pointed toward us, they sped on in perfect formation at an amazing pace with the round incandescent eyes of flame on their tail ends winking at us. I thought I was dead.

There is no mistaking the sound and sensation of being hit. I have been tapped a total of eleven times in my 216 fighter combat missions, and the sensation does not become any less thrilling with repetition. The sound is not as loud as you might imagine, yet it is very precise and definite. I have searched for a good description and the best I can come up with is to take a quarter between your thumb and forefinger and hold it about four inches above a metal surface like a radiator, or even above a hardwood surface like a desk top. Now firmly, but not violently, rap the surface with the quarter. That's the sound, and there is nothing quite like it.

I never worry too much about where on the aircraft I have taken the hit since I have been hit everyplace from the windscreen to the tailpipe, and the specific location is pretty academic. There are four big things you need to know in a hurry. You need to know if the controls are working, and you can check that by simply moving the stick and kicking the rudders to see if the bird reacts. You also have to take a quick look at those hydraulic pressure gauges and see if they are up and holding a steady pressure, because if they are on the way down, there is a good chance that you are also on the way down. Next, you want to know if the mill is still with you, and this you can check by glancing at the engine gauges on the front panel to see if they are in the green and by jazzing the throttle a few times to see if the power follows the throttle. Then you need to see if you are on fire. Theoretically, the two fire warning lights sitting right in front of you will illuminate to give you the word on fire, but I also look around as best I can, and when I have the chance, I take the mask off and sniff for the unmistakable odor of burning aircraft components. This entire check consumes only seconds.

I checked out OK, and John was still on my wing, the target was in front of us, and the bad guys were shooting from the ground. I figured I had come all this way to do a job and that it wasn't too healthy sitting up there wondering how hard I had been hit. I was a bit concerned about putting the extra strain of a high-speed dive-bomb run and pullout on my machine, since the strain might complicate any damage I had taken, but that's the breaks. I had a job to do, and I got on with it and rolled into my run. Those two 3,000-pounders went as directed and we had dirt and buildings flying through the air to spotlight the target for the following flights. My bird recovered from the dive without incident and we charged out of the area and called the Avis wing to give them the go signal, plus a weather check on the target itself. The Avis troops did not fare too well. They had become tangled up with the weather and had been unable to maintain their formation; in fact even some of their four-ship flights were split up. The Migs had also swung in behind them and as they milled about and tried to get organized, the Migs zipped through them and busted their entire effort wide open. Their leadman called their portion of the strike off, and as my machine was still doing OK, I took our flights over to their position and we managed to draw most of the Migs off them as they limped home licking their wounds. I limped back myself with my oil pressure still bouncing and my forward underside peppered by Sam fragments. The mill kept running until I got back to the base, but that was all she ran, and when I shut her down in the chocks she was all through. I got a new engine that night and had some sheet metal work done on my belly and we were ready to go again the next day.

Through the spring and early summer of 1967 there was little significant change in our attack pattern. We continued to work the full spectrum of allowable targets in the North and I managed to get into my favorite hunting grounds fairly often. The activity would vary in intensity from week to week, and the area would light up at one end while slowing down in another section, depending on the weather and the degree of traffic headed for the South, but you could always manage to stir something up if you could spend enough time in there. It was several weeks after my Sam encounter before they got to me again, and sure enough it was right back in my hunting grounds. They sneaked up on me this time and they didn't miss doing me in by very much.

The job for the day was to hit both Viet Tri and Phu Tho, and to see how much damage we could do to the rail facilities and associated equipment between the two towns. They are right on the main rail line that comes from China down through the northwestern portion of North Vietnam, and both spots were quite active. We decided that we could get the best coverage by splitting the strike force into two sections of two 4-ship flights each and letting our Sam hunters take care of both attacks as they roamed the area. I put the second section on Phu Tho and I took the first section to Viet Tri.

There were both good and bad points about taking a strike to Viet Tri. It was not so great in that they had tough gun coverage on the entrance route and there were several Sam sites that had done well around there: they could look across the flat terrain at you all the way, including the actual dive-bomb run itself. They also had a pair of 85- and 100-millimeter batteries that were particularly mean. They were active every time I went up there and, as a rule, they were not afraid to shoot. They usually picked you up just before you rolled in on the rail yard, and they could raise enough fuss to goof up your run. I have personally been on several missions when we dumped many pounds on their heads, but they seemed to come bouncing back with a new crew by the next time we passed their way. I happened to have a good view of one of their rings of gun pits one day

when my number three man put a load right in the middle of
them. One minute you could see them firing, and the next
minute the entire ring was immersed in a fireball of detonating explosives. There is no doubt that he got the gunners but
he obviously didn't kill the guns, so it was nothing but a
messy clean-up job for them and they were ready to go again.
You couldn't ask for a better hit than my number three got
but it didn't really do the job. The answer is obviously better
munitions. If you are going to expose your forces and battle
the guns, you need a munition that will kill the guns as well
as the gunners. You are not going to do it with 1930-style
ladyfingers. A suitable weapon is well within the capacity of
current technology, and as long as we continue to fight
conventional wars we will need such a weapon. The ground
guns are a most formidable threat to mission accomplishment, and unless we get off the dime and do something
constructive to beat these gun systems, other than squashing
them with falling fighter planes, we are going to be in bigger
trouble if we take on bigger enemies. I am not the first to
scream this fact, but like others ahead of me, I have seen
little constructive effort in the antiflak area. In his history of
the fall of Dien Bien Phu, Bernard Fall called attention to the
extraordinary toll of French planes shot down by the Vietnamese
gunners, repeating the success of the North Koreans against
the Americans during the Korean War. Apparently our strate-
gists have still not absorbed these lessons.

Viet Tri was not limited to a couple of large gun positions.
Like so many other areas up there, the guns were spread all
over the complex and they could move freely from day to day.
Looking down on the town you could see sparklers from each
dirt road intersection and from the backyard of every standing building. It is tough to knock out a threat like that unless
you get permission to knock out the entire deserted town.
They had one large complex of buildings just north of town
that was billed as a hospital, and was naturally off limits. If it
was in fact a hospital, it must have been a hospital for sick flak
gunners, because every time we looked at it from a run on
the railhead, it was one mass of sputtering, flashing gun
barrels. Like I said, there is no sporting blood up there.

There were also good things about a strike on Viet Tri.
Most targets in North Vietnam were very tough to pinpoint
from any distance out, and you were fighting right up to the

last second to be sure that you set your pattern of attack properly. But if you had any sort of acceptable visibility and cloud cover, you could plan and implement an attack on Viet Tri from 50 miles out. The landmarks were big and they were easy to read. They went down the line just like a batch of stepping-stones, and where the big hook in the river pointed directly to the target itself, there was even a reservoir directly in front of you to say, "pull up now." The target complex was also large enough so you could pick the most promising impact area with ease. I had picked Viet Tri this time because I wanted to lead the flak suppression flight and get another crack at those two big gun batteries to see if I could beat them.

In an attempt to achieve some degree of surprise, I held the force together until we were almost at the target. When we were nearly ready to race for bombing altitude I swung my Sam chasers out to the side to block for both sections while we bombed. I split my second section on to a slightly divergent course to the right that lined them up with Phu Tho while I pressed straight ahead for the hook in the river. The drill worked like a fine watch and everyone was in perfect position as I started to roll upside down over the real estate occupied by the two big gun batteries so that I could easily let my nose fall through in a good steep bomb run on them the minute they opened up. I had briefed the rest of my flak suppressors to split away from me as I approached the apex of my pull for altitude, and they slid off to other quadrants of the target to cover the threat from all sides, and left me all alone in the ring with the two big gun pits.

I glanced out the side as I rolled, and quickly identified the area, but as I arched upward through 12,000 feet there was no fire from the big guns, only some small stuff from a bit farther north. I couldn't understand this and wondered if we had actually surprised them. I could not hope for a fully effective strike unless the guns showed, by firing at me, where they were and which ones were active that day. I floated a little more and when there was still no appreciable action I wondered if perhaps we had really knocked them out for good on the last trip. I was usually quite comfortable in a vertical rolling maneuver or when hanging upside down looking at the ground through the top of the canopy (probably due to my long tour in front of the Air Force demonstration team, looping and rolling my way around the world), but things got a bit sticky on this one. You can only hang upside down and push up for a limited number of seconds before you run out of everything, including guts. I was running out rapidly, all the garbage, including the bombs, wanted to go down, and it was apparent that I was going to accompany them in that direction before too long. I could have fallen through and hit the general area of the guns but that would probably have been a waste of bombs.

I ran out of everything, with still no show of life from my primary objective and had to make up my head in a hurry. The strike aircraft had been right behind me and had already bombed, and the first billows of smoke and debris from the rail yard testified to their success. While I had not bombed the big guns, I had at least insured their silence while my troops did their job and got out of the way. I found out later that one of my trusty wingmen had knocked out a six-gun 85-millimeter site in one of the other quadrants, while my other two wingmen hammered smaller emplacements, so the suppression job was accomplished. In my awkward position, upside down and with my nose pointed in almost the opposite direction from my preferred attack heading, it would have been most difficult to get a good attack run on those guns even if they opened up at that stage of the game, and the best I could have looked for was a solo recovery going the wrong way back toward Hanoi. I knew I had an instantaneously fuzed load of bombs that would do little damage to the tracks or to rolling stock, but I also knew that there was a dandy choke point with a bunch of transshipment buildings at the far end of the yards that would be ideal targets for this load. I let the nose fall through, a maneuver about which I had little choice, and rolled the wings 180 degrees so that I now faced toward the end of the yards. I could trade some of the altitude gained in my previous gyration for much needed airspeed, and I launched on a dive-bomb run as the choke point floated obligingly up into my sights.

As I floated away from them, those two big sites opened up with all they had and really covered me on my run. Since I had cat-and-moused them until the force was past, they had no other targets, and I think they used their entire daily quota of ammunition on me. It turned into a surprisingly pretty dive-bomb run, and when I looked at some film later I saw that I had a perfect hit that blew the cluster of buildings to smithereens; the walls of one building south of the tracks traveled through the air all the way to the north side. All the troops had done good work and when we compared notes and assessed damage we found that we had started several good-sized fires, triggered three large secondary explosions, destroyed thirty-five railroad cars, destroyed the two largest buildings in the choke point area, cut the tracks in twelve places and knocked out the six-gun 85-millimeter battery. The flights at Phu Tho had also done good work and had closed the choke points at both ends of their yards while saturating the tracks and cars in between. Not bad for the start of a day's work, and we got everybody out without taking a hit.

I was feeling quite satisfied with the drive and precision of my troops as we headed out of the target area and moved toward the south and west. We were fat on fuel, and the weather looked favorable so I decided to take my boys hunting in my favorite area. We were about halfway to Hoa Binh when my Sam chasers, who were still screening between Hanoi and our flights, began to chatter about Sam launches. Three of the four Thuds in my flight had suffered from a lack of Sam warning equipment since takeoff and we were not in the best of shape to take Sam on at this particular moment. When I took a quick glance at the terrain, it was not difficult to see that I was very close to the area where Sam had clipped me before, and I took my troops into an evasive exercise just on general principles. Sure enough, Sam zipped over the top of the spot we had been occupying shortly before and charged on aimlessly to detonate himself in frustration at finding only empty air. I won't swear to it, but I bet he came from the same site that had hosed me before.

We stayed low until we were down around the Black River when I figured we were in position to pick up some altitude and hunt. Then came the Migs to complete our exposure to all the defensive elements for the day. From the various calls on Mig position, the hastily drawn mental picture indicated that we could look for action in our area and it took only a couple of sweeps of the head before I located a Mig, all set up on a quartering head-on pass on us. He had good position and plenty of altitude, and he was really moving as he closed toward firing range from my ten o'clock position. I called the break and started a turn into him that increased the closure rate considerably and compounded his tracking problems to the point that he figured he could not score on that pass. My wingman and my element were up in perfect position and as the Mig whistled overhead, I started a reverse that would allow us to keep him in sight. He used his superior turning capability and pulled up and over in a wingover that put him at about our four o'clock position as he started his second run. Our Thuds, relatively light on fuel, responded well to the full load of coal we poured on them, and as the element crossed underneath me and pulled up into position, the Mig found himself looking right down the axis of the scissors we had prepared for him. He could hardly have pressed the attack on either element without exposing himself to another pair of hungry Thud drivers. It took him only a second or two to realize this and he deferred. He wrapped that little beauty into a diving inverted turn as he disengaged and streaked back for the sanctuary.

It is ultimately frustrating to have them turn you off completely whenever you achieve a setup that might give you a chance to clobber them. Even though we were not about to catch him, we stayed on his tail until we had gone far enough north to insure that all the strike flights had progressed through the area without having him turn on their tails, and then reversed and headed for the road leading from Hoa Binh back through the northwest hill country into China.

I knew this road quite well and had developed the ability to note changes in the overview almost instantly. There were several supply, barracks and transshipment clusters along the route that had been hit, to some degree, during the previous months. Intelligence summaries reported them as unserviceable, but that was just not so. They were used to some extent, depending on the traffic flow down from China or up from Laos, and if you worked the area intently you could spot changes, despite the fact that developments were well hidden just as they were all over the rest of the country. I noted little change in the first few clusters but the third one was different. There were several new buildings and many of the older buildings had been repaired since my last tour of the development. There were several new dirt roads scratched through the complex and the entire operation smelled of activity. As I swung slightly to the north to double back and recheck, I called my element and told them to help me check the development thoroughly, and at the same time I spotted six big fat loaded trucks back at my eight o'clock position. I stroked the burner and called out the trucks as I wheeled hard left across the valley floor and pulled up for altitude to start a strafing pass on the trucks. The element wheeled with me and before I had a chance to initiate my strafing run, I spotted another half dozen trucks on a newly scratched crossroad leading to some of the supposedly abandoned buildings. I knew the element could handle the first batch of six we had spotted, and I called them to take care of them as I pulled around another 90 degrees to go after the second group of six. As I rounded the corner and dropped the nose, the red pipper of my cannon sight climbed lazily to the firing position I wanted, and the trucks looked like six hunched-up brown toads squatting in line. I steadied the pipper out for a second and squeezed the trigger.

The Vulcan cannon barked, and all hell broke loose. The entire valley floor lit up from both sides; I have never seen so much 37-millimeter fire in my life. It came from everywhere. I was already on the run, so I held the trigger down and dispatched the line of trucks, but they zapped me while I was doing it. The white 37 puff balls were so thick it was like flying through a snowstorm and I couldn't get away from them. They hit me hard in the vertical fin with a 90-degree deflection shot and I felt it. They had knocked a huge hole in the fin, taking all the electrical stability augmentation gear along with the surface metal and several supporting members, and the bird went ape. I was still heading down at almost 500 knots, and the loss of the electrical circuits threw her into a wild side-to-side oscillation that banged my head from one side of the canopy to the other. The puff balls still would not go away, and as I bounced harder and harder from side to side as the pendulum effect of the oscillations increased, I knew only one thing—that everything was white, except the green mountains approaching all too rapidly.

My basic problem at the moment was quite simple, but the solution was almost out of reach. The hard hit back in the rear end someplace had deprived me of the normal smooth control forces. Gone were the electrical pick-offs on the control pressures that usually translated themselves into a damping effect to insure smooth control movements and a resulting smooth flight path, and in their place I had a runaway control system that could only interpret and apply full rudder control deflections. The result was a full rudder deflection in one direction that would start the aircraft swinging sideways. As soon as the sick system sensed this swing, it immediately called for full opposite control response; the system was in effect tearing me and itself apart, as it fought to correct its own ever increasing and opposing gyrations.

The second phase of my problem was that I was physically unable to maintain a set position in the cockpit so that I might attempt some corrective action. The buffeting was not only hard on the head and shoulders, it also made it difficult to see properly, and the old headpiece can only take so much rapid swinging before those level bubbles get to be not so level. The G forces were high and getting higher with each exaggerated swing, which meant that my hands and arms were like swinging hunks of lead that I was trying to force to take switch actions within the cramped confines of the cockpit.

Next came the problem of the ground. It rose sharply in front of me into a mountain ridge, and as I had been hit when my nose was pointed down with the speed close to 500, I was still pointed down on a collision course with the base of the mountains. Unless I could stabilize the machine and get that nose up, I was probably going to become a part of the local real estate. The real hooker in the whole thing was that they still had me cornered from the ground. That stuff was detonating all around me like popcorn, and the speed I had plus the wild motions I was going through were the only things that were keeping me from taking more hits. I couldn't afford another hit, and I couldn't afford to pull back on the power or fling out the speed brakes. Either action might give me the change in profile I needed to get the beast back under control, but that would be of little value if I got blown up in the attempt.

I had been this wild control route before. I had an F-106 at 30,000 feet one day and, unknown to me, I had a dandy fire back in the weapons bay where a depot modification team had used a two-cent rivet rather than the ten-cent rivet they were supposed to use. When the fire got to the electrical control components, the stick locked full back and I went from flying at 30,000 feet to stalled out with the nose straight up at 40,000 feet before I knew what had happened. I fought that beauty for thirty minutes before I finally overpowered the

controls and established a rudder exercise stall from 30,000
feet that allowed me to crash onto the runaway at 250 knots.
That one had been different, in that I had lots of altitude and
time to play with. Here, I was running out of both altitude
and seconds, and I was getting shot at.

Ted had my element and when he saw the valley erupt in
ground fire he immediately checked me on my strafing run
and saw my aircraft disappear into the white cloud of flak and
lurch as it took the hit in the tail. He knew I was in trouble,
and he knew that the guns were on me and that he had to get
them off me. It was no trick to establish the fact that those
gunners were plentiful and accurate, but that did not even
slow him down. He lit his burner and pulled himself and his
wingman over the top and onto a strafing run from the other
side of the valley. He knew that the only thing that would
pull the gunners off me, now that they knew I was wounded,
was a big dose of lead in the head, and that is what he gave
them. He picked what looked like the center of the concentration and pulled the cannon trigger and drove right down to
the tops of the gun barrels. When the center section of the
guns faltered with the impact of his first rounds, he stirred
his control stick around the cockpit and he kicked his rudders, and the nose of his aircraft responded by humping,
bumping and swiveling in front of him. The stream of lead
spitting from his Gatling gun followed the nose of the machine and he sprayed ammo all over the area. The impact of
the lead and the sound of his Thud screeching across the gun
pits had the desired effect, and while the central flak battery
went out of business permanently, the rest of the gunners
faltered in their concentration on me.

The first thing I had to do was find a circuit breaker. A
circuit breaker switch in a fighter is an obnoxious little piece
of black plastic that looks something like the eraser and the
top half inch of a lead pencil. When the breaker is pushed in
the system it controls is active. If you pull it out, or if a
malfunction makes it pop out, the system it controls is
deactivated. Each breaker controls one of the many electrical
systems or inputs that makes a complicated weapons system
tick. There are so many of them that the least essential are
not even in the cockpit but are in compartments throughout
the aircraft, where the pilot has no control over them in flight.
If one of the external breakers pops in flight you have lost that

system for the duration. The designers took the zillion most important breakers and placed them in the cockpit, so the pilot could have the opportunity to check and reset some of the electrical systems when necessary. The problem is that there is not enough room for them and they are strung out in lines, globs and little bunches in all the remote corners of the pit that are unusable for other major components. Many of them are on the sides and behind the pilot, and a midget standing up in the seat and looking backward might be able to peer under and behind the seat and armrests and make out the minute lettering and number code that identifies one black pimple from another. When you are strapped in, especially with combat gear on, you can forget all that. Many of them you cannot see, and some of them you can hardly reach. You have to know where they are and, if you can reach them, operate them by feel. While Ted was getting the guns off my back, I was fighting the G forces and the oscillation as I forced my now heavy arm and left hand down and back along the left console panel behind my left hip in search of the stability augmentation switch. If I could find it and disengage it, I would cut out the entire control augmentation system, and while this would give me a spooky set of controls in all the aspects of pitch, roll and yaw, it should at least cut out the frantic and incorrect outputs that were wagging my tail with such alarming force.

I found what I thought was the right one and managed to hook a thumb and finger under its narrow top lip, and I got it out about the time Ted got the gunners' heads down. The instant I got it out I leaned on the right rudder with my right foot, as that was the direction I thought I was swinging toward at that instant. My hope was to lock onto one direction of oscillation and break the swing from side to side, and it worked as the bird slid to the right in an uncoordinated but single direction skid. The instant I felt response I threw out the speed brakes to alter my trajectory, honked back on the throttle, horsed back on the stick, then immediately rammed the throttle full forward and lit the burner as I eased off on the right pedal. She was a long way from being a stable bird, but she responded, and the nose eased up as she waddled and bumped toward the sky above the treetops on the hills that were now under me, and I cleared the mountaintops by less than I like to think about. She was wiggly, but she was flying, and Ted had made it back up from his valley floor excursion.

I had only one of my other flights still working in the area, my Sam chasers, only a few miles to the south and east of me, and they still had a full load of ordnance. I called them into the area. They had no trouble finding the spot and were on the scene by the time I got my now slow-turning beastie around the corner and headed to the west and south. They needed only a quick description of the target, and each one of them picked a separate cluster of buildings and let fly with bombs. The results were spectacular and they got four secondary explosions out of four, with one the telltale white of ammunition, and another the black thick smoke spiral of fuel. That place was loaded. I had to hurry back to the base to report my find and figure out the best way of exploiting it.

Hurrying was not the answer for me for the following hour or so. My wingman had pulled up alongside of me to take a good look at the condition of my tail feathers, and he advised that the hole was huge and was in effect a jagged cut directly through the vertical fin and out the other side. The forward edge of the fin was held on only by the angled leading edge of the fin itself, and wires and loose skin flapped in the hole where supporting members and their covering aluminum skin used to be. His advice was simple, "Slow down before you tear that damn fin off." I would have gone no place but down if I had torn it off, so slow down I did. I would have liked to go home at a comfortable low altitude and a low speed, but we had been working well to the north for some time and I had to have a shot of fuel to make it back. That meant up to altitude for the tanker, and I was a bit concerned about how my charge would handle up there, but we struggled up to 27,000 feet for our tanker. She didn't handle too well, but I figured she was good enough so that a cooperative tanker crew and a good boomer could handle me. I explained my problem to the boomer on the radio, and as I sat behind him, looking like an unhappy worm suspended by a string tied around his middle, he took careful aim and stabbed me the first try. I scarfed up a full load of fuel, just to be sure I had enough in case of any problems in the landing phase, and limped homeward thinking again how lucky we were to have such a good bunch of tanker troops on our side.

The landing was uneventful. I just backed way off from the

runway and came driving in on a flat approach using minimum control pressures. There were many "ohs" and "ahs" as
I taxied in and parked my wounded bird, and we found on
looking at her on the ground that I had taken several small
hits along with the big one. Our information man wanted a
picture of me standing there with my head through the hole
for a news release, and the maintenance guy and the factory
representative wanted one for their bosses, but I refused. I
have never allowed a picture to be taken of me with any one
of my shot-up aircraft. I have had several friends who have
posed for some rather spectacular photos of that type, and an
amazingly high proportion of them are very dead from subse-
quent battle damage. I confined my activities to telling my
crew chief to go steal an aft section off some sick bird that was
down for maintenance, slap it on our rear end and get the
painter to change the numbers. Of the F-105s flying today
there are few that do not exist on parts from other F-105s.

We debriefed very thoroughly to be sure that we had all
seen the same things on the ground and then got the intelligence staff working on all the pictures and background information that they could dig up on the area. What their effort
boiled down to was some third-rate pictures that were extremely old and the information that the area had been a live
target some time ago but had been dropped from active to
inactive because of damage reported in the past and lack of
recently reported activity. We were obviously not up to speed
on developments in that little valley and that made our find
all the sweeter. It might have gone inactive for a while, but it
was obvious from the trucks, guns, buildings and secondary
explosions we had observed that morning that this was no
longer the case. I got on the horn to the big headquarters,
described my find in the most glowing terms I could conjure
up, and asked for permission to take an entire strike wing
into the place the next day to see what I could do about
cleaning all that equipment out while it was still sitting in one
spot. Response was not immediate, but I eventually got the
go-ahead and my wing was delegated to my own control for
only the second time in the entire tour. The headquarters
intelligence types went to work for us also but only managed
to come up with a few more outdated photos of the general
area. I put the planners in my operations section to work,

checked their initial efforts and gave them the go sign, and went about some of my other duties while looking forward to the early morning mission the next day.

We were all hot to trot the next morning and anticipation even took some of the sting out of the two-thirty alarm clock. The plan was simple. We would have two flights of Phantoms in the area and they would patrol between our force and Hanoi so we could feel relatively sure that the Migs would not get in our hair. I wanted to be able to concentrate on getting this job done completely the first time, and for once I was content to leave the Mig-sweep work to someone else. We would refuel and all drop off the tankers together, and I would lead into the area and give a go or no-go on the weather. The rest of the flights would displace themselves behind me so that we would not bunch up in the limited airspace over the valley, and after I had worked I would call the succeeding flights in one at a time. I intended to orbit far enough away from the target to stay out of their way while they were working, but close enough so I could monitor their work and insure that we got the areas I wanted.

I was disappointed that the weather was not holding to the forecast we had received the night before and it did not look too great. At first the headquarters folks did not want to release us, but I got on the horn and was able to talk them into letting us go, and shortly afterward I pulled into the number one spot in the arming area with my strike force in tow.

The arming area is a strange little piece of concrete adjacent to the end of the runway that provides the last respite and physical check of both man and machine before the launch. It is a hectic spot, saturated with ground crews and supervisors who must constantly hustle to insure a smooth flow of aircraft onto the runway. They have to hurry carefully to guarantee that the aircraft is completely ready for the challenge ahead, yet they can't afford any delay in the flow of traffic. A few minutes wasted in this crucial spot compounds rapidly into delayed takeoffs and delayed tanker rendezvous, and can compromise the timing and success of the entire effort. The crew is under the control of a senior sergeant who positions himself midway between the yellow painted lead-in lines that each pilot follows as he places his nosewheel on the spot that will line him up parallel to the next bird, with his

nose pointing out into the boondocks to guarantee maximum
safety should some piece of ordnance misfire during the
arming process. It is always hot out there and as each fighter
swings into and out of the pad, the stinging exhaust from the
tail pipe adds to the heat. The noise and vibration is so
intense that the standard ear protectors provide only minimal
protection to the ground crews working there, and it is
necessary to rotate the arming crews constantly to preserve
their hearing.

As the crewman assigned to each particular spot directs the
pilot into position, the first move is up to the pilot. He checks
all his cockpit switches and when he is satisfied that all
ordnance is in a safe condition, he merely holds both hands
up in the air to say, "OK, men, go to work. I won't shoot you
or drop a bomb on your toes." Once the signal is given, the
ground crew swarms all over the bird. One group checks all
the external weapons to be sure that nothing has vibrated
loose while moving from the parking area to the runway, and
then they pull the safety pins or set the switches that bring
the bombs, missiles and guns to life, ready to detonate on
command. Another crew covers every inch of the outside of
the bird, looking for hydraulic or fuel leaks, loose panels, cut
tires or any little unnoticed flaw that could cost us a man and
machine over hostile territory. If they find something wrong,
it represents the height of frustration to be sent back to the
chocks when you have done all the preparation that is required to get to this point, but in this spot rank means
nothing. If a two-striper says he doesn't like the looks of the
machine about to launch, colonel or lieutenant, back to the
parking area you go. There is no telling how many people and
machines this system has saved for us, as there are many
things that can go wrong with a temperamental machine from
engine crank to takeoff, and the old routine of simply kicking
the tire and lighting the fire is definitely passé.

The pilot is busy during this period racing through the
checklist to be sure he has not overlooked even one small
switch setting, as once he pulls out of this pad it is too late to
worry about details. It is also the spot to take a big suck on
the plastic tube that leads to the thermos full of ice water
behind the seat, and shift into the mental high gear that the
next several hours will demand. This is a serious moment

inside you, too. Fighter pilots are like racing drivers in that disaster always happens to someone else—not them. Yet, here for a few moments things sit still and the immensity of the personal challenge is very real.

Although I never bothered to inquire into the religious habits of my pilots, I was impressed by the numbers who made it to the chapel for one service or another, and I can tell you for sure there are very few atheists in the arming area. When you watch comrades fall from the sky day after day you realize that it is going to take some help and guidance from a level above your own to hack the course.

We always had at least one of our chaplains in the arming area, and day or night, rain or shine, they were there for every launch. While the crews were bustling about the birds the chaplain would move down the line from one aircraft to another, bless the man and the machine and give you a cheery thumbs-up signal. I usually showed the arming area and the launch of a strike to our important visitors, and I was surprised to find that a few of our supposedly more important types found the sweating men of the cloth somewhat hilarious as they moved amid the din of battle preparations. (Many of these visitors were the kind that usually traveled in the back end of a super gooney bird and got only close enough to the war effort to collect the same sixty-five dollars a month combat pay that the fighter pilots earned.) But nobody sitting in the driver's seat of a Thud thought it was at all funny.

Two of our chaplains stood out from the crowd. I confess to being an Episcopalian snob who finds the general run of military chapel activities less than completely attractive, but during this tour I was greatly impressed by a quiet Armenian Baptist and a charging Irish Roman Catholic. They were both very much a part of our operation, and they considered the pilots and ground crew on the flight line their primary charges for the year they worked with us. The Baptist was from California, and like many Armenians from that area epitomized by J. C. Agejanian, automobile racing's most colorful promoter, shared with me an interest in automobile racing. He was the kind of man I liked to talk to, and he seemed to impress all of us the same way. I did not spend as much time with the Roman Catholic, but when things got sticky he was always there to help. I always got a special sense of well-being from their thumbs-up.

My Irish friend was usually quite jovial around the air base, but he was never anything but serious in the arming area. Because it was a bit difficult to get a smile from him at that point, Ken determined to do it one way or another, and he carried an empty beer bottle with him one day as he strapped into his aircraft and taxied into the arming area. When, with his usual stern expression, the father approached in his tennis shoes and fatigues to bless Ken and his bird, Ken feigned a big swig on the empty beer bottle and handed it over the side of the cockpit to the amazed priest, who almost collapsed in a fit of laughter.

I tried to get my Baptist friend a Bronze Star for the tremendous effort he put into his tour, but I ran into trouble from our support headquarters in the Philippines, who could see nothing unusual about his accomplishments. Things are too comfortable down there, and the majority of those people never got with the effort. When he left for the States, he was replaced by a short plump little man, who from our first meeting reminded me of my grandmother. He took over as the boss chaplain and since he couldn't preach, couldn't sing, apparently considered the pilots, the crewmen and the arming area as somewhat bothersome details, and griped constantly about being overworked and persecuted, our relations with the chaplains went downhill. It was a shame, and I understand that my Roman Catholic friend ran head on into his new boss after I left and got hurt in the shuffle. They were great guys, and with their blessing I marshaled my forces on the runway and launched for the area where I had found a superior target the day before, and been hit in the process.

The black takeoff was not too bad, and as we reached altitude, the first light of day was piercing the horizon. The refueling was another story. It was the worst I have ever been through. I had Ken leading my element on his ninety-eighth mission and he has described the refueling as his single most harrowing flying experience. We had huge thunderstorms on all of our refueling tracks and they started on the ground and went up above 35,000 feet, even in the early morning hours.

There was simply no possible way to avoid them, and though I tried desperately to keep the heaving, bouncing mass of fighters and tankers under control, it got pretty well messed up from the start. All of the flight leaders managed to locate their tankers in the rain and clouds, which in itself was quite a feat. It gets real spooky probing through a thick cloud trying to locate another moving object, and neither the tankers nor the fighters are maneuverable enough in the refueling posture to salvage the situation if somebody goofs.

Normally each flight member takes on a load of fuel in 1, 2, 3, 4 order. You burn some fuel while the others are on the boom, so when 4 is full, the flight cycles through once more for a quick top off and a full load before you leave. In bad weather two hookups are plenty demanding, but this day I had to accomplish eight separate hookups before I managed to get all my charges squared away. I don't care if I never have to do that again. The further north we went, the worse the bumps became. We had people falling off refueling booms and sinking into the murk, separated from their flights, and we had entire flights slung off their tankers. There was just no place to go where conditions would be any better and it looked for a while like I would not be able to hold my troops together safely, and that I might have to scrub the mission I wanted so badly to complete. We all had to stay on the same radio channel so we could try to keep track of each other, and since every pilot was having problems, the radio turned into a screaming mess. I was trying to fly instruments, navigate the force, keep track of my tanker, and mentally picture the other tankers and fighters while attempting to figure out how I was going to maintain control of this mess. I had vertigo so many times I lost track of the number, and I repeatedly had to revert to straight instruments to convince myself that I was or was not in some degree of upside-down condition. The tankers were trying to give us all the help they could, but they became confused, and their turns became spastic as they bumped out of unison with us and exceeded the capabilities of our birds heavy with bombs and fuel. The entire situation approached the impossible.

In desperation I told everybody to stay off the radio for a few minutes and suffer in silence, and I contacted the pilot and navigator of my tanker on the radio. I told them that we were just about to blow the entire strike, and on top of that we were liable to run a bunch of us together if we kept lurching about as we were. Since we were the top cell, I told them to keep track of the others on their radar and to start moving up and down, searching for a break between layers of clouds where we could get the force back together. The process of climbing, diving, bending and turning, while we continually cycled off the boom in order to have a full load to be able to take advantage of a break should we find one, was most painful, but we finally stumbled into a clearing between layers that was less than 1,000 feet high and less than 2 miles in diameter. It wasn't a good setup, but it was this or nothing. I told the tanker to wrap it up in whatever turn was necessary to stay in that hole, and while we stood on our ears to stay with him we topped off on fuel once again.

I had little idea of our specific position since I had been dragging around behind my tanker during his gyrations. I called the tanker navigator, who gave me a set of coordinates for our present position which I managed to set into my navigation gear; at least the machine would know where we were. I then told my tanker to get out of the hole and head south, and to call each succeeding tanker and steer him and his fighters into this little clear spot with instructions to fuel his fighters and vacate the clear spot as rapidly as he could. I wrestled with my maps and figured a new course from our new drop-off point to the target and orbited in the restricted clearing until I knew that all tankers and fighters were en route with safe separation between each cell. When the big blunt nose of the second tanker burst through the clouds into my circle, I announced my new course and time on target to all the flight leaders and dumped my nose back into the thunderstorms to let down enroute to the target. What a horrible exercise.

After a bit more bouncing around, we broke through on the other side of the wall of thunderstorms and the air was clear above a low undercast that obscured the ground. All calculations were in the blind now and all I could do was follow my navigation gear and hope that both it and my new computations were correct. After battering us around so badly, the weather finally gave us a break, and as the seconds ticked away and time to target counted down to zero, I was over the desired spot and there was a break in the clouds that centered right over the valley I was looking for. The target complex was in the center of the break that extended from the ridgeline on the north of the target for about two miles to the other ridgeline, on the south of the valley. It was open for a couple of miles to the east and west and we could work, and I could hear the flights behind me breaking out of the thunder-bumps and charging north.

Everything looked just as it had the day before and I knew the precise target that I wanted. My selection of the gun pits that had clobbered me the day before as my target was both personal and professional. I flew east past the road where I had strafed the trucks the day before and placed myself in clear view of the guns that had hit me. I wanted to be sure that the North Vietnamese had not moved them, and I wanted to lure as many gun crews up and on the guns as I could. The gunners responded well, and the valley lit up just as it had the day before, but this time I was ready for them. I made one of the best dive-bomb runs of my tour that day and as I pulled up and looked back over my shoulder, the guns were down, and things were blowing up throughout the gun pits on both sides of the road. I had hit dead center and those guns never fired another round that day. The rest of my flight dropped on separate building clusters and each one of them was right on the money. Earl, my number two man, had the most spectacular drop; the complex he hit must have been loaded with ammunition, as it rocked with one secondary explosion after the other, spewing orange flame and dirty gray smoke skyward. It was still rattling ten minutes later.

I moved to the north of the target and cleared the second flight into the valley which was now well marked with fire, smoke and dust. I moved on an east-west axis that allowed me to observe the work of the succeeding flights as they methodically chewed up the building complexes. I also managed to spot a few new clusters that I had not seen the day before, and all indications were that our find was as good as or even better than we had figured. I swung back to the east from one of these new sightings just about the time my third flight followed my directions to perfection and left another cluster of buildings aflame. The fourth flight was a good minute out, and a small but well-constructed set of buildings followed a straight road now perpendicular to my wing. Why not? I rolled in and strafed the length of the complex with my flight and as we pulled off to the south, the fourth flight rolled in over the top of us and bombed to the north. As they pulled up they rolled into a wingover to the west and strafed what the intelligence people told us might be an early warning radar site in the hills on the northern edge of the valley. It was going like clockwork and I was elated.

As my fifth and last flight pulled off target, the area was pretty well saturated. The count at this stage of the game showed numerous fires burning throughout the area with two large secondary explosions—Earl's ammunition hit, and a fuel hit that lofted black smoke and debris as high as 4,000 feet into the air. The gun positions were silent, and eight large buildings were completely destroyed while twenty-three others were damaged or burning. Eight trucks had been destroyed and left as hulks, and the suspected radar site had been well massaged. As I looked at the valley, I was pleased with the way my guys had worked, but there was one more job that needed to be done. One of the pilots had hit right on the corner of a good-sized complex and cleaned out several buildings, but there were still about a half dozen buildings in that cluster that needed to be hit. As I moved away from the cloud cover to the north I decided to attack these buildings in a high angle strafing pass with my cannon, and I lit the burner and pulled up and over onto a steep strafing run with my flight behind me.

The complex I was after looked like it could be a radar site and, as my nose dropped down toward the target, I was in trouble. I had some hills at my two o'clock position and they led to the site then stretched toward the northern end of the valley. In all of our attacks of the day before and of that day, there had been no fire from that area, but now the air between the green hills and my aircraft was alive with the piercing red balls of tracer ammunition from the ground. There were a lot of them, and they were curling my way. It only takes a few experiences to know when they are on you, and I was afraid that these gunners were on me. I wondered instantaneously where in hell they had come from and then I was in real trouble. My bird lurched to the left with the sickening click of another big hit and before I could even react she lurched and clicked again. Instantaneously the fire light on the instrument panel went to red and the reflexes built up from combat in the Thud threw my eyes to the hydraulic pressure gauges that indicated the number of pounds of pressure per square inch available to move the flight controls. If they went I was done, and there would be no controlling my diving steed. It was the too-familiar pattern that had cost us most of our Thud losses, and my eyes arrived there in fractions of a second only to find the primary system at zero and the indicator needle of the secondary system settling on zero.

I had already lost many of the systems necessary for normal flight and the only thing keeping me under control was the third and weaker utility hydraulic system. The little white needle on that system was already wavering. I was entering my strafing run and I was on fire, and it looked like I was about to become an unguided missile. I thought, What the hell, those lousy bastards may have me but I'm going to get them before I go, and I pressed on, mad and scared. Earl called, "Lead you're hit and on fire with smoke and pieces coming out the back end." I knew it, but I squeezed the trigger for all I was worth and sprayed a stream of lead into the guns and the buildings. If this was going to be it I wanted to get the job done first, and I did. I got about five hundred rounds right in the middle of them, and then it was time to start worrying about the old behind. Very gradually, I started back on the stick with an eye on the utility system. This was it, and if she didn't take now, the only alternative was a high-speed ejection attempt and that was not too promising a prospect. The pressure needle bucked and shuddered even with slight control pressures but she did not fall to zero and the nose started slowly up. I could use all the speed I could get to displace myself from any guns that might still be active, so an easy pullout that just cleared the ground was all I wanted, and that's just what I got.

My gradual pullout had carried me a fair distance to the north of the target area, but in my delicate condition north was not the place I wanted to go. I didn't want to use any greater control pressures than I needed to, as every activation of my one remaining emergency hydraulic system was tempting fate. I had at least one eye on that gauge all the time, and it set up a strange pattern that fascinated yet terrified me. It would hold relatively steady around three thousand pounds for about ninety seconds, then stagger a couple of times and drop down to zero, bounce off the bottom peg and shudder back toward three thousand pounds. If it

stayed on the bottom I was out of flight controls, and each
time it went through its cycle, my hand dropped involuntarily to the ejection handles at the base of my seat. I never
knew if it was going to come back up again and it was most
important that I get south while I was still able. I had to ease
her around to the south and fly right back over the valley that
I had been beating up for two days. Earl had stroked the
burner as soon as he saw my tail light up and he pulled up
close to me as I approached the valley from the north and
said, "Chief, you better get ready to get out of that thing. I
think the rear end is coming unglued and you have lots of fire
back there." Just as he said that the hydraulic needle took one
of its nose dives and for some reason I looked at my clock at
that instant. It was quarter of twelve and I had a very clear
thought, if I have to jump out of this thing right on top of
these bastards I'll never make it even as far as the Hanoi
Hilton. They'll eat me for lunch. The pressure came back up
but I couldn't get the fire out and I was most concerned about
what the fire was eating up in the read end of my bird.

Earl was a pretty cool type and although I never did figure
out whether he did it on purpose or not, he managed to relax
me a bit. He carried a miniature camera with him and as we
crossed the valley he called, "Hey, Chief, how about holding
still for a minute. I want to get a color shot of that mother
bear before it lets go." Fighter pilot humor. He later prom-
ised to send me a print of his picture but I got a letter from
him recently indicating he may not have been as calm as he
thought. It seems that all he got were lots of pictures of sky
and ground as I struggled for altitude and displacement to the
south. His description of the egress is interesting. "For about
sixty seconds that day I wouldn't have given two cents for
your chances of making it at all, to say nothing of making it
back to a forward emergency strip. Here's the incident as I
remember it. You called, 'I'm rolling in on a strafe pass,' and
I followed on the right side. I saw about twenty goof balls
come up in your vicinity—they seemed to come from several
places but were all focused around your aircraft. They all let
loose at the same instant, which was surprising—zap, zap,
zap—and it was over. I pulled up hard, rolled over and
spotted you about a thousand feet below me and a little to my
right and forward. Your aircraft was trailing dark black smoke
for about two thousand feet behind you and there was a

bright orange glow along the right rear side. The smoke lasted about sixty seconds and the glow remained until you had turned southwest and leveled off. The transmissions are hazy, but I remember discussing whether to go direct to the emergency strip or to head for one of the safer bailout areas. I was extremely impressed with the holes in your aircraft and remember thinking it odd that the orange fire from the large hole didn't trail from the forward motion of the aircraft. It sort of licked all around the area like a good fireplace fire. When it would die down momentarily I could see into the tail pipe. Every so often it would flash inside the tail pipe and leave the area a bright red, like a good hot farm stove."

I knew there was nothing I could do to improve the hydraulic situation but that I had better do what I could to get that fire out. Violent control action was out of the question and since the burner had been knocked out with the hit, all I could do was ease up to whatever altitude I could get with normal power and hope that the rarefied air might discourage the fire. I am not sure I would have wanted to pour all that raw burner fuel into the aft section even if it had been working. I felt like I was sitting on a time bomb but I was not about to terminate by jumping out as long as I was still flying. Twenty-three thousand was the maximum altitude I could get out of her, and as I leveled there, Ken pulled up alongside and took over his role as deputy flight lead. I told him I was going to try for the emergency strip and he moved in on my wing as he sent two and four on to a tanker and home. I had enough fuel to get to the emergency strip, if she would keep flying, which was very fortunate as our friendly airborne gas station operators would have been nuts to let a burning aircraft hook up to them. Earl, in two, called the rescue people as he herded four toward their tanker. They scrambled a Spad in no time and headed north to cut me off should I have to step out. The Spad came up on our frequency and talked to me all the way and it was something of a reassurance to know that at least he was ready for what I hoped wouldn't happen.

Once I had leveled off in the rarefied air I started a series of very gentle slips and skids, trying to alter the airflow over the aft section to blow the fire out. After about ten minutes of looking at that ugly red fire-warning light glowing steadily in my face, it flickered on and off a few times. The temptation was great to exaggerate the slips and skids at this first sign of possible success in fighting the fire, but I forced myself to go easy on the remaining hydraulic system that continued to drop my heart into my boots every ninety seconds. (I even took my hand off the stick and regrasped the very top of it with my thumb and forefinger so that I could not possibly manhandle the controls even if I tried.) I continued the gradual slipping and sliding motion and the red light flickered with increasing frequency until when we were about halfway there it went out. Ken confirmed that the rear end looked better and my rescue buddy in the Spad sounded as happy as I was to hear the news that at least the fire was out.

The morning winds had shifted the thunderstorm patterns some, and I was now following a slightly different course outbound from the target as I headed for the emergency strip, but I was still concerned about the weather. Ken and I were able to stay in the clear by altering course and altitude from time to time for the next hundred miles. It was almost imperative that we stay in the clear because my convulsing control pressure could hardly stand the demands I would have to put on it to counteract the bumps and jostling I would encounter if I had to fly through another thunderstorm. Then, with still a hundred miles to go, one of those black monsters stretched across my path and reached from the ground to right out of sight. To enter it was out of the question, but to skirt it meant many more miles of flight while watching that ninety-second gauge that kept telling me this could not go on much longer. There was no choice, and I gently slid my bird to the east and through the rain that hung from the upper deck of the storm. It cost me a hundred miles and it cost me time, but I had to do it. I regretfully advised my rescue companion and he altered his course to remain within striking distance if needed.

As I crept through the peripheral rain and reduced visibility, I contacted the radar ground control people and received two additional surprises. First, I had some difficulty generating the sense of urgency in the ground controllers that I felt in the cockpit. They seemed content to handle me as a routine recovery along with the rest of their traffic and it took a few sharp words to convince them that they had better handle what was left of this bird with kid gloves, or else I would blow up right in the middle of their radar shack if it was the last thing I did. This was probably good for me in a way, as it irritated me so badly it got my mind out of my own cockpit and forcefully into the recovery and landing problem. Second, the man on the radio blithely informed me that I had a 700-foot ceiling to penetrate at the emergency strip. That was all I needed, a little more weather time and an instrument approach, but there was no choice and I did not have the fuel to go anyplace else even if I had wanted to, which I did not. I needed to get on the ground.

Despite his vocal lethargy, my friendly recovery director set me up on a good instrument approach and I guess I have probably never flown a better one. The closer I got to the ground, the more devastating each pressure surge appeared and when I descended through safe bailout altitude I tried to stop looking at the gauge but I couldn't keep my eyes off it. I held my landing gear until I figured I had the end of the runway hacked and then blew them down with the emergency system that worked the first time and showed me the three beautiful green lights indicating landing gear down and locked. When I saw the end of the runway I started to let my bird drop below the glide slope so I could put her down right on the end of the runway. I had no idea how my drag chute and brakes would perform after touchdown and, in fact, did not know what was liable to fall off the bird when I hit the concrete. The two most worthless things to a fighter pilot are altitude above him and runway behind him, and I was going to spot this baby doll right on the end of the runway. This almost got me into trouble, as from Ken's position on my wing it looked like we were awfully low and flat, which we were. He was concerned that I might get too low as I whizzed over the trees on the approach end of the runway and gave me a courtesy call to the effect that I might want to pull it up a bit. I didn't want to, but his transmission was garbled and partially cut out by another transmission and all I got was "up." In a position like that, when you hear the word "up," all you can think about is your landing gear. I knew I had checked my indicators carefully and they said down and locked, but my only thought was that perhaps something in my sick machine had goofed up and that my gear were not properly positioned. I involuntarily jerked back on the stick as my eyes stabbed for the reassurance of my three green gear lights. I got my unnecessary gear-down assurance, but I had overtaxed the extremely sensitive control balance that I was working with and as the pressure needle started down, the controls tightened up and I figured, this is it—got her all the way back to the end of the runway and she's locking up on me. I would have been a big orange ball on the end of the runway if they had locked then, but she struggled back up one more time and I stabbed her onto the concrete.

The drag chute worked and the emergency brakes worked and I even managed to turn her off the runway at midfield. As I cleared the runway I punched the mike button and said, "Thanks a lot, Christ. I'll take it from here."

All the crash rescue troops were there and we got her chocked quickly and I shut down that particular engine for the last time—it grated to a stop. I crawled down the firemen's ladder and took a look at her and she looked bad. She was bleeding hydraulic fluid and fuel and the rear end was burned to a sickly color that failed to hide the more than fifty holes that covered the aft section. One of the functions of this particular strip was the recovery of wounded birds and the boss man of the facility was there to meet me as he had met many others. He gazed at my Thud in disbelief and allowed that it was the worst one that he had ever seen come back. He didn't have to convince me, but I had gotten her back and I had gotten myself back and we would both fly again. I was most thankful. I filled out the usual debriefing forms and bummed a seat on an administrative courier that left for Takhli ten minutes after I landed.

The debriefing and the ride back to Takhli were anticlimactic. I guessed the episode of the past two days might have been good for an award but I was not overly concerned with that at the moment. The three-star commander of our operational headquarters must have thought so as he affixed his signature to an endorsement on a recommendation for my second Air Force Cross that concluded "Colonel Broughton's actions during almost eight hours of combat fighter flying in North Vietnam during this twenty-four hour period represent the ultimate in skill, professionalism and dedication to the detriment of his personal well-being and safety. Through his exemplary leadership and ability, he and his forces destroyed a vital rail link, outmaneuvered a Sam attack, drove off a Mig attack, spotted, identified and diagnosed a significant target complex; planned, coordinated and executed a significant strike; survived perhaps the wildest aerial refueling episode in the history of fighter aviation; regrouped his forces under almost impossible conditions; thoroughly pummeled a major hidden link in the North Vietnamese supply and transportation scheme and recovered two severely damaged irreplaceable F-105 aircraft to fly again. He capped his efforts by attacking the last remnant of his target when his aircraft was on fire and practically out of control. The only thing that he did not do to accomplish his mission was kill himself in the effort; and but for his superior airmanship and guts he would have done that. I recommend that Colonel Broughton be awarded the Air Force Cross."

It didn't work out that way. Two of my majors were accused of strafing a Russian ship near Haiphong as they fought for their lives. I fought for them with all my might and instead of my getting a second Air Force Cross all three of us received a general court-martial. That is quite a story in itself and one of these days I may tell that story too. I haven't decided if I will call it "The Turkestan Incident" or "Hanoi and Back—Six Dollars a Round Trip."

Join the Allies on the Road to Victory
BANTAM WAR BOOKS

SPECIAL
MONEY SAVING
OFFER

Now you can have an up-to-date listing of Bantam's hundreds of titles plus take advantage of our unique and exciting bonus book offer. A special offer which gives you the opportunity to purchase a Bantam book for only 50¢. Here's how!

By ordering any five books at the regular price per order, you can also choose any other single book listed (up to a $4.95 value) for just 50¢. Some restrictions do apply, but for further details why not send for Bantam's listing of titles today!

Just send us your name and address plus 50¢ to defray the postage and handling costs.

We Deliver!
And So Do These Bestsellers.